ANTI-RACISM AND SOCIAL WELFARE

To the memory of Stephen Lawrence

Anti-Racism and Social Welfare

Edited by
MICHAEL LAVALETTE
LAURA PENKETH
CHRIS JONES

NOTTINGHAM UNIVERSITY LIBRARY

Ashgate

Aldershot • Brookfield USA • Singapore • Sydney

© M. Lavalette, L. Penketh and C. Jones 1998

All rights reserved. No part of this publication may be reproduced, stored in a retrieval system, or transmitted in any form or by any means, electronic, mechanical, photocopying, recording or otherwise without the prior permission of the publisher.

Published by
Ashgate Publishing Ltd
Gower House
Croft Road
Aldershot
Hants GU11 3HR
England

Ashgate Publishing Company
Old Post Road
Brookfield
Vermont 05036
USA

British Library Cataloguing in Publication Data
Anti-racism and social welfare
   1. Blacks - Great Britain - Social conditions - Congresses
   2. Blacks - Great Britain - Services for - Congresses
   3. Racism - Great Britain - Congresses 4. Great Britian -
   Ethnic relations - Congresses
   I. Lavalette, Michael II. Penketh, Laura III. Jones, Chris
   305.8'96'041

Library of Congress Catalog Card Number: 98-73763

ISBN 1 84014 507 2

Printed and Bound by Biddles Short Run Books, King's Lynn

Contents

List of Contributors

Paula Asgill is a Senior Lecturer in the Department of Applied Social Sciences, University College of St. Martin, Lancaster.

Gideon Ben-Tovim is a Reader in Sociology at the University of Liverpool.

Claudia Bernard is Lecturer in Social Work at Goldsmith's College, University of London.

Manneh Brown is honorary fellow, Department of Sociology, University of Liverpool.

Dr Dee Cook is Associate Dean of Research at the University of Wolverhampton.

Simon Dyson is Principle Lecturer in the Department of Health and Continuing Professional Studies, De Montfort University, Leicester.

Jennie Fleming works within the Centre for Social Action at De Montfort University.

Cheryl Gore works in the Department of Education, University of Birmingham.

Mark Harrison is the Director of the Centre for Social Action, De Montfort University.

Karen Hassell works in the Pharmacy section at the University of Manchester.

Chris Jones works in the Department of Sociology, Social Policy and Social Work Studies, University of Liverpool.

Paul Kyprianou is honorary fellow, Department of Sociology, University of Liverpool.

Michael Lavalette works in the Department of Sociology, Social Policy and Social Work Studies, University of Liverpool.

Ian Law is Senior Lecturer and Director of the 'Race' and Public Policy Research Unit, School of Sociology and Social Policy, University of Leeds.

Margaret Ledwith is Senior Lecturer in Community and Youth Studies, University College of St. Martin, Lancaster.

Laura Penketh works in the Social Policy section of the Department of Social Studies at the University of Central Lancashire.

Barney Rooney is honorary fellow, Department of Sociology, University of Liverpool.

Rhonda Wattley works within the Centre for Social Action at De Montfort University.

Acknowledgements

We would like to thank each of the contributors for their work and patience in seeing this project through to completion. Ashgate have allowed us to be flexible with our deadlines and have been helpful with our many queries. In particular we would like to record our thanks to Karen McGowan who prepared the script to camera ready standard (and did so while dealing with the demands of a new born baby, Heather).

Michael Lavalette
Laura Penketh
Chris Jones

Dedication

While working on this book the murder of Stephen Lawrence by a group of white racists has been a recurrent item in the national media. The scandal of Stephen's death is not only that such lynchings continue to take place in Britain in the 1990s but that the police and authorities refused to act when informed who the culprits were and whose initial investigations were framed around the idea that Stephen, because he was black, must have been guilty of something. If there was ever a series of events which confirmed the structurally and institutionally racist nature of British society then perhaps this is it. As part of the campaign for justice we dedicate this book to the memory of Stephen Lawrence.

Introduction

Michael Lavalette

The chapters gathered here are developed from papers originally presented to a one day conference on Racism and Social Welfare at the University of Central Lancashire in April 1996. The conference was well attended with 60 papers presented to over 120 participants. The size of the conference reflected the continuing concern with issues of 'race' and anti-racism in the field of social welfare and was helped by the support provided by the Department of Social Studies at Central Lancashire and the Social Policy Association.

In the 1990s racism continues to blight the lives of Black people in Britain. Britain's Black population continue to suffer disproportionately in terms of poverty, unemployment, ill-health, poor housing and inferior working conditions. Racist violence, police harassment and criminalisation remain part of the 'experience' of Black youth. Both overt and covert forms of institutionalised racism relegate or ignore the needs of minority ethnic groups within the full range of social welfare services. While the consequences of the racialisation of political and social life has meant that the Black presence continues to be viewed as a 'problem' for many in authority. The reality is that racist oppression, built into the very fabric of modern capitalist society, affects the Black community on a daily basis. The conference reflected the continuing concern that such structured inequality remains part of the functioning of the 'British welfare state' and that research agendas and praxis which are shaped by anti-racist concerns continue to be marginalised by the political establishment, within welfare services and often within Higher Education establishments: practically orientated research agendas are increasingly marginalised by the restrictions of the Research Assessment Exercise which increasingly blights academic research activity.

1

Yet the reality and consequences of racism are well established. They have been recognised within academic discourse over the last twenty years at least and during this period, policy makers and welfare professionals, have apparently taken cognisance of racism, its causes and consequences. As we approach the new millennium an assessment of the successes and failures of 'race equality' and anti-racist strategies is necessary: how have they improved the lives of Black welfare workers and welfare recipients? Most of the papers, while emphasising the continuing blight of racism, also try to offer an evaluation of various anti-discriminatory policies, locating problems and opening up debate about possible future developments.

The conference reflected a wide range of perspectives on issues of 'race' and anti-racism, a variety which is reflected in the present volume. What brought people together was their commitment to be part of the struggle against racism, in all its manifestations, within the welfare services. This is perhaps emphasised in those chapters that argue for an overtly political stance towards anti-racist research and practice. What unites the contributions is a concern to highlight the continuing injustice and inequality that present social relations create and sustain and the need for academics and researchers to be part of the struggle to create a better and a fairer world (even if there is disagreement about what exactly this will entail!).

The aim of the present volume is to continue the debate on the position of Black people in British society, assess the successes and failures of various anti-racist strategies within welfare institutions and services and raise pertinent issues for those concerned to take research and debate further. In the first chapter Jones 'sets the context' by outlining the increasingly brutal turn within state social policy, both in Britain and the US, and the consequences this has for the Black working class in particular. He locates this general shift within the continuing new right agenda, the 'Americanisation' of social policy under New Labour, and the attempt to deprioritise the social to the needs of economic policy. The new right political and economic agenda, promoted by governments and the various international financial institutions, continues to cause havoc across the globe. Starvation, poverty, unemployment, casualisation, low wages and consequent poor mental and physical well-being are compounded by restrictive and oppressive public and social policies. The brunt of the social consequences fall on the oppressed and exploited across the globe. In extremis it creates the famine conditions in Africa but even within Europe and North America the politics of the new right cause deepening divisions, marginalisation and 'exclusion'. In Britain it meant that one of the achievements of 18 years of Conservative governments was to increase significantly the gap between the richest and the poorest and amongst the poorest Black people are over-represented.

Chapters 2 to 7 deal with various aspects of Black experience and/or responses to racism within Britain. Penketh reviews the experience of CCETSW's anti-racist initiative in the form of the original Paper 30. Paper 30 was, in many senses, a remarkable piece of legislation. Produced by a state agency, it contained a recognition that Britain was a structurally racist society and set out to enshrine anti-racist teaching and practice amongst student social workers. Almost immediately Paper 30 provoked a backlash. Why? In this chapter Penketh sets out the history of Paper 30, the campaign against it from various quarters and its eventual 'replacement'. Tracing this history she asks what general lessons it has for anti-racist activists in the policy field.

Ben Tovim et al. address similar issues in their evaluation of the Third European Anti-Poverty Programme in Liverpool. The programme focused on the poverty and social exclusion faced by Liverpool's Black population in the Granby/Toxteth area. This chapter provides both an overview of urban inequality and racism and an assessment of the 'successes' and 'failures' of the partnership experiment. Although 'including' Liverpool's Black population was one of the objectives of the City Council's programme, the results have been far from successful.

Gore (Chapter 4) and Law (Chapter 3) deal with Black experience in education and housing. Gore suggests 'educational underachievement' of Black pupils is often related to the performance of the schools. School effectiveness is, she suggests, a key element determining how prepared pupils are to undertake public examinations. Her call for increased school inspection may not be shared by everyone, but her data, which shoes how some schools fail Black children more than others, deserves serious consideration. Law looks at the persistence of racial inequality in the housing market. He suggests that while we must acknowledge the role of structural and institutional racism in establishing discrimination there is a need for a more holistic approach which moves beyond what he terms the 'easy' answers. A holistic approach requires acknowledging patterns of housing demand and aspiration, an awareness of general market conditions, an analysis of group need assessment and a recognition of the links between housing and other forms of racist discrimination. From this starting point he proceeds to develop a more complex picture of racial inequality in housing and offer an assessment of policy interventions in this area.

A common theme on racism at work is the apparent concentration of Black workers in poorly paid and less skilled occupations. In chapter 5 Hassell offers a different set of experiences faced by some Black workers in the world of work. In this chapter her focus is the experience of Asian pharmaceutical professionals. The chapter presents evidence from a substantial piece of research which indicates the increasing number of Asians entering the profession (and the simultaneous decline in white male entry).

Cook in an important chapter looks at the racialisation and criminalisation processes involved in the recent legislation to restrict entry to Britain of Black migrants fleeing oppression and exploitation. The Asylum and Immigration Act is, as she notes, a 'draconian' piece of legislation which treats Black people entering Britain as potential 'Bogus' refugees. The Act was brought in by the last Conservative government but it has not been repealed by New Labour. Indeed, the New Labour government were more than happy to use this legislation against Romany travellers fleeing Nazi thugs in Slovakia in the summer of 1997. By late 1997 and during 1998 a number of political refugees were being 'housed' in some of Britain's most notorious gaols and detention centres and a number were forced to resort to hunger strikes to obtain recognition of their status and appropriate living conditions. That such struggles took place under a New Labour government emphasises the bipartisan policy that exists in this area between the major political parties on issues of 'race' and immigration.

The final four chapters address epistemological and methodological issues. The three chapters by Dyson and Harrison, Fleming and Wattley and Asgill and Ledwith all draw inspiration from a broadly 'social action' approach to research and practice. By developing concepts found in the work of (among others) bell hooks, Saul Alinsky and Paulo Freire they argue for an approach to research which is rooted in the practices, struggles and demands of the oppressed themselves rather than the policy driven needs of authority sources. In this perspective, researchers and welfare professionals become facilitators and social educators working with community organisations, various social movements (old and new) and a range of welfare recipients to assert their rights and bring about social change. Finally, the chapter by Bernard deals with the sensitive issue of black mothers' responses to the sexual abuse of their children. Again, she is concerned to address methodological and ethical problems created by undertaking such research and argues for a challenging, Black feminist approach to the research process.

1 Setting the Context: Race, Class and Social Violence

Chris Jones

Introduction

> (Adam) Smith's admiration for individual enterprise was tempered still further by his contempt for the "vile maxim of the masters of mankind: All four ourselves, and nothing for other people" (Chomsky, 1993, p. 19).

I have chosen with some reservation 'setting the context' as the title for this first chapter in this edited collection of papers concerned with various aspects of 'race', racism and social welfare in contemporary Britain. As one reads the various chapters and gains an encouraging sense of the diversity and development of activity and practice with respect to black and anti-racist scholarship in Britain today, it becomes evident that such a title is problematic. The chapters indicate that there is no self-evident single context in this field of activity. They remind us of Sivanandan's rejoinder about the character of anti-racism itself:

> ...there is the misconception that has grown up around the idea of anti-racism itself, viewing it as some sort of ideology, a coherent body of though with its own dogma and orthodoxy. But there is no such thing as anti-racism *per se* - only a thousand ways of combating racism - in different ways in different times (boom and recession) and in differing areas (employment, housing, schools) and different places (inner city, suburbia, rural areas) (Sivanandan, 1998, p. 74).

So let me be clear by what I seek to attempt in this opening chapter. I am concerned to say something about the nature and character of British society at the end of the twentieth century, especially with respect to 'race' and class and thereby set the stage for the chapters which follow. In this task I have an explicit political purpose. It is my contention that the current global orientation of capitalism with its onslaught on state welfare, trade unions, human rights, employment opportunities, its embrace of inequalities and enrichment of the wealthy at the expense of the poor, poses a massive threat and challenge to all those committed to social justice and condemns the large majority of humanity to misery. The weight of this threat is already a reality for millions both in Britain and elsewhere. That 'third' of the society who directly experience the exodus of jobs and meaningful employment opportunities and who on housing estates and in inner city ghettos know what it means to be abandoned by the state include, in disproportionate numbers, the greater part of Britain's black population. For social policy analysts and practitioners these developments, these new social and political realities are of critical importance in setting the general context of our work and should necessarily inform our development and practice in whatever of the thousands of ways or places we choose to struggle for social justice, human dignity and the right to live without fear.

Restating the obvious

"I think we will have to go back to soup kitchens". Then noting Jenkin's reaction, she continued "Take that silly smile off your face. I mean it". (Prime Minister Thatcher speaking to Patrick Jenkin, then Social Services minister, 1979) (cited Davies, 1997, p. 287)

This comment captures something of the tenor of our times. From the late 1970s onwards there has been a decisive shift in the practice, language and ideology of state welfare towards brutalism and ruthlessness. In much of the writing and analysis of state social policy which has drawn attention to the growth of poverty, inequality and social exclusion, there has been insufficient emphasis on this brutalism and its implications. It is almost as if we are fearful of coming to the conclusion that we have political and social elites in our supposedly civilised and advanced nation who have been prepared to pursue policies which in their impact suggest a hatred of substantial segments of the population. Yet how else can we make sense of some of the developments which have taken place and the seeming impunity of government ministers and other influential commentators who can speak of those who have borne the brunt of the neo-liberal revolution as an 'underclass' who are so defective as not really to count as members of the human race. Rather than a cause for compassion and consideration, they are demonised as 'nasty pieces of work' (Kenneth Clarke, then Home Secretary, *Daily Mail*, Feb 22, 1993), as 'vermin' to be driven off the streets (David McLean, then Home Office Minister, *Panorama*, BBC 1, Nov 1st, 1993). Within the black working class such demonisation and the politics of hatred have even longer disgraceful traditions typified by the comments of a Manchester police officer who described the black population of Moss Side and Hulme as 'wall to wall shit' (*Statewatch 1994*, vol. 4, no. 6, p. 3).

In both Britain and the United States, the concept of underclass to describe those segments of the population locked in long term poverty has entered the current vocabulary of domination. It is a particularly vicious concept which marks a return to the eugenicist paradigms of the early years of the twentieth century where the suffering and exclusion of the most vulnerable is unambiguously described as a consequence of their deficient humanity. The term underclass permits governments to sustain policies and ideologies of division and scapegoating. It is a concept which allows the legitimation of massive (and growing) social inequalities and injustices to focus on apparent inadequacies and 'pathologies' of the victims and diverts attention away from any explanations and inquiries which seek to locate these issues in relation to wider socio-economic factors. The concept of underclass bears heavily down on the most impoverished and in particular on the black working class poor where it joins easily with longer traditions of biological racism to justify the enduring plight of so many black peoples. With respect to black Americans, an American criminologist has argued that:

> Though black Americans have long struggled beneath the weight of dominant ideologies, the term 'black underclass' has done much more than past ideologies to dehumanise inner-city blacks (Raup, 1996, p. 163).

This officially sanctioned contemporary politics of hatred and demonisation revealed by the preparedness of the elites to speak openly in derogatory ways of those at the bottom end of the social system, and, most worryingly, with seeming impunity, is starkly illustrated in the raft of social welfare changes which have taken place since 1977 and continue under the government of New Labour twenty years on. This is not surprising given that the discourses of underclass are an inextricable aspect of the neo-liberal onslaught on welfare regimes across the globe over the past twenty five years. The notion that a significant section of the poor and unemployed are there because of supposed inherent deficiencies - are in the language of the Victorian Charity Organisation Society 'unhelpable' - provides a powerful rationale for dismantling and transforming social welfare provision. After all, if this is the case then social welfare directed at this group on the old social democratic assumption that it can lead to human betterment is simply a waste of resource and is actually counter-productive in that it feeds dependency and deviance. The notion of underclass explicitly drives state intervention towards an authoritarian and restrictive stance as the problem of the underclass becomes defined as a problem of discipline and containment and not one of rehabilitation and inclusion. It is also illustrative of the shift towards divisiveness and scapegoating as a means of generating consensus. In the post cold-war world, it is the enemies within who are targeted for creating a spurious moral unity and who are regularly and routinely demonised for the peril they pose to our social fabric and moral order.

The construction of welfare dependency as a problem of and for claimants, and as the key problematic of our so-called welfare state is breath-taking. It is extraordinary the extent to which successive governments with their spin doctors and media allies have pressed the electorate to accept this proposition and to refocus attention on claimants and not on the economic and social forces which have devastated the employment opportunities and standards of living of millions. The implementation of the Social Fund in 1988 (following the 1986 social security legislation) exemplifies the ways in which this ideological construction can lead to the most barbarous of policies.

Prior to the Social Fund, the already parsimonious social security system contained important discretionary provisions that provided some support (after pleading) for claimants in particularly difficult circumstances often related to their health, or when confronted with unforeseen emergencies such as burglaries, fire or flood and storm damage. For some long term claimants, these discretionary payments acknowledged the irregular and specials costs of growing children with their need for shoes and coats. For those claimants with young families, especially with only one principal carer, again encompassing a disproportionate number of black households, these discretionary grants constituted critical sources of support and to a degree helped mitigate the notoriously low level of the core benefit entitlements (see Novak, 1988, for a more detailed discussion). The introduction of the Social Fund in 1988 changed all this. Discretionary payments were abolished to be replaced by loans. Moreover, these loans were now to be drawn from a cash limited fund administered locally. This fiscal discipline ensured that social security officers were compelled to be

8

especially vigilant in the dispersal of loans in addition to the implementation of new regulations which significantly tightened the eligibility criteria. By 1992 these funds had dropped from £504m to £91m. According to Davies,

> Those who were lent money from the Social Fund struggled to repay it. Eventually the system reached gridlock when 116,095 claimants were refused crisis loans to buy cookers or beds or clothing - on the grounds that they were too poor to pay back the money. So the very poor lost their final safety net because they could not afford to pay for it themselves (Davies, 1997, p. 290).

This surreal state of affairs whereby some of the most impoverished are considered to be too poor to take loans from the state's last resort fund has condemned many to new forms of indignity and barbarism, ranging from crime and prostitution, to being at the mercy of those loan sharks who can make fortunes from the most desperate. With banks and insurance companies excluding one in four households from their services the possibilities for such pariahs are considerable.

But the social fund is but one example of the new brutalism and social violence against the poor. There have been countless changes in the social security system over the past thirty years that have either reduced benefits, tightened eligibility criteria or 'reformed' benefits as in the case of the introduction of the Job Seekers Allowance, all of which have contributed to the toughening up of social security. In its totality, there is now no sense whatsoever that the British social security system has any respect for claimants. Rather the inverse is the case. It has returned to the workhouse roots of 1834 in which to be a claimant is taken as proof of unworthiness and a fit candidate for maltreatment with impunity. The same story can be told across the entire sector of state social welfare policies, embracing the health system, schools and schooling, social housing, and the personal social services. In all of these sites of state welfare the same trajectories of reduced services, tougher eligibility levels, overloaded front-line staff, crumbling physical infrastructure can be traced. Collectively they portray the poor and disadvantaged as rapacious and worthless. In the particular case of the black poor, these changes have 'reinforced a climate of opinion where black people are seen as 'outsiders', unwelcome in British society' (Oppenheim, 1993, p. 122). And bizarrely, the injunction of being outwith humanity is directed not at those responsible for this cruelty but at those whose well-being and sense of self worth already battered by the experience of poverty is corroded and undermined when forced into contact with the state.

Everybody knows

> Everybody knows that the dice are loaded...
> Everybody knows that the good guys lost. Everybody
> knows that the fight was fixed: the poor stay poor,
> the rich get rich. That's how it goes.
> Everybody knows.
> (Leonard Cohen, Everybody Knows)

The scale of the damage - of what must be recognised as social violence - done to people who are compelled to rely on the state for all or part of their income can only be guessed at with respect to its enormity. We know that it leads to millions not claiming benefits to which they are entitled; we know that it results in vast numbers of black and white working class children daily experiencing a fundamental disrespect of their ability and value in schools; we know that it makes many families fearful of having contact with state social services because their life styles and arrangements are seen as pathological and expose them to the risk of their children being removed from their care, or their relatives to be 'sectioned' as mentally ill; we know it is a factor in the increasing suicide rates; and we know that the daily experience of being viewed as 'nothing' contributes to an environment of despair in which drug abuse and self-harm flourish (see Wilkinson, 1966, for further details).

The paradox and challenge for those of us who are outraged by this knowledge is that to know is clearly not a sufficient condition for positive action or social mobilisation and agitation for change. Conversations with Liverpool blacks in the Toxteth/Granby area I suspect reveal a common understanding in many black neighbourhoods across the country, namely that no amount of knowing about the devastation of drugs, poverty, racism and discrimination seems to have any effect. Authority appears to take note only when communities erupt in their anger and frustration. At the very least, such a state of affairs poses particular challenges to intellectuals such as ourselves engaged in various forms of social research which have the potential to reveal the dimensions and extent of social violence and the manner in which governing elites attempt to redirect attention and understandings concerning these phenomena.

Any reading of the history of the social sciences (see Abrams, 1968) reveals that authorities have long recognised its possibilities for subversion in presenting insights which run contrary to their world view. Gouldner (1970) amongst others also noted the pressure on social scientists to underplay exploration and interrogation of 'domain assumptions' in favour of middle range theory and investigation which tacitly accepts as a given the existing systems and organisation of society. It must be of some satisfaction to those who benefit most from the existing arrangements that in British higher education today the current research culture actively discourages researchers from publishing their work beyond a restrictive range of 'respectable' academic journals which are largely inaccessible to the wider public and make little impact on popular consciousness and understanding. A key challenge for progressive intellectual workers today is no longer only about 'knowing' but what we do with what know. It raises important question about the sort of alliances we create and the manner in which we do our research which is why the work of the Social Action Centre at De Monfort University is so interesting. We need to consider far more critically how we write and where we publish and our relationships with those whom we research and write about. Simultaneously, we should not forget that those in authority would prefer us not to be engaged in such work which should spur us on to greater effort.

Social violence

The consequences of social violence are not just experienced at a personal level but ripple through society at large. In particular, as investigative journalists such as Davies, Campbell and Pilger have revealed, they are especially devastating in the most hard-pressed working class neighbourhoods and estates which bear the brunt of robberies, assaults, and racial violence. Beyond these areas, the experience of crime and nuisance, and more tellingly the fear of crime as the media perpetuates the threat of the enemies within, has seen the most incredible proliferation of closed circuit cameras and security paraphernalia in homes and public places which heighten the sense of perpetual threat and insecurity. The separation of myth from reality becomes increasingly difficult in such an environment. Nevertheless, as two psychiatrists noted, there appears to be little recognition that "an inescapable truth of human and other higher mammalian relationships is that those who are respectfully treated are more likely to be respectful to others" (Roberts and Kraemer, 1996, p. 5). An

11

escapable truth also noted by Engels in his classic study of the working class in Manchester over 150 years ago, when he stated that if you treat people as brutes do not be surprised by brutish behaviour. Consequently, those who perpetuate the notion of an underclass will never have any shortage of material upon which to base their arguments as long as we have a social system that so thoroughly dehumanises and is so disrespectful of its most vulnerable members.

One of the most disturbing consequences of social violence is the divisiveness and damage it creates within the most disadvantaged neighbourhoods as people struggle to survive - fighting for the crumbs from the tables of the rich. It is a divisiveness that is often actively encouraged by the state and is exemplified by the incentives offered to those who inform on so-called 'welfare cheats'. It is also evident in the complex and often contradictory attitudes taken by the police towards drug trafficking which at times appears to be content to tolerate the destruction of a neighbourhood as long as the consequences of that devastation are geographically confined and don't spill over into 'respectable' society. The same can be said about the activities of loan sharks who in many instances condemn thousands of households to a state little shot of slavery. In recent years the housing policies of housing associations and local authorities especially with regard to the poorest people dependent on rented social housing has done much to confirm the ghetto status of many neighbourhoods (Giles, 1996). The resulting new geographies of deprivation have meant an ever growing concentration of those most disadvantaged being grouped together adding to the instability and degradation of estates. These are but a few examples of the meaning of social polarisation which extend far beyond tables indicating growing income inequalities but determining the very possibilities of a meaningful life.

Racism thrives in such a context. Despite the gains that have been made by some as a result of race and sex discrimination policies at national and local levels, for the majority of black people both in Britain and elsewhere in Europe or the USA their deteriorating social and economic conditions have seen an increase in racism. For as Sivanandan has explained, the battle for survival in a context where to all real purposes the people have been abandoned both by companies and by the state, the possibilities for internecine conflict drawing on centuries of sedimented and constantly renewed ideologies and practices of racism are greatly increased:

Racism and imperialism work in tandem, and poverty is their handmaiden...it is that symbiosis between racism and poverty that, under those other imperatives of multinational capitalism the free market and the enriching of the rich, has come to define the 'underclass' of the United States and, increasingly, of Britain and western Europe. It is not so much a class that is under as out - out of the reckoning of mainstream society: de-schooled, never employed, criminalised and locked up or sectioned off. If they are an under-class, they are an under-class within that deprived, immiserated third of society that monetarism and the market have created - a replica of the Third World within the first. And it is that one-third society, asset-stripped of the social and economic infrastructure that gave it some sense of worth and some hope of mobility, that provides the breeding-ground for fascism. It is there, where the poorest sections of our communities, white and black, scrabble for the left-overs of work, the rubble of slum housing and the dwindling share of welfare, the racism is at its most virulent, its most murderous. And that is the racism which interests me - the racism that kills - not so much the racism that discriminates. Not because racial discrimination is not important, but because it is racist violence that sets an agenda for state racism, official discrimination, in particular (Sivanandan, 1996, p. 67).

Resistances

In presenting this analysis of 'dismal times' it is important to note that there has been resistance at a variety of levels to this neo-liberal onslaught both in Britain and elsewhere. Some of it has been spectacular as in the case of the poll tax rebellion and at moments during the course of the 1984/5 miners' strike. There have also been the momentous uprisings that have punctuated the 1980s and 1990s in Brixton, Toxteth, Newcastle and of course Los Angeles amongst others. With regard to these latter explosions there is still much debate over their meaning with some such as Campbell (1993) arguing that they exemplify the damaged character of abandoned communities rather than an expression of resistance. This is an important rejoinder to those of us who are desperate to identify opposition and possibilities of popular resistance where we can unthinkingly interpret the howls of despair as the growls of resistance.

Nevertheless, in often unpublicised and little commented upon activities there is substantial evidence of thousands of popular developments which do reflect peoples' struggles to transform or improve their circumstances and which counter the state's abandonment of the black and working class poor. Many of these initiatives embody principles and practices which explicitly or implicitly reject those now evident in official agencies. They are often characterised by extraordinary levels of ingenuity and creativity and explode the stereotypes of the underclass with its notions of intellectual and moral depravity. The scope of these initiatives is extensive and includes credit unions, LET schemes, community education and health initiatives, play groups, day centres for older people, youth projects, well women centres, schools, law centres, drama and theatre as well as the more usual residents and community organisations. Together they constitute, despite their sometimes temporary character, a sphere of activity that deserves to be conceptualised as 'popular welfare'. Certainly, many of them in their organisation and concerns with inclusivity, their disdain for bureaucratic and professional forms, their challenge to the statutory systems of welfare agencies and systems that would more appropriately meet human need. Moreover, despite being described as single issue politics - and in so doing being marginalised - many of these community initiatives provide the spring board and infra-structure that allows communities and neighbourhoods to mobilise at times of severe or particular threat or to participate in a wider politics of change. The history of the civil rights movement in the USA in the 1960s, or against apartheid in South Africa highlights the importance of these popular welfare organisations in such developments. Likewise the bulletins of *Statewatch* and the Campaign against Racism and Fascism illustrate their ongoing importance in many British neighbourhoods threatened by fascist and racist attacks where it has been through grass roots community organisations that both black and white people have come together to drive fascists from their streets (see Sivanandan).

The extent of these initiatives has to be considered as remarkable given the uncompromising and difficult circumstances in which they have developed. It must also be noted - and there is insufficient attention given to this - that the daily survival of so many people who daily encounter the social violence of the state the economy without succumbing to the corrosive impact of systemic disrespect, is equally remarkable and is a profound factor informing the sense of historical optimism of those who believe in the possibilities of a future where humanity and social justice will prevail. However, despite this historical optimism, we do need to recognise that we are in the midst of miserable times - not for the first time - where in the words of one of Hollander's protagonists (1997) we are living through a period of 'circumstantial pessimism'. In such a period, popular welfare activity provides in Raymond William's words, 'resources of hope' but on the other hand they too struggle to survive and there is nothing like growing and enduring poverty to exhaust the morale and energy of the most committed activists.

The onslaught

This is most apparent when we look at that bottom third of society in societies such as the UK and the USA. The extent of the onslaught on this bottom third has been dramatic in both its scale and speed. In both societies, and this is true for countless others from Latin America through to Australasia, there has over the recent past been a dramatic redistribution of resources from the poor to the rich. In the British context, Davies notes with respect to shifts in public spending that:

> The financial result of all this activity was stunning. By 1987, Mrs Thatcher's cuts in the welfare state had yielded a total saving of £12 billion. Some of this was used to pay off public debt...Some was used to fund huge increases in military spendings. But most of it - £8 billion -was used to pay for cuts in taxes for the most affluent (Davies, 1997, p. 293).

The Rowntree inquiry group into income and wealth noted amongst its conclusions that in "many areas of the UK living standards and life opportunities of the poorest are simply unacceptably low in a society as rich as ours" (Rowntree, 1995). Likewise, the United Nations Monitoring Committee when looking at the Uk's progress with respect to meeting the requirements of the UN Convention on the Rights of the Child (signed by Margaret Thatcher in April 1990) observed that no country had experienced such an increase in inequality - over 300% between 1979 and 1995 - which was exemplified by the increase in child poverty from 10% to 31% of all children over that period. The monitoring committee further noted that this was not a reflection on the enrichment of the wealthy simply increasing relative poverty. Rather, the poorest in 1995 had 17% less resource in absolute terms than they had in 1979. As Peter Townsend observed, this dramatic redistribution from the poor to the rich "is the biggest single recent change in British society, and it has many ramifications: it has to be given priority in political discussion" (1995, p. 145).

Within this overall development, the position of the black working class and poor has markedly worsened:

> Blackness and poverty are more correlated than they were some years ago. In spite of government concern with racial disadvantage, and the undoubted limited success of positive action and equal opportunities in helping to create a black middle class, the condition of the black poor is deteriorating (Amin and Leech, 1988, cited Oppenheim, 1993, p. 115).

Oppenheim (1993) succinctly highlights this critical racialised dimension to poverty in Britain - the manner in which black workers are squeezed further out of secure employment and into the increasingly insecure low waged sectors of the economy such as hotels and catering; their disproportionate experience of long term unemployment; and the discriminatory systems of state welfare. Thus, although Britain may now have a black middle class, may have some network of equal opportunities policies, and may have some sort of black presence in key institutions, this should not be allowed to disguise the more pertinent facts that as a whole, the plight of Britain's black population is significantly worsening.

Relying on repression

> We are in the grip of the post-modern vagabond. We have expensively constructed slums full of layabouts and sluts whose progeny are two-legged beasts. We cannot cure this by family, religion and self-help. So we will have to rely on repression. (Bruce Anderson, advisor to Conservative prime ministers during the 1980s and 1990s, cited Davies, 1997, p. 303).

As indicated above, the responses to these dramatic social developments at the level of the state, especially in the UK and the USA, have been and continue to be authoritarian rather than compassionate and humanitarian. Within the US/UK capitalist axis, in contrast to the capitalisms of continental Europe, the years of the social democratically informed welfare state are rapidly coming to be seen as an aberration. In this sphere of capitalism, the political elites whether under the aegis of Thatcher and Reagan or now Clinton and Blair, have expanded much effort in decrying this earlier welfare settlement as being largely worthless for the new realities, as well as being deeply flawed on its own terms. Much use is made of globalisation to justify this shift. It is presented as an almost immutable externality over which nation states have little purchase and which must be accommodated to if future prosperity is to be assured. As Massey noted:

> Globalisation in this version is a *deus ex machina*, and we had just better get used to it...And this in turn has further effects. For this discourse of inevitability serves to hide two things. First, it hides the possibility that there may be alternatives. And, second, it hides the agencies and thus

the interests, involved in the production of globalisation in this form (Massey, 1997, p. 9).

That other comparable societies including Japan and much of continental Europe have not shown such a thirst to dismantle their state social welfare provision or to embrace new forms of social violence as a key strategy for managing the ramifications of deepening social polarisation is largely and conveniently ignored. Instead, we find in both the UK and the USA, political leaders and social commentators vilifying the social democratic welfare system for its expense and its assumed capacity for demoralising the poor by undermining their desire for waged work through inducing welfare dependency. Threaded through these accounts is what Massey discerned as 'heroic impotence' (1997, p. 9). which is largely a new spin on Margaret Thatcher's refrain of there being no alternative. In the new global context where competition is all, Britain, we are told, can no longer to spend so much on social welfare. Quite simply, this is a travesty of the truth.

Threaded through these generalised accounts we are presented with case studies of black welfare mothers in the US who are 'looting' Aid for Families with Dependent Children (AFDC), their counterparts in Britain who despite their many assumed inadequacies are experts at manipulating the welfare state to secure housing and benefits, working class male youth who have lost the will to find a job and so forth, all of which are presented as 'proof' of the need to reform welfare. According to Frank Field, who was appointed as Minister for Welfare Reform in the new Labour Government of 1997, the 'old' welfare state had created a "nation of cheats and liars" (cited Novak, 1998, p. 6) whereas for Clinton it was a system which "pay(s) people for doing nothing" (cited Sklar, 1995, p. 124).

A number of writers have drawn attention to the ruthlessness of Anglo-American capitalism as one of its enduring and distinctive characteristics. Chomsky for example, in his powerful critique of Angle-American conquest, chillingly demonstrates the extent to which "savage injustice" has been a hall mark of its 500 years of global domination (1993, p. 5). Likewise, in her short account for UNICEF of child neglect in rich nations, Hewlett concluded that it was possible to discern an Anglo-American cluster of societies in contrast to continental Europe and Japan with respect to policies supportive of children and families. In the former she observed, an "anti-child spirit is loose in these lands" (1993, p. 2) and locates this in large measure as a consequence of the idolisation of free markets.

Throughout the Anglo-American world the pattern is the same. Unfettered markets do not seem to work on either the social or the economic front. After approximately a decade of market forces, growth rates in the increasingly 'private' economies of Australia, Canada, New Zealand, the United Kingdom and the United States stubbornly lag behind the supposedly welfare-ridden, inefficient economies of Europe...Any nation that allows large numbers of its children to grow up in poverty, afflicted by poor health, handicapped by inferior education, deserted by fathers and cut adrift by society, is asking for economic stagnation and social chaos, and will get it - richly deserved (Hewlett, 1993, pp. 53-4).

It is beyond the scope of this chapter to detail the specificities of this brutalising heritage or the reasons for the collapse and discrediting of social democratic welfare regimes in the Anglo-American world. But it is nevertheless important to recognise that there is a dreadful continuity within these societies in their tendency to revert to authoritarianism and violence in the management of social division, inequalities and injustice. This is especially evident when the influence and countervailing forces of what can loosely be described as the labour movement and other progressive social forces are so weak as has been the case over the last quarter of the twentieth century. Both objectively and subjectively, this period can be characterised as a period in which the class forces are in favour of capital as against labour. It is this configuration and relationship, exemplified by decisive shifts in the waged labour market - unemployment, lower wages, casualised and part-time work, insecure employment - which allows capital to 'win back' welfare concessions made earlier in the century and to introduce wide ranging legislation intended to shackle and diminish the influence of workers' organisations. Furthermore, in their pursuit of political power, all the major political parties that once claimed some relationship with the more powerless in their societies have moved decisively to the right. In so doing, and this is exemplified by New Labour in Britain and the new Democrats in the USA, they have clearly abandoned the poor in their pursuit of middle England (white and middle class) and middle America (white and middle class).

Recent developments within the labour market have given rise to a social and political terrain in which capitalism in its core centres can no longer use steadily rising incomes and prosperity as a means of securing social cohesion. This is simply not considered possible in a world where technological developments, globalised communication and productive forces contribute to the creation of large sections of the able-bodied adult

18

population who, to all intents and purposes, are defined as surplus to requirements. And unlike earlier phases in the historical development of capitalism, there is no longer any anticipation of a future that will need this surplus. Thus, there is no longer the same imperative to maintain and sustain the surplus in a state of physical, social and political readiness to 'rejoin' the market. Of course, all of this reasoning is within the paradigm of Adam Smith's 'vile maxim of the masters' which does not countenance the possibility that the wealth of nations could possibly be managed or even imagined in accordance with other more human principles. The words of Keynes in his *Essays in Persuasion* come to mind here when he described capitalism as that 'extraordinary belief that the nastiest of men for the nastiest of motives will somehow work for the benefit of all' (cited Hewlett, 1973, p. 51).

We now confront a strange paradox whereby the Anglo-American political elites have determined that the future for the new surplus should not be secured through state welfare policies but through waged work - welfare to work - at a time when what work is available is commonly low paid, insecure, part-time and generally mind numbing. Political leaders, with little challenge in their debating chambers of in the media, are proceeding to dismantle welfare entitlements on the grounds that paid work is more dignifying and a route out of long-term welfare dependency. But what paid work? under what conditions and at what rates of remuneration? In both the US and the UK we are witnessing a major reduction in manufacturing employment - the highest paid and most secure sector of the economy. In its place is the service sector, notorious for its low pay, insecurity, dangerousness, anti-union, and mindless employment. Contrary to statements about the future of work being all about high tech work for an increasingly educated workforce, the reality is that the projections for the greatest expansion in employment is in poorly rewarded, part-time and highly exploited work including nursing assistants, waiters and waitresses, security guard, cleaners, caretakers, cashiers and sales clerks (Hollander, 1997, p. 225). Employment in these jobs may take a person off the welfare roll but it will not necessarily lift them out of poverty and on to the promised land of dignity and well-being.

Welfare to work offers a most limited and pessimistic vision for the future. There can be no illusion that a part-time job at an out of city shopping complex is the route for overcoming social exclusion and alienation. To have any hope at all of becoming a meaningful policy for managing the plight of those deemed to be 'surplus to requirements' the alternatives have to become ever more draconian - how else to make work in a fast food outlet remotely attractive? Hence the attention to recasting the welfare entitlements where benefits are not simply reduced but are made more and more unpleasant to claim (the revamping of the 1834 Workhouse test). It also helps to explain the quite dramatic expansion of the prison system in both the US and the UK.

The Gulags of the West

> But in their eagerness to outdo one another on law and order toughness, the politicians have not only ignored the expense and injustice of their prisons policy, but also over-estimated its effectiveness...There is little proof of any simple connection between imprisonment rates and crime (*Economist*, 15th March 1997).

In both countries the 1990s have seen dramatic increases in the prison population. Since coming to power in 1992, Clinton has overseen the prison population rising from 1.2 to 1.8 million. Currently, six million Americans are under the supervision of the criminal justice system - in prison, on probation, awaiting trial or on the run, including 40% of all young blacks in Washington DC (*Observer*, 8th Feb 1998, p. 28). A similar trajectory is evident in Britain with the prison population at new record levels at nearly 64,000 having risen from 40,000 in just over five years (*Observer*, ibid.). With the British prison population increasing by 1,000 a month it is now estimated that a new prison is required every fortnight. In both societies, despite disquiet in their respective prison services about their capacity to manage these increases in a context of ensuring that the prison experience is felt as punishment by those inside, there is no widespread sense of outrage as to what is happening. Instead the discourse is predominantly one of prison 'working' with the demand from the popular press that judges and courts should continue to imprison offenders. Prison it appears works in that it takes the criminal 'out' of circulation; it is not a comment about the rehabilitative effectiveness of prison where there is considerable realism that it has a largely negative impact.

These developments are as highly illustrative as changes in the welfare system of the manner in which the centre-right governments of Britain and the USA are seeking to manage their surplus populations who constitute the vast majority of prisoners. The rapid expansion of imprisonment is unambiguously authoritarian and targeted quite deliberately at those who are deemed to be the most troublesome, namely young black men. What Marable notes for the US is equally true for Britain;

The racial oppression that defines US society as a whole is most dramatically apparent within the criminal just system and the prisons. Today, about one-half of all inmates in prisons and jails - or more than three quarters of a million people - are African-American (Marable, 1997, p. 44).

Black people (are) seven times more likely to be imprisoned than white people; 547 per 100,000 compared with 77 (per 100,000) for whites in England and Wales. (*Guardian*, 9th April 1994).

According to the *Observer* columnist Nick Cohen, 'it is not too fanciful to talk of a prison state in the land of the free' and he continues,

New Labour says it wants to imitate Clinton's success in reducing unemployment. It doesn't seem to understand that Clinton is keeping the jobless figures low by jailing the poor instead of supporting them (*Observer*, 8th February 1998, p. 28).

Such is the scale of investment in prisons that one is tempted to suggest that on current trends that we shall soon be describing the British and American economies as prison/industrial complexes. Whatever gains they bring to those private corporations now given such a prominent role in the building and running of prisons (see Marable, 1997, p. 44), for the dispossessed they epitomise their abandonment as human beings. The conditions in which they are housed, their vulnerability to arbitrary violence and abuse, are symptomatic of their perceived worthlessness. In the US moreover, we are seeing new brutalisms as increasing number of states introduce three strikes and out measures which condemn offenders to life in prison with no hope of parole. Then of course there is the growing use of executions, which have every possibility of being extended as the costs of imprisonment increase. In the process, the notion that prisons are only for the worthless - Anderson's post modern vagabonds - is reinforced and the public is further exposed to the idea that the only response to such a threat from within is through the most pitiless punishments.

This increasing use of prisons and the ongoing onslaught on welfare entitlements are part and parcel of the new politics of repression and pessimism by which we are encouraged to understand the most impoverished and vulnerable as being beyond redemption and that their position in society is an accurate reflection of their worthlessness. We are encouraged in this thinking by endless rounds of scapegoating and demonising in which specific groups are highlighted for castigation and rejection. In all of these discourses that of racism is never far from the surface, and in attacks on lone parent families in the USA, and on young male offending in both Britain and America has been explicit. The consequences are however consistent in suggesting particularities instead of similarities, of focusing attention downwards rather than upwards. As Sklar has argued:

> Racist and sexist scapegoating make it easier to forget that the majority of poor people are white. Scapegoating makes it easier to treat inner-city neighbourhoods like outsider cities - separates, unequal and disposable. Scapegoating encourages people to think of 'the poor' as the 'other America'. Them and not US. That makes it easier to divide people who should be working together to transform harmful social and economic policies. makes it easier to write off more and more Americans as Untouchables. makes it easier to leave unjust economic practices untouched.

> Many white men who are 'falling down' the economic ladder are being encouraged to believe they are falling because women and people of colour are climbing over them to the top or dragging them down from the bottom. That way they will blame women and people of colour rather than the system (Sklar, 1995, p. 117; see also Kushnick, 1997, p. 182).

The fissures of racism, sexism and intra-class division are singly or in combination being ruthlessly exploited and worked on to divide and fragment those who have suffered most. The evidence of increased race and gender violence are but two of the more salient indicators of this damage. Some might wish to argue that this is an over-exaggeration, after all have we not seen in these societies legislation and commissions created to progress equal opportunities and combat racism and sexism? But as Sivanandan observed:

> In some senses, this is true. There has indeed been some sort of economic and social mobility for African-Caribbeans and Asians in the middle tranches of society. Equal opportunities and the Race Relations Act have worked for them.
> But, in the deprived and inner-city areas, on the dilapidated housing estates, in that third of society which has been socially and economically excluded for almost a generation, racism has got worse. There, racial

22

attacks are on the increase, racial harassment is commonplace and fascism finds ready recruits. People who have defended their communities or themselves against such attacks, like Satpal Ram, are themselves arrested and arraigned - while the murders of promising youngsters like Stephen Lawrence and Manish Patel go unsolved and unpunished. And, in schools, young black boys are excluded at a rate four times higher than white boys (Sivanandan, 1998, p. 73).

These are but some ramifications of the neo-liberal project that flow as surely as night follows day from the new brutalities of capitalism. Broad swathes of our society are now compelled to live in third world conditions competing to survive and make sense of their lives as the state withdraws an already minimalist network of welfare resources; where the prospects of secure and meaningful employment are scarce; where the physical infrastructure crumbles and decays; and where the prevailing dominant set of explanations identifies and scapegoats vulnerable single mothers and young men (black and white) as some of the chief culprits.

Conclusion

They are in the deepest sense redundant. Looking at them from a strictly economic point of view, these former workers and their families are worthless. More than that, they are an expensive burden- at least they will be if they are to be properly housed and clothed and fed, if they are to be given decent schools and hospitals. So, why bother?...From an economic point of view, they are worth nothing, they will be given the bare minimum. For these redundant humans, the creation of poverty is the final solution (Davies, 1997, pp. 299-300).

There is much in this chapter which needs further elaboration and consideration and, given its scope and unrealistic ambition there are a number of inexcusable omissions especially in relation to exploring the gendered experience of and relationship to poverty and social violence. Much of the terror of poverty falls on women. They are seen by some such as Charles Murray as the cause of the underclass and unmarried mothers in particular have been singled out for blame and condemnation as a consequence. It is still largely women who try to manage the consequences of poverty and deprivation in households, starving themselves in some cases, in order to feed their partners and their children. It is the women who overwhelmingly stay with children when relationships fail and who are beaten and degraded as the social violence of poverty and despair is turned inward. This gendered dimension is also of particular importance when one begins to explore that cluster of activities which I have conceptualised as 'popular welfare' for women are commonly at the forefront of these initiatives (see Campbell, 1993).

With probably insufficient evidence in parts, the chapter has attempted to convey something of the contemporary context of race and class. It implicitly takes issue with those traditions in social policy writing that ignore the dimensions of human misery which lie behind the tables and charts which plot the parameters of poverty and inequality. It seeks to use words such as violence and hatred that are common in some psychology writings in this area (Hollander, 1997) but rarely appear in books on social welfare. I have done this not to be sensational but because I think such concepts accurately portray what is happening.

My main concern has been to convey a sense that at the end of the twentieth century we have particularly in the USA and Britain a process underway with respect to the management of surplus/residual populations which is highly disturbing in its ruthlessness and barbarism. It is a process which is targeting the so called failures - those whose relationship to the economy and to all mainstream institutions is marginal, largely as a consequence of the circumstances of their birth. In the USA the discourse of social violence is heavily racialised whereas in the UK this is more discrete, yet in both societies the condition of the greater proportion of the populations of people of colour is deteriorating. It is an aspect of the new ruthlessness that the primary explanations of this worsening plight are laid at the doors of its victims, who in turn are deemed increasingly to be beyond redemption. Locking them up in prison and throwing away the key exemplifies this approach.

Overall, it is a context that ought to provoke deep anxieties amongst those who are committed to social justice and human dignity. The dehumanisation and demonisation of the new surplus populations create an environment in which it is possible to cultivate and create ever more punitive policies and practices. The resources of authority are considerable in this respect and the discourses of racism which are so pervasive in both Britain and the USA can be expected to be increasingly drawn upon. At the same time, it is evident that there are many who are becoming increasingly concerned about deepening inequalities and poverty. In our different places and in our different ways we must continually dedicate ourselves to confronting these injustices and policies of hatred. Above all, the seriousness of the situation we now confront must more clearly inform our activities and ideas to ensure this period of circumstantial pessimism is quickly brought to an end.

References

Abrams, P. (1968), *The Origins of British Sociology 1834-1914*, University of Chicago Press: Chicago.

Amin, K. and Leech, K. (1988), 'A new underclass: race and poverty in the inner city', *Poverty*, No. 70.

Campbell, B. (1993), *Goliath*, Methuen: London.

Davies, N. (1997), *Dark Heart*, Chatto and Windus: London.

Giles, C. et al. (eds) (1996), *Living with the State*, The Institute for Fiscal Studies: London.

Gouldner, A. (1970), *The Coming Crisis of Western Sociology*, Heinemann: London.

Hollander, N.C. (1997), *Love in a Time of Hate*, Rutgers University Press: New Jersey.

Hewlett, S.A. (1993), *Child Neglect in Rich Nations*, UNICEF: New York.

Kushnick, L. (1997), *Race and Class*, Rivers Oram Press: London.

Marable, M. (1997), *Black Liberation in Conservative America*, South End Press: Boston.

Massey, D. (1997), 'Problems with globalisation', *Soundings*, Issue 7, pp. 7-12.

Novak, T. (1998), 'Poverty as a Relationship', unpublished paper presented to the Rowntree Conference, March 1998, York University.

Oppenheim, C. (1993), *Poverty the Facts*, CPAG: London.

Raup, E. (1996), 'Politics, Race and US Penal Policies', *Soundings*, Issue 2, pp. 153-168.

Roberts, J. and Kraemer, S. (1996), 'Introduction: Holding the Thread', in Kraemer, S. and Roberts, J. (eds), *The Politics of Attachment*, Free Association Books: London, pp. 1-20.

Joseph Rowntree Inquiry Group (1995), *Income and Wealth*, Joseph Rowntree Foundation: York 1995.

Sklar, H. (ed.) (1980), *Trilateralism: The Trilateral Commission and Elite Planning for World management*, South End Press: Boston.

Sklar, H. (1995), 'The dying American dream', in Berlet, C. (ed.), *Eyes Right!*, South End Press: Boston, pp. 113-134.

Sivanandan, A. (1996), 'La trahison des clercs', *Race and Class*, Vol. 37(3), pp. 65-70.

Sivanandan, A. (1998), 'The making of home to the beat of a different drum', *Race and Class*, Vol. 39(3), pp. 73-75.

Townsend, P. (1995), 'Persuasion and Conformity: An assessment of the Borrie Report on Social Justice', *New Left Review*, No. 213, pp. 137-150.

Wilkinson, R.G. (1996), *Unhealthy Societies*, Routledge: London.

2 Anti-racist Policies and Practice: The Case of CCETSW's Paper 30

Laura Penketh

Introduction

This chapter aims to explore the development of the Central Council for Education and Training in Social Work's (CCETSW's) anti-racist initiatives as outlined in the 'Rules and Requirements for the Diploma in Social Work' (Paper 30) (CCETSW, 1989a). The main purpose of this exploration is to analyse this development as an example of a 'top-down' policy initiative which attempts to deal with issues of inequality and racism. Paper 30 was in many ways a remarkable initiative. It emanated from a government agency and contained within its remit a recognition that Britain was an institutionally racist country, and that social work education and training should, as a consequence, be structured by anti-racist concerns. For academics, practitioners and anti-racist activists, such a clear statement represented a significant and important step forward.

The aim of the chapter is not to dismiss this initiative, but rather, to look at how it came about, how it fared in practice, what barriers it came up against, what reaction it generated and what political response it produced. Thus, the chapter will analyse CCETSW's Paper 30 as an anti-discriminatory initiative which attempts to deal with the manifestation of racism in social work agencies by imposing legitimate modes of practice onto social work students and practitioners from 'above', by regulating training and assuming this will filter through to practice. One of the major concerns of the chapter will be to look at the successes and failures of this policy, and barriers which prevented its constructive implementation and operationalisation. An analysis of these developments will be based on research which was undertaken at the University of Central Lancashire between 1990 and 1992 which, in the context of CCETSW's anti-racist developments, explored the implications for social work education and training by interviewing a number of black and white students and their respective practice teachers on placement in social work agencies.

In concluding the research it became evident that whilst anti-racist initiatives are clearly relevant to social work education and training in a society structured by inequality, policy initiatives by themselves do not necessarily invoke change in institutions such as social work agencies. It also became apparent that such policies are always vulnerable to counter-policies from political opponents hostile to anti-racist perspectives. As such, 'top-down' policy initiatives are relatively limited in the extent to which they alone can develop anti-racist practice within welfare agencies which themselves operate in ways that reflect and embody institutional racism. Consequently, I argue that, in order to be effective and fully integrated into practice, policy prescriptions need to be located more fully within wider counter-structural movements against racism. That is, they must be more fully integrated with the struggles of the oppressed against all manifestations of structural and institutional racism.

Setting the context

Initially, it is worth analysing why an anti-racist commitment should have been incorporated within social work education and training at a time when the Thatcherite project was apparently in full swing (Hall and Jacques, 1983, Gamble, 1988). According to Gamble (1988), part of the Thatcherite political agenda was to establish a new hegemony around a commitment to the free economy and the strong state, and for Hall (1985) central to obtaining such hegemony was the development of an authoritarian populist ideology, within which were implicit references to the 'traditional values' of family, nationhood and 'race'. Thatcherism clearly represented a new political formation, drawing on the tradition of 'organic, patriotic Toryism' combined with a 'virulent brand of neo-liberal economics and an aggressive religion of the market' (Hall, 1985, p. 16), and was a relatively successful attempt to move mainstream political thinking in this direction, shaping a new party political consensus. However, it was never the case that these ideas and values were unproblematically accepted *in toto* by the majority of the population. First, the rhetoric of Thatcherism masked the reality, which often represented a much less dramatic break within economic and social policy than the claims would lead us to believe (Johnson, 1990). Further, as Curran made clear in his critique of hall's thesis:

Hall's contention that Thatcherism has undermined "the popular case for welfare socialism" and "displaced reformist politics" is contradicted by extensive survey data. A recent survey report (*British Social Attitudes: the 1984 Report* edited by Roger Jowell and Colin Airey) reveals, for example, that the overwhelming majority of people oppose reduced spending on health and education (85%), oppose development of a two-tier health service (64%) and...those who think that benefits are too high and discourage people from looking for work (35%) are outnumbered by those who think that benefits are too low and cause hardship (46%) (quoted in Callinicos, 1985, p. 151).

Even at its height, Thatcherism generated significant popular political opposition (for example, the Miners Strike of 1984/85 and the Poll Tax rebellion, 1989/90). One form of opposition to the Thatcherite project was the growth of a 'reformist left solution' in and around the Labour party. The early 1980s saw the growth of a new 'local socialism' when a number of left-wing Labour councils attempted to use their local base to promote alternative, non-market based political solutions to local problems (Boddy and Fudge, 1984, Anderson and Cochrane, 1989). At the same time, the growth of both Women's and Black Sections represented an important political development within the Labour party. In some senses these developments represented conflict over strategy within the New Social Movements. During the 1960s such groups had been much more concerned with politics outside Parliament and the development of alternatives to mainstream politics. In the 1970s organisations like the Anti-Nazi League, Rock against Racism and the Campaign against Racism and Fascism similarly looked to changes outside dominant political structures, and were relatively successful in uniting black and white youth against racism and nazism. By the early 1980s, the growth of womens' and black sections represented both an acknowledgement of issues of gender and 'race' inequality by the Labour party, and an accommodation with the Labour party by a number of activists from these movements.

Nevertheless, this led to a situation where issues of gender and racism became more visible in Labour Party discussions and documentation, and where Labour controlled councils increasingly adopted Equal Opportunities statements. These developments coincided with the growth of the 'race relations industry' (Sivanandan, 1991), and led to a situation where, despite the ascendancy of the Conservative Party under Margaret Thatcher, there was a developing political culture within the Labour party, local government and the equal opportunities community which stressed the racist nature of British society. This culture, which was to be influential within and upon CCETSW is one factor which helps to explain why, despite a political climate apparently hostile to progressive politics, CCETSW could make a commitment to anti-racist social work education and training. Also, from the mid-1980s onwards, progressive authorities such as Hackney were pressing CCETSW about the inadequacies of much professional social work education in preparing social workers for anti-racist practice.

A second major element in the process was the role played by black activists and academics in the welfare field. In the 1940s and 1950s Britain was a hostile, unwelcoming environment steeped in the ideology of racial superiority, and black organisations were formed around the need to protect black communities (Miles and Phizacklea, 1984). A variety of black organisations were set up during the early 1960s to organise against both discriminatory legislation and racist practices, and the 1970s witnessed an increase in the number of black organisations and pressure groups around the country. Black groups continued to expose the discriminatory practices which the black community faces at the hands of the British state, revealing the racism which young black people endure at the hands of the police and the courts (Gilroy, 1987, Denney, 1983, NACRO, 1993), and resisting discriminatory and negative social welfare developments. For example, during the 1970s and 1980s, black women in particular were involved in tenant's and squatter's campaigns and in struggles against the abuses of the education system (Bryan et al., 1985). The black press, for example *The Voice*, was also influential in the 1980s in documenting the social and economic deprivation and discrimination faced by black families.

Thirdly, and finally, the resistance to discriminatory welfare legislation also manifested itself in the social work arena, where black organisations and black practitioners had, over the years, been increasingly critical of the nature of social services provision for the black community. This was the result of increasing concern that 'patterns of discrimination and disadvantage seem to be reproduced and reinforced within the operations of social work, rather than being compensated for by its provision' (Ely and Denney, 1987, p. 99). During the 1970s black social workers began questioning the content of social work, its relevance to the black community and its ethnocentric nature. This was starkly revealed by the under-representation of black clients in the caring and preventive elements of social work provision (Bryan et al., 1985, Duncan, 1986, Ahmad, 1990), and their over-representation in its controlling side (Dominelli, 1988, Ahmad, 1990, Thompson, 1993). Black people's behaviour and family life were judged particularly harshly by social work professionals, especially in terms of mental health and child care. Black parents were more likely to have their children removed and placed in residential and foster care (Bebbington and Miles, 1989), and to receive more severe diagnoses of mental illness and confinement under the Mental Health Act (Francis, 1991).

Black social workers and black voluntary groups have, over the years, fought to expose the fact that these disturbing trends are a consequence of unacknowledged and unintentional racism based on negative stereotypes and assumptions of black groups. For example, Afro-Caribbean families are often pathologised, with mothers seen as being too strong, whereas the Asian family is seen as problematic because the mother's position is considered weak and uninfluential (Dominelli, 1988, Skellington et al., 1992). Black groups have been instrumental in exposing the destructive effects of these incorrect and negative interpretations of black behaviour and family structures in areas such as child protection (CCS, 1982, Roys, 1988), and in highlighting the need to confront the ethnocentricity which informs the professional judgement of social workers (Arnold and James, 1988). They have also demonstrated the negative effects for the black community of stereotypes expressed in positive terms such as 'Asians look after their own' (Cadman and Chakrabarti, 1991). As a result, much of the work done to make social services accessible and appropriate to the needs of the black community has been done by the black community itself. As Dominelli stated:

It has been black people writing from a black perspective rooted in their experience of racism in Britain that has begun to shift the eyes of white academics and social workers towards racism as a structural phenomenon which permeates every aspect of social work intervention and is reflected in all white social worker's individual practice (1988, p. 400).

So, in terms of contextual setting, we can see that it was a combination of struggle by black social workers and students, in an atmosphere of both a growing awareness and critique of institutional racism within welfare agencies, and the rise of a counter-Thatcherite political opposition within the Labour party, local government and the equal opportunities community which created the 'space' for CCETSW's anti-racist initiatives to develop. These initiatives constituted a systematic attempt to create a set of anti-racist policies for social work education and training by introducing specific anti-racist requirements into the Diploma in Social Work. These requirements in turn had fundamental implications for academics and practitioners involved in social work training, who were now formally required to address issues of racism and demonstrate competence in implementing anti-racist practice. During this period, there were also important staff changes in the upper management of CCETSW. For example, Tony Hall, who came from the British Association of Adoption and Fostering, which had developed progressive anti-racist policies, became a director. Such staff changes made CCETSW particularly receptive to pressures from sections of the profession keen to promote and establish anti-racist policies and practices.

CCETSW - Paper 30

CCETSW responded to the criticisms of welfare practice and the structure of British society by looking at its own role in social work education and training. In general, a number of anti-oppressive initiatives were developed, and although space does not allow us to explore all CCETSW's recommendations, it is useful to outline some of the key developments. These were important, as they demonstrated a serious commitment to look at routes to anti-racist social work practice, and began to question seriously why social work practice was so deficient in anti-racist initiatives.

In November, 1988, the Central Council formally adopted an anti-racist policy which stated that:

> CCETSW believes that racism is endemic in the values, attitudes and structures of British society including that of social services and social work education. CCETSW recognises that the effects of racism on black people are incompatible with the values of social work and therefore seeks to combat racist practices in all areas of its responsibilities (CCETSW, 1991, p. 6).

The Diploma in Social Work (Paper 30) further stipulated learning requirements in relation to anti-racist social work which include:

> Recognising the implications of political, economic, racial, social and cultural factors upon service delivery, financing services and resource analysis;

> Demonstrating an awareness of both individual and institutional racism and ways to combat both through anti-racist practice;

Developing an awareness of the inter-relationships of the processes of structural oppression, race, class and gender, and

Working in an ethnically sensitive way (CCETSW, 1989a, pp. 15, 16, 19).

Paper 30 also included requirements for programmes leading to the Diploma in Social Work. For example, programme providers must develop:

Clear and explicit anti-discrimination and anti-racist policies and explicit practices and procedures which provide evidence that these policies will be implemented and monitored in all aspects of the programme (CCETSW, 1989a, p. 22).

Paper 26.3 (CCETSW, 1989b) which governs the Council's approval of agencies for practice learning and its requirements for the accreditation and training of practice teachers, is an integral part of a commitment to improve the quality of placements for students. Practice teachers, according to this paper, must have the ability to enable students to undertake anti-racist and anti-discriminatory social work and link theory to practice, and practice teachers must keep up to date with current debates. Thus, CCETSW's approval of agencies for practice learning insisted on the provision of learning opportunities within an environment which encouraged anti-discriminatory practice. In 1988, CCETSW also launched its five year Curriculum Development Project (CDP) which included meetings with black students and an all-black conference of students and workers from the North of England. A key factor in the creation of this Project was the Cental Council's concern to meet the complaints from some sections of social work education that there were no relevant texts or curriculum materials through which to deliver anti-racist social work education. The CDP set itself the task of meeting this criticism through the production and publication of anti-racist literature, created by the joint work of students, practitioners, tutors and researchers using a wide pool of knowledge and skills.

The above developments all constituted an attempt by CCETSW to make anti-racism a central requirement of social work training and a central component of good social work practice.

It was in the context of such developments that in 1990 the Department of Social Work at the University of Central Lancashire instigated a piece of research to explore the experiences of black and white students on social work placements. During this period the department of social work had begun to place greater emphasis on and integrate anti-racist education into the social work curriculum, and had taken steps to increase the intake of black social work students. However, these steps had led to the emergence of two fundamental problems for black students in the department. Initially, there was increasing conflict between and amongst black and white students in relation to issues of 'race' and racism, and secondly there was a growing awareness that black students were experiencing substantial difficulties whilst undertaking social work education and training, particularly in the area of practice placements. These difficulties were influential in determining that research was needed to attempt to offer explanations as to why this situation existed, and to increase awareness of and uncover previously unexplored areas of the black student experience. However, it is worth recognising that, during this period, the Department of Social Work was more active and committed to anti-racist practice than other academic institutions in the region. In this respect, its anti-discriminatory initiatives were not typical of developments in other social work departments.

The research project was carried out over a period of two years from 1990 to 1992, and involved interviewing eight black and white students in 1990 (four first year students and four second year students), with six of the first year students interviewed again during their second year in 1991. In 1990 each student was interviewed three times whilst on placement and in 1991 each student was interviewed twice. Students' respective practice teachers were also interviewed once during the course of each placement.

Evidence from the research project began to reveal the pervasiveness of racism within social work agencies and the need for anti-racist policies to counter incidents of racism, the research also exposed the difficulties encountered in implementing anti-racist policies and procedures. The accounts of black students reflected the concerns which had been raised by other black social workers over the years regarding the ignorance, indifference, disinterest and inertia in most social work agencies in relation to 'race' and anti-racist practice. They also revealed the persistence of racist and ethnocentric ideas and practices which have serious implications for the experiences of black students on placement. For example, there is often a failure to recognise or legitimise the racism that they experience which results in the 'de-racialisation' of their experiences. As such, they are somehow expected to reconstruct or forget the racism which is a reality of their personal and professional lives. The accounts of black students also demonstrate that in social work agencies racist incidents are not isolated but occur with alarming frequency and that racism is not only overt, but is reflected, for example, in the attitudes and assumptions of other social work professionals and in the under-representation of black staff and clients.

Below are a representative sample of black students' accounts regarding their experiences of racism whilst on placement and the difficulties in dealing with it. In terms of overt racist comments, one black student was called 'darkie' by an elderly male client who also made derogatory comments about Asian countries. Another student who was involved in a football with other social workers was called 'black bastard' whenever he received the ball, and another stated that 'my practice teacher keeps making subtle racist and sexist jokes'. None of these students felt that their experiences were taken seriously or that they were supported constructively in agencies, and some of the responses made by their respective practice teachers demonstrated how attempts are often made to 'de-racialise' such experiences. For example, in relation to two overt incidents of racism, responses were as follows. One practice teacher responded by saying:

Well, I told the student that you are not always the person that clients expect to see. I also told her that I used to be discriminated against because I look younger than I am, so I have experienced discrimination too.

Another practice teacher 'explained' a fellow social workers' racist comments as follows:

He didn't mean any harm, it's just the sort of bloke he is. He's quick-witted and he thinks that he is being funny.

Responses such as these from practice teachers which undermine black students' experiences of racism in agencies, also diminish students' confidence in raising issues again. As a result, the racism which they experience on placement is often hidden, and students are left to deal with it individually.

Black students also criticised assumptions which were prevalent in agencies regarding the black population. For example, one black student

35

was concerned at the lack of social work provision for black clients and stated that:

> About 20 years ago, you could have said that Asians looked after 'their own', but the younger generations have been brought up here. Yet, if they need help, social workers are still saying "Oh no, they don't need our help, they will resolve the problem within the family network".

Another commented:

> My practice teacher asked me what I would think if they acquired a golliwog doll in the agency and I told her that I would find it offensive. Although there is nothing wrong with the doll itself, it is how it is perceived and what those perceptions have become to mean. My practice teacher has no idea about such issues.

One student was questioned about her ability to work with clients by an associated professional who said:

> Where do you come from? You won't really have any idea or knowledge about the way we live will you?

To which the student replied:

> I have lived in this country for over 20 years and I have been educated here and have worked in social work for quite a while.

These incidents demonstrate the added pressure which black students are subject to whilst on placement, due to inaccurate assumptions which negatively impact on their experiences. They reveal that students are often placed in the stressful situation of having to inform and 'educate' social work staff regarding issues of 'race' and racist practice. Conversely, when a student felt unable to, or chose to ignore discriminatory comments or assumptions, they were often left feeling guilty and inadequate.

Although placements are crucial to the successful completion of social work courses, the research exposed the continuing difficulties which black students have in obtaining placements, and the problems which they encounter whilst placed in agencies. As a result, placements often became a daily struggle for survival, and black students and a minority of white students who challenged racism were often accused of 'being kill joys' or 'having a chip on their shoulder'. Black students were expected to 'fit in' to white eurocentric organisations and prove their ability to work with white clients, whereas white students did not fail on anti-racist criteria and were rarely assessed on their ability to work with black clients. As there had never been any compulsion until CCETSW initiatives in the late 1980s and early 1990s for agencies or practice teachers to address anti-racist issues, black students were often expected to initiate and sustain change around issues of 'race' and racism, whilst being denied the structures, influence and support to make such changes possible.

For example, one black student spoke about attempting to deal with racism whilst on placement. He said:

> I do think it could threaten my placement success, and if other black social workers started challenging the ways of this building then their progress would be seriously undermined. But if they seemed to be getting on with everyone and kept quiet about racism then their chances of success and promotion would be greater.

Another stated:

> As a student you are in a vulnerable position and you really need to put things constructively if you raise issues around racism. You have to do it in a way that doesn't sound like general moaning...if you do feel confident in raising issues then you need someone to back you up as it is impossible when you are a lone voice.

The concept of racism has developed progressively over the years from individualistic explanations based on personal attitudes and behaviour, to a recognition that racism is a phenomenon that exists, and is structured within the practices of all British institutions, including social services departments, local authorities and higher education institutions. This reconceptualisation of racism highlights the manner in which individuals who may be genuinely opposed to racism can behave in ways which inadvertently discriminate against black people by following uncritically, the activities, 'norms' and unquestioned assumptions of the institutions within which they are located. In the research project practice teachers (who were all white) often appeared hostile to, threatened by, and defensive towards anti-racist developments.

For example, one practice teacher spoke of his relationship with a black student as follows:

...it may well be that because this student has been black all her life she has learnt a range of mechanisms for coping with it, and it may not be a problem for her. I think she presents herself in a way that is not a problem for anyone else. But I do know a man who has a problem, and he becomes a problem for other people.

This implies in other words, that being black and assertive over issues of anti-racism is viewed as a problem, whereas racism itself is not.

When questioned about anti-discriminatory issues, and his ability to implement anti-discriminatory supervision, another practice teacher supervising a black student stated quite forcefully:

I am sick to death of apologising for what I am. I have to make all sorts of sacrifices for the sake of being referred to as some kind of social leper.

This response is characteristic of individuals and professionals who resent having to implement anti-discriminatory practice and procedures, and who feel unfairly attacked when asked to do so.

A practice teacher who was supervising a white student made overtly disparaging remarks regarding anti-racist practice when he commented that:

It would be damn well impossible to implement anti-discriminatory practice here, you would have to send students to Bradford...if a black face knocked on a clients door here they would probably be highly suspicious and would wonder whether to let them in.

Yet another practice teacher spoke to his student about the manifestation of racism in the agency in which he was placed. He observed:

There are racist staff in this office, but it is not always blatant racism as we are supposed to be a caring profession. However, there are individuals here who you could call blatant racist bigots, but it is never taken seriously.

It seems that some social workers find it hard to come to terms with the fact that, on the one hand they perceive themselves as working against social injustice, whilst on the other they may be perpetrating it through racist practices. This often contributes to their difficulties in acknowledging the persistence and pervasiveness of racism in social work agencies, and acts as a barrier to implementing anti-racist initiatives. However, it is also

38

necessary to recognise that, during the 1980s, social work as a profession was negatively affected by Thatcherite welfare developments. In a period characterised by widening inequalities and increased poverty in Britain, social workers had to meet expanding need in a climate of severe financial restraint, and at the same time were being undermined professionally (Jones, 1996). In this climate, there was often resentment regarding CCETSW's anti-racist initiatives, especially as social workers and practice teachers were given little preparation or support in enabling them to facilitate such practice.

The research revealed three institutional indicators as being instrumental in determining black students' experiences of anti-racist social work practice. These were the representation of black clients within agencies, the representation of black staff and the effectiveness of anti-discriminatory policies.

An exploration of issues relating to the representation of and resources for black clients was characterised by an enormous disparity in the responses of black and white students. Whereas black students gave in-depth, lengthy and knowledgeable responses and analyses in relation to questions around black client representation, white students' responses tended to be short, patchy, and lacking in critical analysis. Black students were alert to the fact that there were often few or no black clients represented in social work agencies and they analysed this in relation to the inadequacy of resources available and the impact of negative stereotypes on the black population.

Black students made comments such as:

I have been communicating with a client in Gujerati who has problems with post-natal depression...my black clients feel comfortable with me and I can speak their language. I feel I can see their problems from their perspectives and can offer them relevant alternatives. The staff here have been very impressed with my multi-cultural work.

Last year I worked with black clients and although some people felt they could respond to me better than to a white social workers, on the other hand, the Asian children saw me as a threat because I am a professional yet I don't dress like white people do. I think the teenagers in care thought I was trying to convert them back, but if I was going into a family situation then they would open up to me because of the way I dress and because I am educated. In this respect they would think I could give them more help, and the women in particular would be able to relate to me.

Black students also spoke of their overt experiences of racism whilst on placement. For example, a student undertaking a probation placement said:

> I hear racist jokes (in the agency) but I just keep my mouth shut although I do not think that it is acceptable. But I am not surprised to hear them. I have had racial taunts from prisoners, but I can accept that from them more than I can from professionals.

Another female student stated that:

> My practice teacher makes subtle racist and sexist jokes, and at first I got really paranoid about it. He just gets away with it, because people say that "it's just his personality". I used to pick him up on things at first, but as a student you are vulnerable, and then he started saying things like "oh, I don't know if you are going to pass your placement", and then I felt even more vulnerable.

There were a small minority of black students who did have more positive experiences in relation to anti-discriminatory practice, and in these instances, the support and commitment of their respective practice teachers was fundamental.

For example, one student gave the following account:

> I knew early on that I would be fine with this practice teacher. She telephoned me before I came here and she knew I was black and we discussed black issues. I brought the issue of dealing with racism up at the pre-placement visit and was assured that they would be behind me all the way. Also, there is another black worker in this building and I know that they have also supported another black social worker who experienced racism from a client.

Although many white students were less concerned regarding anti-racist practice, and their accounts were much less detailed and revealing, there were a small number who demonstrated a political commitment to anti-discriminatory practice, and their responses were more detailed and revealing than those of white students less knowledgeable, committed and concerned about such practice.

There was a simple disparity when students were questioned regarding black staff representation in social work agencies. Most black students were aware of the general under-representation of black staff, and of their marginalisation when employed in agencies, a situation which acts to

40

facilitate and reinforce dominant white definitions of professionalism in the social work arena. The research revealed, that for a few 'experienced' black social work students, the 'professionalisation' had led to an identification with dominant institutional values that reflected the attitudes of white social workers towards issues of racism and anti-racist practice. This tended to be a result of the overwhelming pressure for unsupported black social workers to conform to dominant 'norms' whilst working in social work agencies.

A number of black students responses to questions around black staff representation were as follows:

> Where I worked before the qualified workers did literally look down on section 11 workers.

> There is a black chap here who is qualified and people are very wary of him and do not make remarks because they know he has got a 'piece of paper' like they have and so he has proved that he is competent. I think he is more accepted because of that.

> It would help to have more black staff but they would have to be the right sort of black worker, in the way that good black workers can give off positive images and get cooperation, then a bad black worker can take it all away again. There are certain ways of trying to change things. If you have a 'bull in a china shop' approach on 'race' then you get people's backs up and they put the shutters up even more than they do now.

With regard to the effectiveness of anti-discriminatory policies in affecting the experiences of social work students whilst on placement, their accounts demonstrated that most social work staff are either unaware or only vaguely aware of such policies. As a result, they were totally ineffective as a tool for exploring anti-racist practice, or for helping students to deal with the racism which they experienced whilst on placement. In spite of this, black students expressed an awareness of the potential value of anti-discriminatory policies, but recognised that, in order to be effective, they need to go beyond rhetoric and be constructively implemented. However, a number of white students and practice teachers appeared to be of the opinion that anti-discriminatory policies were not really important unless there were black clients represented in social work agencies.

Again, below are a representative sample of black students' responses:

I did ask about policies when the placement started, but no one seemed to have any information. There is a lot of talk about 'equal opportunities' but very little in practice and policies are not used.

I have seen some anti-discriminatory policies but they are not implemented and monitored. If policies were used then they would give students confidence.

They may have things on paper but it doesn't mean they take things seriously. I have worked in places where a lot of it comes down to the attitude of workers who will ignore any policies and do what they want to do. It would be nice if people did take them on board, but I know that they are not worth the paper they are written on.

The failure of agencies to recognise and validate the range of racist experiences which were identified whilst they were on placement led to a situation where they experienced racism, yet were then denied any mechanisms or support to deal with it in an effective or constructive manner. This led to feelings of great insecurity and vulnerability for many black students who feared that challenging racism could negatively affect their relationships with other social work staff, and could jeopardise the successful completion of their placements. However, there were differences amongst black students in terms of the way they did deal with racist incidents and attitudes. Generally, those students with the most extensive social work experience in white statutory agencies and/or those students with particularly strong personalities, were the most confident in dealing with racism, although they were still affected by feelings of anxiety in doing so. Black students who lacked previous social work experience and/or lacked personal confidence found it much more difficult to question or challenge racism in social work agencies. In attempting to counter racist stereotypes and assumptions whilst on placement, many black students were also under pressure to play an educating and advisory role in agencies, and were often perceived as being 'experts' regarding issues of 'race' and racism. This ignores and undermines differences amongst black students/the black population, and does not take into account other factors such as class and gender which impact on professional relationships.

In being placed in a situation in agencies where they experienced racism, yet were not afforded any institutional support in dealing with it, the ability of black students to cope with racism, and white students to incorporate anti-racist practice became greatly influenced by their relationships with their respective practice teachers. For example, with a supportive practice teacher who was receptive to issues of 'race' and anti-racist practice, even the most insecure students with limited professional backgrounds were able to raise the issues in a relatively secure and confident manner. Conversely, those students with extensive social work experience and strong personalities struggled to raise issues with an unsupportive practice teacher who was hostile to or defensive about anti-discriminatory practice. In this respect, practice teachers had a great deal of power in determining whether anti-racist practice reached the placement agenda and to what extent. The research project identified three general categories of practice teacher. First, a minority who were receptive to progressive social work developments and the implementation of anti-racist social work practice, who were willing to recognise gaps in their own practice and learn from the ideas which students brought to agencies. Second, a minority who were hostile to such developments and expected social work students to practice in a way which was compatible with established (often racist) 'norms'. Finally, the majority, who felt fearful and defensive regarding the imposition of anti-racist learning requirements due to their lack of personal experience, knowledge, education and training, and who as a result, felt vulnerable, threatened and confused in relation to black student supervision. As a result, most practice teachers were unable to facilitate anti-racist education and training, and failed to support black students constructively whilst they were on placement.

Although academic tutors are involved in supporting and guiding students whilst they are on placement, and also have the responsibility of liaising with practice teachers, there is little evidence that they played a significant role in reassuring students during this period. In some cases, this appeared to be a result of their fears of jeopardising placement opportunities, which made them hesitant and insecure when raising anti-racist initiatives, and they seemed to be aware of the divergence between anti-discriminatory academic input and agency practice.

The evidence presented above demonstrates that, despite CCETSW's anti-discriminatory initiatives, there are fundamental institutional barriers which prevent students from exploring and implementing anti-racist social work practice. The manifestation of institutional racism also contributes to the often negative and disabling experiences of black students whilst on placement. However, as well as barriers within social work agencies to implementing anti-discriminatory practice, there are also 'outside' pressures which can be detrimental to the successful development of anti-racist initiatives. The next section will go on to explore how political pressures in society in the early 1990s also began to negatively impact on the constructive implementation of CCETSW's initiatives.

Backlash: CCETSW's anti-racist policy under attack

Although evidence from the research highlighted the need for CCETSW's anti-racist policies to be sustained *and* developed, constructive implementation of the recommendations has been seriously impaired due to a backlash against such initiatives, and a denial that racism is endemic in British society. Anti-racist social and political developments have been challenged by right-wing gurus such as Charles Murray, who identified anti-racism as left extremism, and who promoted the view that the left are threatening the 'genuine concerns' of the majority in acting in the interests of the minority (Murray, 1990, Searle, 1989). Murray and Hernstein (1994) also attempted to resurrect biological determinism, by reintroducing biogenetic theories which suggest that intelligence and non-conformist and anti-social behaviour are genetic in origin.

Right-wing critics have also been involved in an ongoing assault on CCETSW's anti-racist social work developments, strongly denying the destructive nature of racism in contemporary society. There have been increasing calls for a return to 'traditional' social work skills which deny the need for any fundamental change in social work practice and fail to acknowledge the institutional nature of racism. Black struggles and black experiences are undermined and denied political legitimacy by those who see no need for the development of anti-racist social work practice.

In 1992, Virginia Bottomley, the then Secretary of State for Health and Social Services, took CCETSW to task for too great an emphasis on anti-discriminatory practice in qualifying agencies, and in Autumn 1993, Jeffrey Greenwood in taking over as Chair of CCETSW, defined himself as a supporter of equal opportunities whilst publicly committing himself to 'rooting our politically correct nonsense' (quoted in *The Independent*, 29th August 1993).

The issue of anti-racist social work developments gained substantial press coverage during August 1993, particularly in *The Independent* and *The Observer*. As Jones (1993) stated:

> Over a period of four days, Melanie Phillips in The Observer, Robert Pinker in the Daily Mail and Brian Appleyard in the Independent all had major articles virtually a page in length to lambast social work courses and portray CCETSW and Paper 30 as the cause of doctrinaire and abusive anti-racist perspectives (p. 10).

There were mixed responses in the Letters page of *The Observer* (8 August 1993) to the debate. One contributor stated that:

As a social worker for 16 years I wish I could indignantly deny the allegations about political correctness in social work training made by Melanie Phillips (last week). However, they struck me as all too true, not just at the training level but as management policy in the practice of social work. I am torn between shame on behalf of my profession and relief that its present slavish adherence to rigid dogmas at the expense of intellectual open-mindedness has been exposed.

Another letter (*The Observer*, 8 August 1993) criticising anti-racist social work education came from the Director, Plymouth Guild of Community Service who argued that:

Melanie Phillips is to be congratulated for drawing attention to the takeover of the social work training council by a group of fanatics and zealots, obsessed only with race and gender issues and politically correct expressions. Both the training council and institutions running social work courses seem to have lost sight of what social work is all about.

There were also two letters from those who supported CCETSW's developments and a letter from Tony Hall, then Director of CCETSW, stressing that the developments were not concerned with 'political correctness', but were seeking to ensure that qualifying social workers were able to work effectively in a multiracial and multicultural society. The same debates were also taking place on the letters page of *Community Care* and *Social Work Today* and demonstrate the highly charged and controversial nature of the subject of anti-racist social work.

In spite of evidence citing the persistence of racism in society and in social work agencies and growing media attention to the increasing evidence of escalating racist violence in Britain and the rest of Europe (Patel, 1991), criticisms of anti-racist developments resulted in moves to undermine their relevance and importance in relation to social work education and training, and led to a review of Paper 30. These changes were seen by the government as a triumph of 'common-sense' over 'left-wing politically correct' ideology, and constituted a dilution of CCETSW's commitment to anti-racist practice. Since then, black groups have increasingly voiced their concern that, because of such developments, 'race' issues have been pushed further down the agenda of social work departments, and as a result, are failing to have any lasting impact on social work practice. Their grave concerns regarding the failure of

CCETSW's anti-racist initiatives are given legitimacy by recent social services research which demonstrates that:

41% of black staff, social workers in particular, said they had experienced racism from service users or relatives

27% of black staff said they had experienced racism from colleagues or managers

Most of those affected by racism had not received adequate help and support from their department (Balloch et al., 1997).

At the same time, other important political developments were also undermining the implementation of anti-discriminatory education and training in social work departments. Social workers, students and practice teachers were being affected by moves to weaken and narrow the profession's education and research roots (Jones, 1996), by an increasing focus on the importance of competency based social work training; a development associated with government policy to develop the role of the National Council for Vocational Qualifications. This has led to concern that 'person and social-based knowledge, experience and skills are being redefined in terms which reduce their value and which make social workers and their tasks more easy to manage in the workplace' (Canon, 1995, p. 15). As a result, there is increasing disquiet that these changes will involve the transmission of knowledge and skills for utilitarian objectives devoid of any critical reflection (Humphries, 1993), making it even more onerous for students to implement anti-racist practice whilst on placement. The majority of students participating in this research project found it extremely difficult, and in some cases impossible to challenge white views of professionalism, and changes which reinforce the transmission of dominant values will increase their vulnerability.

Conclusion

This chapter has attempted, in the context of examining CCETSW's anti-racist policy developments, to demonstrate that 'top-down' policy initiatives to deal with issues of inequality are, by themselves, relatively ineffective. It reveals that, whilst anti-racist initiatives and teaching are clearly relevant and necessary in a society structured by inequality, mere policy initiatives do not by themselves necessarily invoke change in the world of work and welfare institutions. They are vulnerable to counter-policies from political opponents hostile to anti-racist perspectives and are relatively limited in the extent to which they alone can develop anti-racist practice within welfare agencies which reflect and embody institutional racism.

The development of Paper 30 and Paper 26.3, demonstrated CCETSW's commitment to developing and facilitating anti-racist social work education and training, revealing a serious attempt to look at routes to anti-racist social work practice. However, the implementation of these policies was influenced by the fact that social work as a practice and social work agencies as state institutions, incorporate a range of contradictory processes and elements. On the one hand, social work pathologises the poor, often limits client access to services, works within government imposed financial limits, and discriminates between the deserving and the undeserving poor. At the same time, social workers intervene in the lives of the most oppressed groups in society, often providing resources and support, and attempting to alleviate their disadvantage and deprivation. Social workers themselves reflect a range of values and assumptions about the nature of society and the causes of its ills, and tend to operate broadly within a range of models which reflect their social values and principles, and consequently their understanding of social work activity. As 'ideal types', these models can be categorised as the conservative, the social-democratic and the radical approach to social work. It is in this context, of social work as a contested and contradictory activity open to a number of interpretations in practice (all be it, within the limits imposed by agencies) that CCETSW's anti-racist initiative can be located as an example of a progressive top-down model for change.

The vast majority of social policy developments are 'top-down policies' which attempt to utilise various forms of legislation, agency rules, institutional working practices and procedures to impose change 'from above'. They are policies which attempt, in different ways, to alter the social world or aspects of social behaviour, in order to establish particular 'norms' and 'goals'. However, in the vast majority of cases such norms represent the dominant assumptions of modern British society. They *assume*, for example, that women will primarily be carers in the home, that gay families are 'illegitimate', that working class families (especially mothers) whose children break the law are bad parents and need lessons in parenting, that working class youth, both black and white, are unruly and need to be controlled, and that black migration (and not white racism) is a social problem. The 'goals' they are trying *to achieve* are 'social harmony and stability', where, as a by-product, people accept their location in the class structure, racism, sexism and homophobia, as natural and inevitable aspects of social life. In this perspective, such acceptance brings stability which, it is thought, allows economic development to proceed relatively unhindered, and with economic advance, there will be a general improvement in the living standards of all. The reality may be somewhat different, but this perspective reflects the goals, or partial goals, of most policy developments.

The label 'top-down' encapsulates two aspects of this model for change. First, it assumes that the social problems of society can only be judged and resolved by the 'far-sightedness', and the political commitment of a particular elite, although 'the elite' may change. For example, it may be the state bureaucracy, a section of the ruling class, a section of the intelligentsia, or more widely a political party. Thus, top-down policies are the norm in a whole range of political regimes, and in this sense, are not necessarily progressive or regressive. Secondly, they are top-down policies because their view of social change is one that relies on the actions and activity of an 'enlightened minority' to improve social life or aspects of social living, by imposing rules and regulations onto the behaviour, actions and activities of the vast majority in society. This in turn, is a political project in two aspects. First, because what 'improving social life' actually means and entails will reflect a variety of political interpretations, values and commitments. Secondly, because it is a model of social change that excludes the majority in discussion, debate and the solutions of social problems, except as mere passive consumers or recipients of policy procedures and change. In this respect, they are the 'acted upon', but not active collective agents in the process of social change (Callinicos, 1985). Thus, what top-down models have in common is their rejection of collective action shaping the world, in contrast to models of change 'from below' which assume the self-emancipation of the oppressed and exploited as central to their political project (cf Draper, 1966/1997). However, what separates various top-down models is the political values they embody and the type of social world they are trying to create.

Although CCETSW's anti-racist policy emanated from the demands of many social workers, black activists and academics (reflecting the demands of individuals and groups 'from below'), it utilised a top-down policy model (albeit a progressive one), whose intention was to impose change in social work education, training and practice. The aim of the policy was to challenge all manifestations of racism in social work (and in some accounts, to challenge all aspects of racism in the social world, cf Mullard, 1991).

In identifying racism as a structural and institutional phenomena built into the historical development of British society, CCETSW's anti-racist

48

perspective reflected a number of radical social work values. However, the perspective was to be adopted and implemented in a hostile political environment (at the general level, in the sense of existing in a society structured by exploitation and oppression, and in the specific circumstances of 'Thatcherite' domination), and in social work agencies structured around institutional racism. It also attempted to impose particular forms of social work practice onto 'conservative' and 'social-democratic' social workers, rather than engaging politically with these workers to win them to anti-racist perspectives *politically*. Therefore, CCETSW's anti-racist initiative was a progressive but politically charged development which was introduced into often hostile agency environments. These were important factors in determining how anti-racist practice fared and progressed in relation to social work education, training and practice.

The research has emphasised the fact that institutional racism remains a key feature in social work agencies. It operates within social work agencies and detrimentally impacts on black workers, students and clients. Further, it is clear that racism as a structural and institutional feature of modern British society, operates in all areas of social life. Thus, there is a clear need for an appropriate anti-racist strategy. However, the findings from research carried out at the University of Central Lancashire clearly question the suitability of a strategy based on the imposition of policies, practices and procedures 'from above' onto workers in the field, and onto agencies which operate in racist ways. The research suggests that the top-down anti-racist model did not enable professionals to practice anti-racist social work, but instead increased their anxieties and vulnerabilities over this particular activity in the wider political climate of the time.

In this sense, the future of anti-racist social work must take a step back. Although anti-racist policies are significant statements of intent and must be supported, they should not be left as an abstract social policy blueprint. Anti-racist statements are necessarily political statements that encapsulate a view of what the world is like, and it is incumbent upon anti-racist activists to engage with those around them to convince them of the validity of their perspective. A perspective based on winning over increasing numbers of social workers to anti-racist practice, of breaking down barriers between social work agencies and the black community, and showing the relevance of anti-racism to social work intervention, has a greater chance of establishing a set of procedures and practices that are 'owned' by social workers who are convinced of their necessity and value as a central tool of the social workers armoury.

References

Ahmad, B. (1990), *Black Perspectives in Social Work*, Venture Press: London.

Anderson, J. and Cochrane, A. (1989), *A State of Crisis: The Changing Face of British Politics*, Hodder and Staughton: London.

Arnold, E. and James, M. (1988), 'Finding families for black children in care: a case study', *The Jewish Journal of Sociology*, Vol. 30, No. 2, December.

Balloch, S. et al. (1997), *The Social Services Workforce in Transition*, National Institute of Social Workers: London.

Bebbington, A. and Miles, J. (1989), 'The background of children who enter Local Authority care', *British Journal of Social Work*, Vol. 19, No. 5.

Boddy, M. and Fudge, C. (1984), *Local Socialism? Labour Councils and New Left Alternatives*, Macmillan: London.

Bryan, B., Dadzie, S. and Scafe, C. (1985), *The Heart of the Race*, Virago: London.

Cadman, M. and Chakrabarti, M. (1991), 'Social work in a multi-racial society: a survey of practice in 2 Scottish local authorities' in CCETSW (1991).

Callinicos, A. (1985), 'The politics of "Marxism Today"', *International Socialism*, 29.

Canon, C. (1995), 'Enterprise culture, professional socialisation and social work education in Britain', *Critical Social Policy*, 42, Winter 1994/95.

Central Council for Training and Education in Social Work (CCETSW) (1989a), *Rules and Regulations for the Diploma in Social Work (Paper 30)*, CCETSW: London.

CCETSW (1989b), *Regulations and Guidelines for the Approval of Agencies and Accreditation and Training of Practice Teachers (Paper 26.3)*, CCETSW: London.

CCETSW (1991), *One Step Towards Racial Justice (the teaching of anti-racist social work in Diploma in Social Work programmes)*, CCETSW: London.

Centre for Contemporary and Cultural Studies (1982), *The Empire Strikes Back: Race and Racism in 1970s Britain*, Hutchinson: London.

Denney, D. (1983), 'Some dominant perspectives in the literature relating to multi-racial social work', *British Journal of Social Work*, Vol. 13, No. 2.

Dominelli, L. (1988), 'An uncaring profession? An examination of racism in social work', *New Community*, Vol. 15, No. 3, April.

Draper, H. (1966/1997), *The Two Souls of Socialism*, Bookmarks: London.

Duncan, D. (1986), 'Eliminate the negative', *Community Care*, 5th June.

Ely, P. and Denney, D. (1987), *Social Work in a Multi-Racial Society*, Gower: Aldershot.

Francis, E. (1991), 'Mental health, anti-racism and social work training' in *CCETSW* (1991).

Gamble, A. (1988), *The Free Economy and the Strong State*, Macmillan: London.

Gilroy, P. (1987), *There Ain't No Black in the Union Jack*, Hutchinson: London.

Hall, S. (1985), 'Realignment or What' in *Marxism Today*, Vol. 29, No. 1.

Hall, S. and Jacques, M. (1983), *The Politics of Thatcherism*, Lawrence and Wishart: London.

Humphries, B. 'Are you or have you ever been...', *Social Work Education*, 12 (3).

Johnson, N. (1990), *Reconstructing the Welfare State*, Harvester Wheatsheaf: Hertfordshire.

Jones, C. (1993), 'Distortion and demonisation: the right and anti-racist social work education', *Social Work Education*, Vol. 12, No. 30.

Jones, C. (1996), 'Anti-intellectualism and the peculiarities of British social work' in Parton, N. (ed.), *Social Theory, Social Change and Social Work*, Routledge: London.

Miles, R. and Phizacklea, A. (1984), *White Man's Country*, Pluto: London.

Mullard, C. (1991), 'Towards a model of anti-racist social work' in *CCETSW* (1991).

Murray, C. (1990), *The Emerging British Underclass*, Institute of Economic Affairs: London.

Murray, C. and Hernstein, R. (1994), *The Bell Curve*, Hernstein Scribner, New York.

National Association for the Care and Resettlement of Offenders (NACRO) (1993), *Awaiting Trial - The Final Report*, NACRO: London.

Patel, N. (1991), 'The curriculum development project: model and process 1988-1990' in *CCETSW* (eds) (1991).

Roys, P. (1988), 'Social Services' in Bhat et al., *Britains Black Population*, Gower, Hants.

Searle, C. (1989), *Your Daily Dose - Racism and the Sun*, Campaign for Press and Broadcasting Freedom: London.

Sivanandan, A. (1991), 'Black struggles against racism' in *Northern Curriculum Development Project* (eds), CCETSW: London.

Skellington, R. and Morris, P. (eds) (1992), *'Race' in Britain Today*, Sage: London.

Thompson, N. (1993), *Anti-Discriminatory Practice*, Macmillan: London.

3 Sharpening the Conceptual Tools: Racial and Ethnic Inequalities in Housing and Policy Intervention

Ian Law

Introduction

The character and extent of racial discrimination in the various sectors of the housing market constitute one of the most well established aspects of racial inequality in modern Britain. The significance of such discrimination in accounting for and explaining the reproduction of racial inequality has, however, frequently been overstated, with a tendency for such arguments to slip into mono-causal accounts which emphasise the structural determination of such practices in limiting provision, or supply, in the housing market (Ginsburg, 1992). Here, the operation of racism, elaborated in its subjective, institutional and structural forms, provides an 'easy' explanation for the development and persistence of racial inequality. The development of a more complex and holistic account of racial inequalities in the housing market must also address a range of other factors, as studies by Sarre et al. (1989), Smith (1991) and Harrison (1995) illustrate.

1   Firstly, the complexity of patterns of demand needs to be taken into account with consideration of preferences, aspirations, choices and household strategies.
2   Secondly, general questions of prevailing market conditions, patterns of housing finance, investment and legislative and policy interventions must be analysed and their differential impact on racialised groups needs to be assessed.
3   Thirdly, linkages between housing and other structures of racial inequality needs to be made, particularly the labour market, education, health, wealth and political power.

This wider perspective will inform the following discussion which will seek to open up the range of issues involved in the operationalisation of the concept of racial inequality in housing and in assessment of policy interventions.

A key concern here is to call for a fresh injection of intellectualism into policy analysis and discussion. Constant critical reflection and checking that our conceptual tools are sharp and 'fit' for the task are required as simplistic or sloppy theorising can undermine our substantive understanding and impede policy intervention. The certainties of previous decades are being swept away; the simple construction of black unity, the primary and determinate effects of racist ideologies, the underlying liberalism of 'race' relations policy, the evidence of black 'under-achievement' and traditional representations of ethnic identity have all been the object of critical reflection. Reflections on the 'end of anti-racism', the 'crisis of anti-racism' and the 'glaring lack of serious debate' over the effectiveness and appropriateness of anti-racist policies and initiatives all indicate the need to focus attention on and improve our analytical understanding of the underlying processes at work. These conceptual and theoretical concerns have emerged alongside increasing recognition of the failure of 1970s race relations legislation in tackling racial discrimination, the failure of 1980s municipal anti-racism in tackling racial inequalities (particularly in the context of growing social inequalities) and the failure of national and international political institutions in halting the rise of racism across Europe in the 1990s (if indeed it is a 'rise' that we have been witnessing). Perceptions of such 'failure' can often be misleading and incorrect. The problems of sloppy, damaging and inaccurate conceptual and empirical analysis which frequently give rise to poor policy is a common theme which is explored in this paper. The complexity of trends and related explanations is often forgotten and misrepresented. Both the increasing inner city concentration and increasing suburbanisation of black minority households belies simple analysis. Social, racial and ethnic inequalities in income and wealth are increasing at the same time as the educational qualifications gap is closing. Minority ethnic groups are travelling along differing and diverging socio-economic trajectories at the same time as there is increasing socio-economic differentiation occurring within specific minority groups. The 'fit' between ethnic categories and inter-subjective ethnic identities is in many cases weak, as perceptions of ethnic and cultural identity change.

But, prior to addressing the concept of racial inequality in housing consideration needs to be given to the extent and effects of embedding notions of 'race' in policy debates.

The use of 'race' in policy discussion

The concept of racialisation, which was first developed by Fanon (1967) and subsequently elaborated by Miles (1989) refers to a dynamic process, an extension or resurgence of racist statements and related behaviour where 'race' is used to perceive and define boundaries between groups of people, for example in British parliamentary discourse where debates from the early 1900s onwards over immigration policy showed such characteristics. In Lloyd's case, the concept is applied to the other central plank of British policy in this field, 'race relations' legislation, and those agencies and institutions concerned with promoting and enforcing related policies. So, racial divisions are seen to have been actively created by policies which have been concerned to challenge racism and racial discrimination. This is seen as resulting from the persistent use of the notion of 'race' in bureaucratic, technical, academic and political discourse. 'Race' has been given an official reality in race relations legislation, race relations policies, race relations courses and programmes of study, and party political agendas. The cumulative effect of which is, for Miles (1993, p. 47) to:

> implicitly (and often explicitly) endorse common sense, and hence sustain an ideology which Barzun called a 'Modern Superstition' (1938) and which Montagu described as 'Man's [sic] Most Dangerous Myth' (1974).

In other words, the continued use of the 'race' idea is seen as reinforcing dominant common-sense ideas that different 'races' exist and have a biological reality. The connection between such scientific racism, with its emphasis on the natural reality of racial difference, and social scientific analysis is quickly condemned when this forms part of a right-wing discourse, e.g. propositions about the lower intelligence of the black underclass by Murray and Hernstein (1994), but tends to be ignored in left-wing discourse, e.g. Sivanandan (1990) attributes 'race' with an independent reality not only in his writings but also in the journal he edits, *Race and Class*.

The rejection of 'race' as an analytical tool in this way raises a number of problems. Firstly, thorough critique of the mythical notions of 'race' and 'race relations' implies that not only are there no real relations between 'races' but that it is meaningless to search for equality or justice between 'races'. Are we to reject these ideas as well? How far should political calculation of the potential effects of using such terms, or indeed research to establish the previous impact of 'race' discourse be considered before use of such terms is dismissed. Secondly, the assumption that challenging racial inexplicitness, or the denial that racism exists, through explicit use of the 'race' idea will inevitably and automatically increase divisions, which previously existed, between racialised groups is highly suspect. The 'race' idea can be employed to articulate strategies of liberation and emancipation, such as black power, and to highlight existing racial divisions in order to facilitate political mobilisation, or policy intervention, without necessarily increasing those divisions. Indeed, it may be established that such action achieved its objective of a reduction of some aspects of racial divisions, for example in political participation. The value of such 'strategic essentialism', where categories of 'race' may be invoked in political struggle cannot be theoretically assumed to have a racist political effect. Is anti-racist work in Britain, however weak, ineffective or constrained to be dismissed because it explicitly uses notions of 'race' in its campaigns, policies and arguments? This argument comes close to the attacks on anti-racism by the New Right (Flew, 1987) where the 'race relations industry' is seen to be actively exacerbating racial conflicts.

The questionable use of the 'race' idea and its deployment in representation and discussion of social and public policy can be resolved if it is seen as with the concepts of ethnicity and nation as having *no necessary political belonging* (Rattansi, 1994, p. 56-57). The use of particular concepts and their discursive articulation with others, e.g. biology, sexual difference, or rights, will determine their political and policy implications. So, it cannot be assumed that the concepts of 'race' and nation will only be used to articulate domination and exclusion or that ethnicity will only be used to articulate cultural pluralism. The problematic nature of the 'race' concept is acknowledged but its use in policy analysis may be sustained where it is treated by social actors as a real basis for social differentiation. It may be used strategically to mobilise a 'black', 'white', 'ethnic' or 'national' constituency and it provides a totem around which racist discourse and discriminatory behaviour may be sanctioned. Its explicit employment, therefore, needs to be treated with suspicion in policy analysis, whether in the simplistic and mythical construction of 'race relations' or in the presentation of evidence of the 'black-white' divide, which Modood (1994) has called 'worse than meaningless' in the reductionist aggregation of ethnic difference. Denial of the explicit use of the 'race' idea in policy making, for example in France, has not stopped racism permeating significant arenas such as immigration policy, urban policy and labour market policies. The political manipulation and mobilisation of 'race' may bear fruit for those with widely differing perspectives, but its use mis-represents and mystifies and as such requires critical analysis. This points to a set of analytical concerns as the object of study. These include, firstly the active construction of the social world by those who articulate racism, secondly the political, economic and ideological processes which have determined the use of 'race' to comprehend patterns of migration and settlement, and thirdly analysis of law, policies and practices which have drawn on ideas of 'race' and which have been concerned to respond to or regulate such real social processes.

The meaning of racial inequality in housing

It is important to acknowledge the contested and differing conceptions of the general idea of equality and, by implication, the meaning of inequality which underlie discussion of 'race' and ethnic divisions. These conceptions include ontological equality, equality of opportunity, equality of condition and equality of outcome. In addition, three problems with these conceptions can be identified; inherent mutual incompatibility, the massive social and political regulation required for policy implementation and conflicts between group equality and individual liberty. In the field of 'race' and housing the implications of these problems and issues have rarely been adequately considered. As Smith has remarked,

> There is too often a tendency to aspire to some abstract state of 'racial equality' without specifying how this might be recognised (1989, p. 186).

The ontological view of racial equality stresses the belief that all people are of equal moral worth. People who are different are recognised to be equal in their fundamental worth. Hodge (1990) elaborates this position but does not address questions of policy or measurement. Ideas of sameness, commonality or proportional views of group equality conflict with this position. The moral notion of equality underlies arguments for universal equal rights of citizenship and equal rights before the law. The dangers of universalist approaches, in a nation where discourse of citizenship have been operationalised in an ethnically differentiated form so as to construct and entrench racialised boundaries, for example in immigration law. Racialised immigration controls have had direct effects on exclusion from social housing as this has created a class of black and minority ethnic people who are legally resident on the condition that they do not have any recourse to public funds (Gordon, 1991). Given the frequent use of universalist discourse to articulate and construct racial exclusion, notions of 'race' specific group equality have often provided a more effective political terrain for the elaboration of anti-racist perspectives. Housing policy in Britain, particularly that determined by local authorities, housing associations and the Housing Corporation, has provided one of the most important arenas for the development, implementation and management of group-based racial equality strategies.

The quality, condition and value of the housing stock across Britain varies enormously. To achieve racial equality, in terms of housing outcomes, would require massive redistribution of wealth particularly in terms of property ownership, major structural changes in political control of housing policy and control of housing institutions and producers, and massive bureaucratic regulation of peoples' access to housing. Yet, this broad, grand notion of racial equality is frequently operationalised as a yardstick to assess overall patterns through measurement and evaluation of indicators of housing outcomes such as tenure and physical and social housing conditions. Measures of housing deprivation are themselves used to indicate socio-economic disadvantage or income differentials, and in local authority resource allocation, for example in the determination of standard spending assessments. Should the goal of racial equality policies be aiming to equalise the representation of ethnic groups across different forms of housing tenure and across the quality range of Britain's housing stock? If observed differences are taken and defined as inequalities then clearly the answer must be yes. But, are we to disregard ethnic differences in tenure preferences? Table 1 indicates tenure outcomes for ethnic groups and preference for a particular type of housing is one of a complex of factors which determines this pattern.

The marked reluctance of Indian, Pakistani and Chinese households to enter or apply for local authority housing may be interpreted as resulting from a combination of negative perceptions of a residualised sector (Habeebullah and Slater, 1990), aspiration to home ownership and avoidance of perceived discrimination and racial attack. Perceptions of the negative utility of council housing may then, for some households, outweigh or override the experience of living in poor physical and social housing conditions, which would itself give priority in terms of entry into social housing if an application was made. For those who measure inequality in terms of differences in outcomes in the housing market, the low level of some minorities in the local authority sector has led to the construction of such differentials as a social problem requiring policy intervention. This leads to consideration of a perennial housing management problem which has surfaced in the literature from the 1960s onwards, how can black and minority ethnic groups be encouraged to move to predominantly all-white housing estates? Whereas from the perspective of these minority group households a move into council housing may be perceived as leading to a significant reduction in the general quality of life, particularly if it is perceived to involve a move to estates where the risks to personal safety are greater and the opportunities for participation in social and community activities are reduced.

Table 3.1
Housing tenure by ethnic group in Great Britain, 1991

Ethnic Group	H'holds (000s)	Owner occupied (%)	Local authority (%)	Rent from Housing Assoc. (%)	Rent from Private L'lord (%)
White	21,026.6	66.6	21.4	3.0	7.0
Ethnic Mins	870.8	59.5	21.8	5.9	10.8
Black	*328.1*	*42.3*	*36.8*	*10.1*	*9.2*
Black-Carib	216.5	48.1	35.7	9.7	5.6
Black-Afr.	73.3	28.0	41.1	10.8	17.8
Black-Other	38.3	36.7	34.5	11.2	13.6
Sth. Asian	*357.2*	*77.1*	*11.1*	*2.5*	*7.6*
Indian	225.6	81.7	7.8	2.2	6.5
Pakistani	100.9	76.7	10.4	2.2	9.6
B'gladeshi	30.7	44.5	37.0	6.1	9.6
Chinese	48.6	56.1	13.1	3.5	17.0
Oth. Asian	59.0	62.2	13.6	4.4	24.5
Other	77.9	53.9	19.3	6.2	18.2
Total	21,897.3	54.0	21.4	3.1	7.1

Source: *1991 Census Local Base Statistics*, in Owen, 1993, p. 8.

Overall, there are broadly the same proportion of white and minority ethnic households in council housing, but most South Asian and Chinese groups are under-represented and black households are significantly over-represented in comparison to white households. It is certainly questionable to use the white norm as the yardstick for assessing inequality, in that consideration of housing provision in relation to housing needs for each ethnic group may be a more appropriate measure of equality. This involves treatment of households with equal respect but with differing levels of need rather than equal treatment of groups that are assumed to have similar levels of need. In general terms, black and minority ethnic households are in poorer quality housing and are in greater housing need than white households (Owen, 1993). Therefore, evaluations of housing outcomes which do not take into account differences in housing needs will underestimate the level of inequality. This has particular importance for the construction of equality targets in housing policies. The greater dependence of Bangladeshi and black households on the council sector is a reflection of these differing levels of housing need which combined with the residualisation or restriction of this sector to poorer households raises concerns over the reproduction of social inequalities more generally for these groups. The development of an account of housing in primarily, ethnic or cultural terms, comes to grief in the consideration of the location of Bangladeshis and Pakistanis given their similar backgrounds yet widely different representation in council housing. Here, differences in housing needs are paramount, higher levels of homelessness and poverty have combined to override negative perceptions of council housing to a greater extent amongst Bangladeshis. The move into social housing by Asian households generally is in the process of expansion particularly through the development of black-led housing associations who are increasingly acting as an accessible 'doorway' to social housing for these groups. The redistribution of households across the existing quality range of the present housing stock in terms of ethnic representation involves securing entry of some black and minority ethnic households into higher quality properties across all tenure sectors, and a displacement of white households into poorer quality properties. Sharing out the misery of poor quality housing is one of the outcomes of racial equality policies which restrict themselves to questions of housing consumption and ignore questions of housing production, investment, repair, rehabilitation and improvement. This has been a fundamental weakness of many local authority 'race' and housing strategies which have focused in great detail on questions of allocation and access to council housing with little consideration of the 'big picture' of housing investment from the Housing Corporation, the Department of the Environment, the private sector as well as through the local authority's own housing investment strategy and the overall impact on the housing conditions of local black and minority ethnic communities (Mullings, 1991).

To establish racial equality, in terms of equality of access, does not require consideration of racial and ethnic differentials in housing conditions, except in so far as they affect access to housing, but it does require consideration of inequalities in income and wealth. Over a third of those classified as non-white, in the 1990 General Household Survey, are in households with gross incomes (adjusted for family size) in the poorest fifth, compared to 18% of whites (Hills, 1995). The higher probability of low incomes amongst non-whites is particularly striking given the relatively small numbers of pensioners in this group (as they tend to have low incomes generally). Bangladeshi, Pakistani and West Indian households, in declining order of probability, are particularly likely to be on low incomes. Analysis of 1991 Census data show that over half of Bangladeshis were living in wards which were in the most deprived tenth nationally ranked by unemployment, economic inactivity or lack of car ownership (Green, 1994). Levels of car ownership can also be used to indicate income and Census data show that Indian and Chinese households had higher rates of ownership than whites (76.8% and 70.6% compared to 67%) with very low rates amongst blacks (44.9%) and Bangladeshis (39.1%). The widening in income inequalities over the last two decades is evident across minority ethnic groups with Indian and Chinese households diverging in their socio-economic trajectories from the position of Bangladeshis, Pakistanis and black people. In addition, the widening of income inequalities within each of these groups is likely to be occurring and at differing rates. (Evidence on ethnicity by income is poor, the Family Expenditure Survey does not collect ethnicity data, the General Household Survey collects ethnicity data but minority ethnic samples are too small for reliable analysis of individual groups and the DSS Family Resources Survey which will provide some useful data is not yet available). As regards marketable wealth, this correlates positively with income and age and given the concentration of minorities in the lower end of the income distribution and in the younger end of the age structure we can propose a similar complex pattern of wealth inequalities across ethnic groups to that of income with the condition that generally wealth inequalities are much greater (Joseph Rowntree Foundation, 1995).

The question of racial equality in access to housing also involves consideration of questions of demand and supply. Inequalities in ability to pay and the impact of the income tax and social security system on housing expenditure, in terms of housing benefit and mortgage tax relief, together with differences in basic knowledge and general perceptions of available housing opportunities will all influence the pattern of demand in the housing market. Reproduction of racial inequalities in income and wealth will therefore reproduce racial inequalities in housing which in turn will affect access to other services and opportunities, e.g. education, health and leisure. Ethnic differentials in the knowledge and perceptions of different forms of housing tenure will also affect demand. We would therefore expect that, where the supply of housing is not affected by direct or indirect discriminatory practices or distorted by the operation of racism and racist behaviour, there would be considerable inequalities in access to housing due to these demand factors. Discrimination in the supply of housing has taken a variety of forms. Blatant exclusion, the 'steering' of housing choices of minority households and discrimination in the provision of information about housing opportunities by estate agents, accommodation agencies and housing managers has been well documented. The operation of indirect discrimination in the regulation of access to council housing, housing association properties and mortgages has also been well documented (Skellington, 1992, CRE, 1983, 1984a, 1984b, 1985, 1988a, 1988b, 1989a, 1989b, 1989c, 1989d, 1990a, 1990b, 1990c, 1991, 1992, 1993a, 1993b, 1993c).

What is most remarkable in this field is the prevailing acceptance and acknowledgement of general racial inequalities of condition amongst many housing professionals and the recognition, most notably by the Housing Corporation, that group-based redistributive policies are justified. The impact of over thirty years of research and campaigning has been successful in this respect. The building of alliances between key agencies, individuals and the expanding black housing movement has been a crucially important factor facilitating this process. Despite questions of assigning greater importance to group membership than individual rights, a climate of decreasing financial resources for social housing, the potential for increased racial conflict and the way in which such policies sustain the social reality of 'race', the Housing Corporation's strategy for black and minority ethnic housing began in 1986 with explicit goals for positive discrimination in capital allocations (this is discussed below). However problematic, the vague notion of 'racial equality' is, it has provided an effective conceptual tool in the development of policy strategies. Indeed, its vagueness and generality have enabled it to evade the difficulties that more specific concepts, such as indirect discrimination, have encountered when deployed in individual cases and policy contexts. This position has been supported by predominantly structuralist accounts of racial inequality in housing, but, there is a need to examine both household strategies and the resulting process of increasing ethnic segmentation in housing markets in order to improve our understanding of the likely impact of policy interventions.

Ethnic segmentation of housing markets

These limits and constraints on access to housing are compounded by avoidance strategies and territorial defensiveness which may be of particular significance in accounting for the entrenchment or maintenance of racial inequalities in both access to housing and housing outcomes but they are less well-documented. Action to pre-empt the opportunity for racial discrimination to take place by a housing institution may occur by a household restricting its search for housing and avoiding parts of the housing market. The development of ethnically or racially differentiated sectors in private rented housing, council and housing association housing and in owner occupation provide some evidence of the impact of the process of dynamic racist ideologies - racial discrimination and harassment - previous experience and perceptions of anticipated discrimination and harassment - responsive strategies of avoidance, accommodation and resistance. Overall, this then leads to the hardening of ethnic and racial boundaries through the increasing concentration of minority households in particular streets and estates, particularly those who have less ability to buy there way out of perceived danger, and associated low-level defence of these neighbourhoods. This process appears to be operating at the same time as parallel residential dispersion into 'safer' areas for those minority households who are living on higher incomes. Research by Virdee (1995) and analysis of the 1992 British Crime Survey data by Mirlees-Black and Aye Maung (1994) have both shown the range of different forms of adaptation minority households have made to their lifestyles in response to fear of racial violence, including restrictions on the choice of where to live, where to go, how to travel and when to travel. They also document the personal refusal of others to let the fear of racial violence and harassment affect the way they lead their lives. The development of avoidance strategies has been highlighted in research which has shown the establishment of 'dual markets' (Smith, 1989), particularly in the private rented sector. Here, from the 1960s onwards only a small proportion of white tenants were renting from black landlords and only a small proportion of black tenants were renting from white landlords. Hence, households restricted their access to housing controlled by a particular group of landlords and thereby chose from a lower quality range of properties in a restricted range of locations. Ethnic segmentation of housing markets is probably a better way to conceptualise the pattern particularly given the role of informal community networks in influencing perceptions of housing agencies and in the provision of information about housing opportunities. The dependence of Asian owner occupiers on finance from friends and relatives, informal property exchanges and Asian estate agents which frequently restricted housing options to the cheaper, older, residual end of the property market as shown in Cater's study of Bradford (1981) further exemplifies this pattern. The racialised perceptions of local authority housing estates held by applicants, tenants and staff combined with the marked increases in minority ethnic concentrations in this sector, due to a variety of factors, have frequently determined the estate choices of black and minority ethnic households and their acceptance of tenancy offers (CRE, 1984a). In the housing association sector, the emerging network of black-led housing associations are rightly seen as offering better access to housing than white-led housing associations which in some areas, for example in Leeds (Law, Phillips and Harrison, 1995), produces similar ethnic segmentation in the pattern of demand. Here, black applicants were less likely to register on the waiting list of a white housing association than a black association; which then restricts housing options. Although, the implications of such a process for housing quality are less clear cut, particularly where minority access to a significant proportion of new build rented housing in the locality has been secured. The operation of local housing markets is heavily influenced by government housing policies and the extent to which ethnic segmentation has been exacerbated by housing investment policies is considered below, with research material drawn from a case study of Leeds.

Housing investment

The extent to which government and local authority programmes of housing investment reduces, maintains of increases the evident racial and inter-ethnic inequalities in physical and social housing conditions is of key importance. This section aims explore the ways in which these programmes impact on black minorities. Firstly it may be useful to consider the underlying arguments that characterise debates for policy intervention. There are four strong themes which have been and should continue to be emphasised in justifying the call for positive intervention in the reduction of racial inequalities in housing. All have their difficulties and drawbacks which may arise in their deployment during contestation, in local and national arenas, over what should or should not be done to tackle racial inequalities in housing.

There are three key programmes of public sector housing investment; Housing Corporation Capital Allocations which fund the development of new rented housing association homes and smaller homes for sale schemes, Local Authority Capital Expenditure on the Private Sector Stock which particularly funds urban renewal through improvement grants for inner city owner occupiers and Local Authority Capital Expenditure on the Public

Sector Stock which funds the repair and improvement of council houses. To indicate broad trends in the impact of this housing investment on minority ethnic households assessment of the largest element in each of these three programmes in the context of a Leeds case study will be carried out. The particular elements to be analysed will be Housing Corporation allocations for new build housing association properties for rent, Housing Renovation Grants and Council Housing Improvement programmes.

Justificiations for Positive Intervention in Racial Inequalities in Housing

1 *Compensatory* arguments emphasise the value of obtaining 'redress' for 'historic inequalities'.
   - Criticism of this view stresses that those who are *not* responsible for past discrimination may be the people who suffer.

2 *Empowerment* arguments emphasise the importance of seeking to expand the 'opportunities for black minority ethnic people to have control' over aspects of their daily lives, the experience of individuals being involved in attempts to introduce consultation, participation and empowerment has sometimes resulted in the reinforcement of feelings of marginalisation.

3 *Individual rights* arguments emphasise the importance of eradicating racial discrimination, securing 'access to social rented housing' according to housing need and equal treatment in obtaining access to other forms of housing, the rhetoric of housing need e.g. in council housing and housing association allocations policies has frequently failed to deliver increased opportunities particularly where explicit minority ethnic targeting has been absent.

4 *Utilitarian* arguments emphasise the increase in aggregate welfare to be gained through reducing racial inequalities and ethnic boundaries and encouraging cultural diversity. Similar arguments may equally be used to argue that aggregate social welfare benefits from an absence of ehtnically specific positive intervention or indeed explicit racial exclusion e.g. 'immigration control is good for race relations'.

Leeds case study of Housing Investment Data

Housing Corporation capital allocations

Special tabulations and reports have been provided by the Housing Corporation which give details of allocations and completions in Leeds. The evaluation of the effectiveness of the strategy of targeting black and minority ethnic households rests on the use of investment codes which are not monitored. The 1993/94 Policy Statement (p. 36) sets a target of 25% of rented housing for black minority ethnic households. This is reflected in the Council's Housing Strategy for 1993/94 (p. 27) which sets a target of 25% of new housing association development for rent or low cost purchase to go to such households. Analysis of Housing Corporation figures for rented completions in 1993/94 using ethnicity as specified in the investment codes confirms the target in the 1994/95 Allocations Statement (p. 22) that about 24% of rented homes completed have gone to black and minority ethnic households. Comparison of investment codes with actual lettings shows that schemes targeted at white households, such as The Ridings' Roberts Avenue and Haigh Rd., have had up to 10% of their lettings to black households, and equally schemes targeted at some black households, such as Sanctuary's Farm Rd., had no black households rehoused there, or, as with Unity's Devon Rd., rehoused more white households than anticipated. Overall, the anomalies cancelled each other out as, for the period March 1993 to April 1994, 24% of black and minority ethnic households were housed. But, two areas of concern are evident, Unity (the local black-led housing association) rehoused 70% of the black households, hence without Unity, the Council and the Housing Corporation would not have met their targets and 'under-performance' by mainstream associations appears to be a cause for concern. Also within this overall target there is a disparity for Asian households, 11.7% of new rented homes were targeted for them but only 5% were rehoused in new lets.

It is clear from the table below that the bulk of Housing Corporation capital allocations are spent on homes for rent. This has been a declining proportion of the allocation in both percentage and real terms, but in 1994/95 it was stretched with free land valued at 3 million transferred through Leeds Partnership Homes. Black minority ethnic households are benefiting from this investment through effective targeting. On the assumption that 24% of the homes for rent allocation directly benefits such households this amounts to just under 4 million in 1993/94 and 1994/95. The extent to which black minority ethnic households are benefiting from the Homes for Sale, Tenants Incentive Scheme, Do It Yourself Shared

66

Ownership and other Housing Corporation programmes is not monitored and requires further investigation.

Table 3.2
Capital allocations in Leeds ('000s)

	1992/93	1993/94	1994/5
Homes for Rent	20,018	15,895	12,614
	(81.5%)	(73.8%)	(73.4%)
Homes for Sale	887	1,195	821
TIS	626	924	732
DISYO	1,120	1,800	1,360
Mini-HAG	790	413	382
Misc.	1,129	1,909	1,275
Total	24,570	21,536	17,184

The findings and implications of this data for policy are summarised below:

1   Black minority ethnic households are generally benefiting from the investment in housing for rent through rather general targeting, and the key role played by the only black-led housing association in Leeds; Unity Housing Association;

2   Targeting may be improved by the introduction of 'minimum shares' for different minority ethnic groups within an overall target, and by the monitoring of multiple rather than single types of housing need;

3   The ethnic origin investment codes should be used to review and monitor schemes after letting has been completed, particularly to ensure that all schemes targeted at black minority ethnic households are actually let to those households;

4   'Under-performance' in the allocation of black minority ethnic households by mainstream housing associations is a cause for concern, particularly where such households are not being nominated by the local authority to these associations, and where these associations are failing to allocate homes to black nominees and applicants in a fair and equitable manner;

5   The low level of access by Asian households to new build rented housing is a cause for concern, the development of both minority group-specific targeting, in terms of allocation share, and the development of more specific schemes to meet the needs of Bangladeshi, Pakistani and Indian households would assist in

resolving this problem;

6   The extent to which black minority ethnic households benefit from Housing Corporation programmes, other than homes to rent, requires evaluation, particularly whether any programmes are or could facilitate access to owner occupation for black minority ethnic households in suburban areas.

Local Authority House Renovation Grants, 1994/95

The largest programme of investment in the local authority's private sector renewal and rehabilitation strategy is on a range of grants that collectively are called House Renovation Grants. Over 6.5 million was spent on these grants in 1994/95. The data produced through ethnic monitoring of House Renovation Grants indicates a number of issues;

1   lack of applications from Chinese and Vietnamese households (0.1%) across all types of grant;
2   low level of minority ethnic households (2.9%) receiving disabled facilities grants, whereas 4.5% of applications were received from such households during this period which indicates the likelihood of increased completions next year;
3   the importance of house renovation grants to minority ethnic households in general, who received about 32% of completed renovation grants and 16% of minor works grants, and Asian households in particular, who received 26% of completed renovation grants.

To assess the financial benefit black minority ethnic households receive from renovation grants, disabled facilities grants and minor works grants calculation of average payments and numbers of completions was made. This produced an estimate that approximately 22%, or about 1.5 million, of the overall expenditure on house renovation grants was spent on private sector renewal which benefited black minority ethnic households.

The findings and implications of this data are summarised below;

1   Private Sector Housing Renewal, through the provision of house renovation grants is the largest and most important source of housing investment for Asian and Chinese households;
2   Effective targeting of resources in the inner city has ensured that black minority ethnic households benefit from renovation grants;
3   The low level of housing investment in Chinese and Vietnamese

households in the private sector was evident in the low level of grant applications;

4   A low proportion of disabled facilities grants by black minority households was evident;

Table 3.3
Ethnic Monitoring of House Renovation Grants, 1994/95

	White (%)	Black (%)	Asian (%)
Grant enquiries (n=1566)	70.6	7.3	19.5
Grant approvals (n=478)	60.0	6.1	28.0
Grant completions (n=408)	65.9	5.4	26.2

(Note: Cases where ethnic origin not known have been excluded)

Local Authority Council Housing Improvement Programmes, 1994/95

The largest source of public sector housing investment is the local authorities public sector capital programme, being about 35 million in 1994/94 compared to about 17 million housing association capital allocation and a 6.5 million private sector capital programme. The impact of investment in council housing raises two sources of concern.

Firstly, the persistently low proportion of Asian and Chinese households in council housing and the lower level of demand from these groups for this form of tenure disproportionately excludes these groups from benefiting from housing investment, when considered overall, despite the disproportionately greater levels of housing need.

Secondly, the general pattern of housing investment within the council housing sector in Leeds does not appear to be commensurate with the levels of housing need found amongst black minorities. Although further research work is required to establish the benefit black minority ethnic households receive from various elements of this capital programme there are aspects that substantiate these concerns. The local authority Housing Strategy, 1994/5-1996/7 (p. 22) reports the finding of the Stock Condition Survey that investment is concentrated on older inter-war dwellings. This same report, as noted previously, found black minorities to be concentrated not in these properties but in pre-1919 housing stock. The largest element of the capital programme is concerned with Estate Action which accounts for approximately 47% of the total programme, as the table below shows, only a small proportion (2.7%) of this money improved the housing conditions of black minority ethnic households. This is likely to over-estimate the benefit received as it assumes a similar tenure pattern between black minority and white households which is not the case.

Table 3.4
Impact of Estate Action on Black Minority Households, 1994/95

Area	Capital (000's)	% black minority h'holds (NHO figs)	% of capital allocation
Belle Isle North	4,978	1.4	69.7
Ebor Gardens	6,100	4.1	250.1
Gipton South	2,954.8	3.4	100.5
Halton Moor	2,421.5	1.1	26.6
Total	16,454.3		446.9 (2.7%)

In comparison, the element of the capital programme of most benefit to black minority ethnic households was concerned with improving pre-1919 miscellaneous properties. This accounted for approximately 2% of the overall programme (694,500) of which just over 30% improved the housing conditions of black minorities.

The findings and implications for policy of this data are summarised below;

1   Asian and Chinese households are disproportionately excluded from benefiting from the public sector capital programme due to their pattern of housing tenure;

2   The public sector capital programme does not effectively target the housing needs of black minority ethnic households, particularly in comparison to the other two forms of housing investment considered here, and although the opportunity to address racial inequalities in this programme is limited in the coming years, the development of targets for allocation share by minority ethnic group should be considered;

3   The opportunity to encourage the rehousing of black minority households into Estate Action areas needs to be considered, particularly in the context of the development of minority ethnic

group targeting in council house allocations;
4   The impact of council housing improvement programmes on black minority ethnic households requires further research.

Case study conclusions

In conclusion, the effective implementation of group-specific racial equality targeting has been established in the housing association sector, the effective implementation of inner city targeting of private sector housing renewal programmes has been seen to be of important significance, particularly to Asian households, and the failure to operationalise any form of targeting in the council housing sector promotes the widening of racial inequalities in housing conditions. The serious and sustained concern for action to tackle racial inequalities in housing in Leeds, particularly amongst key officers and certain councillors in the past decade, prompted by sporadic community pressure, has produced significant results but it has been constrained by a number of wider factors. Firstly, the general and persistent decline in Housing Corporation capital expenditure and local authority capital programmes due to Government restraint on public expenditure has a highly significant effect on black minorities due to their poorer housing conditions. Secondly, in the context of tight resources the politically-driven rather than needs/stock condition-driven nature of council house improvement programmes has frequently disadvantaged black minority households due to their lack of local political power.

Research and policy intervention

The review of research and policy relevant issues has highlighted a number of themes. Firstly, the 'worse than meaningless' (Modood, 1994) aggregation of data into a simple black-white divide obscures the true extent of racial disadvantage and inequality between minority ethnic groups and is a blunt instrument for the comparative analysis of need. Analysis of *ethnic differentiation in housing need, household formation, residential settlement, tenure preferences and perceptions of housing agencies* is required for any serious mapping of racial inequalities and for the development of housing strategies. Census data can be used to establish broad patterns in the first three aspects, data from local housing agencies will help to map needs and area preferences and research work is required to assess differing perceptions of tenure and housing agencies, and actual patterns of demand.

71

Secondly, the degree of support for racial equality targets in housing allocations and Housing Corporation strategy and its broadly successful implementation, as shown from recent research in Leeds, with little public hostility is remarkable. This is not to deny the range of difficulties that have been encountered in its achievement or that may beset the successful maintenance of such a programme. Julienne (1994) envisages a realistically ideal future of ten to fifteen large black associations and seventy five to a hundred smaller ones, with the black housing movement running 40,000 to 55,000 homes nationally. But, falling grant rates, the shift to sale and incentive schemes and reducing capital allocations are seen to be likely to lead to a reduction in the diversity of provision found particularly amongst the smaller associations. At present, targets do not acknowledge that ethnic diversity. The arbitrary nature of these targets requires that thought be given to the development of a well-reasoned and more detailed understanding of what racial equality in the housing market might actually look like. If one accepts that different minority ethnic groups will have different housing needs, tenure preferences and area preferences then *racial equality targets should be replaced by racial and ethnic equality targets which embody an uneven proportional representation of minority groups which reflects differential positions and preferences, and which reflect both racism and minority ethnic exclusion.* Moving the debate towards this objective requires good information, qualitative fieldwork, consultation and negotiation.

Thirdly, the *construction of housing choices, acceptance of particular offers and decisions to stay in a particular location* involve a complex set of processes which need to be disentangled. The representation and policy discussion of such processes amongst minority ethnic groups is often confused, ambiguous and contradictory and as a result easily leads to the reinforcement of ethnic stereotypes and the development of housing policy and practice on the basis of those stereotypes. The hardening of ethnic boundaries, due to the racialised territorialisation of residential space, has been a common finding in studies of racial harassment (Webster, 1995). Yet, this process, which may be happening in particular inner city areas or housing estates, may not necessarily be restricting the movement of black minority ethnic households into better quality residential areas. Here, the connection between overt racist behaviour and achievement in the housing market cannot be assumed to have an overall determining effect. The dual processes of increasing concentration and uneven dispersal of black minority ethnic households throughout Britain clearly contradict any simple statements about where such households want or do not want to live. Similarly, the reduction of the housing choices of such households to consideration purely of racism or cultural preference is highly suspect.

Fourthly, the extent to which the *total picture of housing investment and finance*, including mortgage tax relief, housing benefit, improvement grants, local authority and Housing Corporation housing investment and private sector housing investment increases, maintains or decreases housing needs amongst black and minority ethnic households requires further research. The detailed discussion of access of such households to social rented housing in the CRE, NFHA and Housing Corporation literature often appears to take place with no cognisance of the way in which these other factors are operating. The complex network of housing markets and housing agencies appear to be increasing racial and ethnic inequalities, in terms of housing outcomes, both within and between ethnic groups. Increasing homelessness, particularly amongst young black people, increasing concentration in poor quality properties across all forms of housing tenure and failure to benefit from the advantages of owner occupation are some of the general themes which have been identified.

Fifthly, the complexity of factors also requires a *'life course perspective'* as Smith (1991) and Harrison (1995) have argued. Changes in access to council housing, the development of segmented markets across different forms of housing tenure and the effects of housing policies have changed the opportunities and housing outcomes for black and minority ethnic households over time. How the life paths of households and individuals interacted, and how they gained and lost, within this changing pattern of opportunities and constraints has not been adequately evaluated and requires further research.

Note

A previous version of this article is published as Chapter 3 Racial inequality in Housing: meanings and interventions in Law, I. (1996), *Racism, Ethnicity and Social Policy*, Prentice Hall/ Harvester Wheatsheaf: Hemel Hempstead. The full report of the Leeds case study can be found in Law, I., Davies, J., Phillips, D. and Harrison, M. (1996) *Equity and Difference, racial and ethnic inequalities in housing needs and investment in Leeds*, RAPP, School of Sociology and Social Policy, University of Leeds, price £4.50.

References

Anderson, I., Kemp, P. and Quilgars, D. (1993), *Single Homeless People*, HMSO: London.

Atkinson, R. and Durden, P. (1994), 'Housing Policy since 1979: Developments and Prospects', in Savage, S., Atkinson, R. and Robins, L., (eds.) *Public Policy in Britain*, Macmillan: London.

Bannister, J. et. al., (1993), *Homeless Young People in Scotland*, HMSO: London.

Barnado's/Ujima Housing Association (1991), *Young, Black and Homeless in London*, Barnardo's: Ilford.

Ben-Tovim, G., Gabriel, J., Law, I. and Stredder, K. (1986), *The Local Politics of Race*, Macmillan: London.

Cater, J. (1981), 'The impact of Asian estate agents on patterns of ethnic residence: a case study in Bradford', in Jackson, P. and Smith, S. (eds.), *Social Interaction and Ethnic Segregation*, Academic Press: London, pp. 163-183.

Commission For Racial Equality (1974), *Unemployment and Homelessness*, London.

Commission For Racial Equality (1983), *Collingwood Housing Association Ltd., Report of a Formal Investigation*, London.

Commission For Racial Equality (1984a), *Race and Housing in Liverpool, A Research Report*, London.

Commission For Racial Equality (1984b), *Race and Council Housing in Hackney*, London.

Commission For Racial Equality (1985), *Race and Mortgage Lending*, London.

Commission For Racial Equality (1988a), *Racial Discrimination in a London Estate Agency: Report of a Formal Investigation into Richard Barclay and Co.*, London.

Commission For Racial Equality (1988b), *Homelessness and Discrimination: Report into the London Borough of Tower Hamlets*, London.

Commission For Racial Equality (1989a), *Racial Discrimination in an Oldham Estate Agency: Report of a Formal Investigation into Norman Lester and Co.*, London.

Commission For Racial Equality (1989b), *Racial Discrimination in Liverpool City Council: Report of a Formal Investigation into the Housing Department*, London.

Commission For Racial Equality (1989c), *Racial Discrimination in Property Development: Report of a Formal Investigation into Oaklawn*

Developments Ltd. Leicestershire, London.

Commission For Racial Equality (1989d), *Race Relations Act 1976, A Guide for Accomodation Bureaux, Landladies and Landlords*, London.

Commission For Racial Equality (1990a), *'Sorry Its Gone' : Testing For Racial Discrimination in the Private Rented Sector*, London.

Commission For Racial Equality (1990b), *Code of Practice in Non-Rented (Owner Occupied) Housing, Consultation Draft*, London.

Commission For Racial Equality (1990c), *Out of Order: Report of a Formal Investigation into ths London Borough of Southwark*, London.

Commission For Racial Equality (1991), *Code of Practice in Rented Housing*, London.

Commission For Racial Equality (1992), *Racial Discrimination in Hostel Accomodation; Report of a Formal Investigation of Refugee Housing Association Ltd.*, London.

Commission For Racial Equality (1993a), *Housing Associations and Racial Equality in Scotland: Report of a Formal Investigation*, London.

Commission For Racial Equality (1993b), *Housing Associations and Racial Equality: Report of a Formal Investigation into housing associations in Wales, Scotland and England*, London.

Commission For Racial Equality (1993c), *Room for All: tenant's associations and racial equality*, London.

Craig, G. (1991), *Fit For Nothing?*, Children's Society: London.

Dalton, M. and Daghlian, S. (1989), *Race and Housing in Glasgow: The Role of Housing Associations*, CRE: London.

Davies, J., Lyle, S., Julienne, L., Kay, H., Deacon, A. and Law, I. (1995), *Homeless Young Black and Minority Ethnic People in Britain*, Research Report, University of Leeds.

Doling, J., Karn, V. and Stafford, B. (1985), 'How far can privatisation go?', *National Westminster Bank Quarterly Review*, August, 42-52.

Elam, G. (1992), *Survey of Admissions to London Resettlemet Units*, HMSO: London.

Ford, J. and Vincent, J. (1990), *Homelessness Amongst Afro-Caribbean Women in Leicester*, Foundation Housing Association Ltd: Leicester.

Garside, P., Grimshaw, R. and Ward, F. (1990), *No Place Like Home : The Hostels Experience*, Department of the Environment: London.

Ginsburg, N. (1992), 'Racism and Housing: Concepts and Reality', in Braham, P., Rattansi, A. and Skellington, R. (eds), *Racism and Antiracism: inequalities, opportunities and policies*, Sage/Open University: London.

Gordon, P., 'Forms of exclusion: citizenship, race and poverty', in Becker, S. (ed.), *Windows of Opportunity, Public Policy and the Poor*, CPAG:

London.

Green, A.E. (1994), *The Geography of Poverty and Wealth: Evidence on the changing spatial distribution and segregation of poverty and wealth from the Census of Population 1991 and 1981*, Institute for Employment Research: Warwick.

Greve, J. and Currie, E. (1990), *Homelessness in Britain*, Joseph Rowntree Foundation: York.

Habeebullah, M. and Slater, D. (1990), *Equal Access: Asian Access to Council Housing in Rochdale*, Community Development Foundation: London.

Harrison, M. (1992), 'Black-led housing organisations and the housing association movement', *New Community*, Vol. 18, No. 3, pp. 427-437.

Harrison, M. (1995), *Housing, 'Race' and Empowerment*, Centre for Research in Ethnic Relations/Avebury: Aldershot.

Hendessi, M. (1987), *Migrants : The Invisible Homeless*, Migrant Services Unit: London.

Hendessi, M. (1992), *4 In 10*, CHAR: London.

Hills, J. (1995), *Inquiry into Income and Wealth, Volume 2*, Joseph Rowntree Foundation: York.

Hodge, J. 'Equality: Beyond dualism and oppression', in Goldberg, D.T., (ed.) *Anatomy of Racism*, University of Minnesota Press: Minneapolis.

Housing Corporation (1992), *An Independent Future, Black and Minority Ethnic Housing Association Strategy, 1992-1996*, London.

Housing Corporation (1993), *North East Policy Statement 1993/1994*, Leeds.

Ivegbuma, J. (1989), 'Local Authorities and Black Single Homelessness', *Black Housing*, Vol. 5, No. 5.

Jones, T. (1993), *Britain's Ethnic Minorities*, Policy Studies Institute: London.

Joseph Rowntree Foundation (1995), *Inquiry into Income and Wealth*, York.

Julienne, L. (1994), 'The Housing Corporation's Black Housing Strategy Review', *Black Housing*, May/June, pp. 13-16.

Law, I. (1985), *White Racism and Black Settlement in Liverpool: A study of inequalities and policies with particular reference to council housing*, Unpublished Ph.D Thesis, University of Liverpool.

Law, I., Harrison, M. and Phillips, D. (1995), *Racial and Ethnic Inequality, Housing Needs and Housing Investment in Leeds*, Phase 1, School of Sociology and Social Policy Research Report, University of Leeds.

Law, I., Davies, J., Phillips, D. and Harrison, M. (1996), *Equity and*

Difference, racial and ethnic inequalities in housing needs and investment in Leeds, RAPP University of Leeds.

Leeds City Council (1993), *Housing Association Strategy 1993/1994*, Leeds.

Leigh, C. (1993), *Right to Care*, CHAR: London.

London Against Racism in Housing (1988), *Anti-Racism and the Private Sector*, London.

Lyle, S. (1995), *Youth Homelessness in the UK, Interim Report*, University of Leeds.

Mirrlees-Black, C. and Aye Maung, N. (1994), *Fear of Crime: findings from the 1992 British Crime Survey*, Home Office Research and Statistics Department: London.

Modood, T. (1994), *Racial Equality, Colour, Culture and Justice*, Institute for Public Policy Research: London.

Mullings, B. (1991), *The Colour of Money, the impact of housing investment decision making on black housing outcomes in London*, London Race and Housing Research Unit: London.

Niner, P. and Karn, V. (1985), *Housing Association Allocations: Achieving Racial Equality - A West Midlands Case Study*, Runnymede Trust: London.

Owen, D. (1992), *Ethnic Minorities in Great Britain: Settlement Patterns, 1991 Census Statistical Paper No. 1*, Centre for Research in Ethnic Relations, University of Warwick: Warwick.

Owen, D. (1993), *Ethnic Minorities in Great Britain: Housing and Family Characteristics, 1991 Census Statistical Paper No. 4*, Centre for Research in Ethnic Relations, University of Warwick: Warwick.

Peach, C. and Byron M. (1993), 'Caribbean tenants in council housing: 'race', class and gender', *New Community*, Vol. 19, No. 3.

Randall, G. (1992), *Counted Out*, CRISIS and CHAR: London.

Randall, G. and Brown, S. (1993), *The Rough Sleepers Initiative : An Evaluation*, HMSO: London.

Sarre, P., Phillips, D. and Skellington, R. (1989), *Ethnic Minority Housing: explanations and policies*, Avebury: Aldershot.

Smith, J. and Gilford, S. (1993), *Birmingham Young People in Housing Need Project*, Barnardos: Ilford.

Smith, S.J. (1989), *The Politics of 'Race' and Residence*, Polity Press: Oxford.

Smith, S.J. with Hill, S. (1991), *'Race' and Housing in Britain, a review and research agenda*, University of Edinburgh: Edinburgh.

Strathdee, R. (1992), *No Way Back*, Centrepoint: London.

Strathdee, R. (1993), *Housing Our Children*, Centrepoint: London.

Virdee, S. (1995), *Racial Violence and Harassment*, Policy Studies Institute: London.

Webster, C. (1995), *Youth Crime, Victimisation and Racial Harassment*, Paper in Community Studies, Bradford and Ilkley Community College: Bradford.

4 Inequality, Ethnicity and Educational Achievement

Cheryl Gore

Introduction

This chapter details a piece of research which illustrates the way in which inequalities within the British education system act to produce differential educational achievement for pupils of different ethnic origins. This topic calls forth two ongoing (usually separate) debates. One of these is the debate which centres upon the so-called 'underachievement' of pupils of African Caribbean, Bangladeshi and Pakistani origins. The second is the debate which is concerned with school effectiveness in terms of achievement in public examinations.

The problem of 'underachievement' of pupils of African Caribbean, Bangladeshi and Pakistani origins is usually depicted as an 'ethnic problem'. This led in the past to the proposal of both biological and cultural explanations for the low achievement of pupils of these ethnic origins.

There is evidence to suggest that which school a child attends plays a major role in determining achievement in public examinations; for example, Rutter, 1979, Smith and Tomlinson, 1989, Nuttall and Goldstein, 1989. However whilst these studies recognised the differences between schools in average levels of achievement, like most previous research the only comparisons of pupils of different ethnic origins made, were overall comparisons. That is, no within-school comparisons were made. In addition, the question of how pupils of different ethnic origins were distributed among schools of varying degrees of effectiveness was similarly not taken into account.

Britain's black[1] population is not evenly distributed throughout the country. For example, 54 per cent of Britain's black population resides in the south east of the country (Jones, 1993). Even within regions black people are not evenly distributed. Certain ethnic groups in particular tend to be concentrated in inner city areas. This of course has implications for the type of schools children of these origins are likely to attend.

If inner London is taken as an example, it can be seen that whilst 4 per cent of the total population of Britain is to be found in inner London, 33 per cent of Britain's African Caribbean population and 40 per cent of Britain's Bangladeshi population reside in inner London (Jones, 1993). In 1992 the proportion of pupils in inner London boroughs gaining five or more A to C grades at GCSE was 23 per cent. The national average, in the same year, was 38 per cent. Similarly, only two, out of a total of over 100 state schools in inner London in 1992, gained an average A level score which was greater than or equal to the national average.[2]

National comparisons of the public examination results of pupils of different ethnic origins do not appear to be valid when the facts that schools differ greatly with respect to the public examination results they achieve and that black pupils are not evenly distributed throughout the country are taken into account.

For example, in a study by Eggleston et al. (1986) a breakdown of examination entries and results by local education authority (LEA) was provided. Of the LEAs in the study Birmingham and the Inner London Education Authority (ILEA) were found to come off worst in terms of examination results. For example, the mean number of O level passes in Ealing (an outer London borough) was found to be three times that in Birmingham and almost three times that in the ILEA. It should be taken into account that 73 per cent of the African Caribbean pupils and 43 per cent of the Asian pupils in the study attended schools within the ILEA and Birmingham, in comparison to 27 per cent of the white pupils. Therefore the African Caribbean and Asian pupils in the study were over-represented within the LEAs which achieved the poorest examination results. When Eggleston et al. compare the examination results of pupils of different ethnic origins *within* Birmingham and the ILEA, African Caribbean pupils were found to have slightly higher examination attainments than the white pupils; and little difference was found between the Asian and white pupils within Birmingham LEA. (The sample of Asian pupils within the ILEA was too small for such comparisons to be made.)

Since such differences can be seen to exist between LEAs, the implication is that it could be useful to examine achievement patterns at the level of individual schools. In the same way that Eggleston et al. compared examination results between LEAs and results by ethnic group within LEAs, it would be useful to compare average examination results between individual schools and results by ethnic origin within individual schools.

There is also the question of why black pupils of certain ethnic origins are achieving at higher levels than others. In general, pupils of East African Asian and Indian origins appear to be achieving better results than those of African Caribbean, Bangladeshi and Pakistani origins. For example, a study carried out by the Policy Studies Institute (Jones, 1993) found that amongst 16 to 24 year olds, whilst 20 per cent of young white people left school without any qualifications, this applied to 18 per cent of young people of Indian origin and 22 per cent of young people of East African Asian origin. The figures for young people of Pakistani and Bangladeshi origins however, were found to be 48 per cent and 54 per cent respectively.[3] I have focused here on differences between different Asian groups as differential achievement between Asian and African Caribbean pupils could possibly occur as a consequence of different racist stereotypes which abound within society. So why then do these variations in achievement exist even between different Asian groups?

Social class has been suggested as a likely causal factor (Reeves and Chevannes, 1981, Rattansi, 1992). There have been differences found in the socio-economic composition of different black ethnic groups. For example, Labour Force Survey figures for 1988-90 show that 27 per cent of white male employees fall within the 'top' socio-economic category, similarly 27 per cent of male employees of East African Asian origin and 25 per cent of male employees of Indian origin also fall within this category. However only 12 per cent of male employees of African Caribbean, Bangladeshi and Pakistani origins fall within this category. (The categories employed were: professional, manager or employer; other non-manual; skilled manual; semi-skilled or unskilled manual.)[4]

This difference in the socio-economic composition of different ethnic groups has implications for the sort of areas in which members are likely to live and consequently the type of school their children are likely to attend. Rattansi (1992, p. 18) writes of the 'significant absence' of social class from ethnic monitoring. He goes on to predict, on the basis of ethnic monitoring recommendations (both in schools and elsewhere), that official information on the achievement of pupils of minority ethnic origins will continue to suffer from this lacuna.

Prior to concern with 'black underachievement', debate in Britain centred upon 'working-class underachievement'. Numerous studies found children from working-class backgrounds to be achieving at lower levels than those from middle-class backgrounds. However the question must be asked, as to whether it is social class in itself which determines achievement, or a class-related factor, such as the school attended.

Previous studies have failed to examine the representation of children of different ethnic origins within schools which achieve varying degrees of academic success. Also, little prior research has incorporated a comparison of the achievement of pupils of different ethnic origins *within* schools. If these factors are included in studies concerned with educational achievement, they may aid in the quest to ascertain why pupils of African Caribbean, Bangladeshi and Pakistani origins are underachieving in comparison to national averages. As Drew and Gray (1991, p. 171) say, 'To date we lack a study...covering a sufficient range of variables... combining both qualitative and quantitative forms of data-gathering...'.

In the past, many who have put forward theories aimed at explaining 'underachievement' have spent little, if any, time in the schools attended by black pupils. Therefore the lack of insight which is evident in many theories is not surprising, as it is likely that they are no more than attempts to guess at the processes which bring about the 'underachievement' of pupils of certain ethnic origins. More research time needs to be spent in schools, in order to study the ethos of different schools and to determine what it is which causes some schools to be more academically successful and others less so. At the same time it would also be possible to investigate the way in which black pupils are treated in different schools. As Parekh says (DES, 1985, p. 5), 'much of the debate is conducted at too abstract a level to connect with the reality of the school or the child, or to permit sensible discussion, or to have clear policy implications...'. The importance of such research is that there is a need to discover the real cause, or causes, of 'underachievement' so that an appropriate solution can be found.

The research

The research which I carried out focused primarily on Birmingham. However I have also collected quantitative data from other local education authorities (LEAs). There were several main aims of my research. The first of these aims was to examine differences in average achievement in GCSE and A level examinations between schools in Birmingham. I was able to achieve this aim by using the government's league tables. My second aim was to examine the distribution of pupils of different ethnic origins among schools in Birmingham. I obtained information on the ethnic composition of schools in Birmingham from Birmingham LEA. Achieving these two aims meant that I would be able to determine how evenly, or unevenly, pupils of different ethnic origins were distributed among schools with higher or lower average levels of achievement. I also wanted to compare the achievements of pupils of different ethnic origins *within* each school. This would enable me to determine whether or not there was any relationship between ethnicity and achievement within schools. I therefore also obtained data on the average 'score' for GCSE of pupils of different ethnic origins within each Birmingham school from Birmingham LEA.

Another of my aims was to discover which school processes might be responsible for any differences in achievement in public examinations. My main aim was to concentrate on processes which produced differences in achievement between different schools. At the same time, however, I was also interested in trying to detect any processes which might cause a differentiation of pupils of different ethnic origins within schools. In order to examine the processes which occur within schools I carried out observation in three schools.

I chose one school, School A, because it was an independent school and also because it had obtained some of the highest results in the country during the past two years. School A was a single-sex, girls', 11-18 school. I chose the second school, School B, because it was an 'inner city' school, which had achieved relatively poor academic results for the past two years. Another reason which I had for choosing School B was that it had substantial proportions of pupils of different ethnic origins. School B was an 11-16, coeducational, state comprehensive school. I chose a third school, School C, for observation because it was a state comprehensive school which had achieved relatively good academic results for the past two years. School C was also chosen because it had substantial proportions of pupils of different ethnic origins. School C was a single-sex, girls', 11-18 school. Ideally I would have liked to have observed a school which fulfilled the same criteria as School A, but which was more ethnically mixed; however I was unable to find such a school. (This did not really surprise me.) As School B had no sixth form, I also used a fourth school, School D, for the purpose of carrying out research with sixth form pupils and teachers. School D fulfilled the same criteria as School B; but it was an 11-18 school.

I observed Year 11 and Year 13 lessons during the last few months of teaching leading up to GCSE and A level examinations. (Year 11 and Year 13 are the year groups which were previously called the fifth year and the upper sixth respectively.) I spent full days in each of Schools A, B, and C so that I was able to observe the whole school day. I carried out observation in the schools from late February until early May. (I did not observe lessons in School D as I encountered problems when attempting to gain access.) I carried out the observation by sitting amongst the pupils in their lessons. On the whole, I assumed the role of a silent observer; but I did ask teachers and pupils some questions during lessons; and I also spoke to pupils and teachers during breaks.

In addition I wanted to obtain information on: the pupils' perceptions of the expectations of parents and teachers; the influences on the pupils' educational and career aspirations; how well prepared pupils were for their upcoming public examinations and the pupils' expectations about how they would do in their examinations.

I obtained this information by using questionnaires and conducting interviews. I administered questionnaires to all pupils in Year 11 at each school during the week after their Easter holidays. I later followed up the questionnaires with interviews, taking a sample of pupils from Years 11 and 13. I conducted the interviews during late April and early May. The interviews were semi-structured. They allowed me to gather more detailed information than was possible with the use of questionnaires. They also allowed a greater degree of free response and enabled interviewees to raise issues which had not been previously addressed. At Schools B, C and D, I selected the interviewees to represent a range of ethnicities. I also aimed to represent male and female pupils from the main ethnic groups within Schools B and D. At School A the pupils were predominantly white pupils of UK origins and all female, so pupils were selected for interview completely at random. Some of the pupil interviews were group interviews and some were individual.

Finally I wanted to obtain information on the perceptions, and academic expectations which the teachers had of the pupils. Therefore I also carried out interviews with teachers. In each school, I interviewed senior teachers, or teachers who had taught in the school for a long period of time (often the same teachers). I conducted interviews with teachers who taught a range of subjects at each school. For example, I interviewed one mathematics teacher, one English teacher and so on. The interviews were once again semi-structured, but this time they were all individual interviews.

The findings

This chapter reports upon work in progress. That is, whilst I have finished conducting the fieldwork, and have collected the necessary statistics, as yet I have not finished analysing all of the data. The statistical data has not yet been analysed. I have however analysed the findings of the observation which I carried out; and I have transcribed the interviews which I conducted with the pupils. In addition, I have analysed the questionnaire

84

data. The two main school processes which have emerged from my research which appear to be related to achievement, are those of teacher perceptions and expectations of pupils; and the way in which pupils are prepared for their public examinations.

Teacher perceptions and expectations of pupils

Teachers at the different schools appeared to have very different perceptions of the pupils within the schools, and also quite differing expectations of the public examination results pupils would obtain. Teachers and careers officers, similarly, had differential expectations of pupils in the different schools, with respect to their future careers.

Examination results

At School A, the teachers had very high expectations of the pupils with respect to the GCSE and A level examination results which they expected them to gain. Pupils tended to be expected to gain at least a B in each subject at GCSE. Pupils at School A usually took ten or eleven GCSEs. (Only one pupil in the year group in my study had been entered for less than ten GCSEs.) I was informed that no pupil at School A had ever been entered for less than eight GCSEs.

The following extract from an interview with a Year 11 pupil at School A was typical of the sort of answers pupils gave when questioned about their teachers' expectations of their examination results.

CG: What sort of [GCSE] results are you expecting?

Kate (white girl): I'd like to get eleven As. I don't know whether I will. I hope I do. In one or two subjects I'd like to get an A*.

CG: Do you know what sort of expectations your teachers have?

Kate: Probably the same. I should imagine that they're hoping that I'll get all As.

[A* was a new grade introduced in 1994. It is higher than an A.]

At School B, the teachers had a tendency to have very low expectations of the pupils in terms of the GCSE examination results which they expected them to achieve. Most pupils were not expected to obtain a grade above a D in any of their subjects. In contrast to School A, 80 per cent of the Year 11 pupils at School B were entered for less than nine GCSEs.

The following is an excerpt from a group interview with Year 11 pupils at School B:

Clare (white girl): They [the teachers] say,"I couldn't care what you get. It's my job. I've just got to teach you this and that."

CG: They actually say that to you?

Clare: Yes. Exactly.

The next extract is from an interview which I carried out with five African Caribbean girls who were Year 11 pupils at School B:

CG: What about your teachers, what do they expect?

Justine: "You're not going to get anywhere in life." Mr Jones sometimes does that to people. He didn't do it to us, but he does it to other people. Like Neil, remember Neil wanted to be a pilot? And he said [Mr Jones, the teacher responsible for careers], "I don't think so," and embarrassed him. And Lyndon wanted to be a paramedic and he [Mr Jones] goes, "No way are you going to get the grades to be a paramedic." And Lyndon really felt small.

[Neil and Lyndon were both African Caribbean boys in Year 11.]

In another interview the pupil's answer related more directly to GCSE grades:

CG: How do you think your teachers are expecting you to do?

Tariq, Year 11 pupil (Asian, Muslim[5] boy): Medium

CG: What's medium?

Tariq: Ds or Es.

At School C, teachers had relatively high expectations of the pupils in terms of achievement in public examinations. There was some

86

differentiation however within the school, in terms of expectations of pupils in 'upper' or 'lower; ability bands.

> Kulvinder, Year 11 pupil (Asian, Sikh[6] girl), "Upper Band": Well they're [the teachers] quite confident for us.

A Year 11 pupil (white girl) told me, whilst I was carrying out observation in the school, that the teachers expected her to do well in the subjects in which she had been placed in 'Set 1', but not in the other subjects.

Future careers

The following table shows the perceptions which pupils had of their teachers' expectations of them, in terms of the level of education which they expected them to achieve.

Level of education which pupils perceived that teachers expected them to obtain

Table 4.1
Pupil Perception of Teacher Expectation

	School A	School B	School C	School D
GCSE	0	40.5	19	20.5
A Level	4	25	28	23
Degree	92	12.5	24	36
Not clear	4	22	30	20.5

Figures are percentages of pupils.

From the table above it can be seen that there were striking differences in the pupils' perceptions of their teachers' expectations of them at the different schools. For example, at School A, 92 per cent of pupils felt that their teachers expected them to eventually obtain a degree. However at School B, only 12.5 per cent of pupils felt that the teachers expected them to obtain a degree. Similarly none of the pupils at School A felt that their teachers only expected them to gain GCSEs, without continuing to study for other qualifications after completing Year 11. However 40.5 per cent of pupils at School B indicated that teachers only expected them to obtain GCSEs, and not any higher level qualifications. (The figures at Schools C and D were 19 and 20.5 per cent respectively.)

At School A, all pupils were generally expected to stay on at the school into the sixth form, to pursue A level courses and eventually to progress into higher education. For example, once whilst I was observing a Year 11 English lesson at School A the teacher (white female) told the pupils that they must get used to writing notes as they would need to do this when they undertook 'A level and university courses'.

The following statement was made by a Year 11 pupil at School A when she was talking about the A levels which she had chosen to undertake the following year:

> Alex (white girl): The careers adviser, Mrs Carr, she said that a lot of universities would accept double maths.

The careers adviser in this school therefore appeared to be having discussions with pupils with a view to them going on into higher education.

At School B pupils were not generally expected to progress to study for A levels or to enter higher education.

The following excerpt is from an interview which I carried out with five African Caribbean girls in Year 11 at School B:

> CG: Were you influenced by anybody when you were deciding what to do?

> Kirsty: No, the careers adviser always tries to put you onto a training scheme.

> Justine: And what they try to do, they always try to say that you can't do what you wanted to do. That you're not going to get it. Or, "Do you know that you have to go to university?"

> Marsha: The first thing they say is they put you off. No the first thing they say is,"Have you ever considered Training Credits?" And I say, "No thank you ." Then they go,"bye."

> CG: What do they say when you tell them what you want to do?

Marsha: "Are you sure you don't want to go on Training Credits?"

Justine: Everything is Training Credit.

[Training Credits are part of the current Youth Training.]

Another pupil at School B had this to say:

Zahid, Year 11 pupil (Asian, Muslim boy): I don't think I'm going to go to university.

CG: Why's that?

Zahid: University is just like - it's for really clever people. That's what I think.

CG: What about if you do well in your GCSEs?

Zahid: I'm more practical than academic.

CG: What makes you think that?

Zahid: Most of my teachers.

Whilst I was carrying out observation at School B, Birmingham University had an open day. I went to collect a poster from those involved with the administration for the open day. They told me that they had sent out information packs, including posters, to all schools which had requested one. School B was not one of these schools, therefore I told the Headteacher about the open day and gave him a poster with details about it. As far as I know he did nothing to advertise the open day within the school and I never saw the poster again.

I found pupils whom I interviewed at School B to be lacking in knowledge with respect to higher education. For example most pupils had never seen a university; and at least two of the pupils whom I interviewed did not know that there were any universities in Birmingham, whilst there are actually three universities within the city; with another three universities within daily commuting distance.

The following excerpt is from an interview with one of the aforementioned pupils at School B:

CG: Do you see university as a place that you would or could go to?

Tariq, Year 11 pupil (Asian, Muslim boy): I don't want to go out of Birmingham.

CG: You can go to university in Birmingham.

Tariq: There isn't one.

Another pupil at School B had this to say:

Zahid, Year 11 pupil (Asian, Muslim boy): In university you have to go by the rules, and it's more strict than colleges.

CG: What kind of rules?

Zahid: Well, in universities you have to attend...and if you miss a few days you get suspended.

The following is an extract from a group interview which I conducted with five African Caribbean girls, who were Year 11 pupils at School B:

CG: What sort of image do you have of university?

Sherice: Study, study and more work.

Kirsty: A lot of studying and more work.

Hazel: Some difficult problem solving.

Marsha: Financial hardship.

Pupils at School A had very different perceptions of university however. The following excerpt is typical of the responses which pupils at School A gave:

CG: What image do you have of university?

Alex, Year 11 pupil (white girl): Basically I really want to go to university. It seems really good fun. Both my brothers said that they - they both went to Oxford actually, and my other brother is now at university in America. But he said that at first, he just didn't do any work for the first year, or year or two, and then when it got down to it he just scraped through the end of year exams, so that, you know, he stayed in, and then he just worked really hard. I mean he got a good mark in the end...so I'm hoping to have a lot of fun. I've visited them at university a few times and I love the life...I'm sure a lot, the majority of young people want to...go on to university because of the idea that - well my parents said that it was the best time of their lives...

In addition, pupils at School B appeared to perceive university students as being quite different to them. For example:

Clare, Year 11 pupil (white girl): The impression I get of people in university is that they're really snobby, but they live in like down-and-out flats and stuff. And they stay up until about four o'clock and they say, "Oh yah and x= bla, bla, bla."

At another stage during the interview Clare imitated the sort of thing she thought somebody who was at university might say.

Clare: "Shakespeare is such a wonderful person, I knew him personally." [With an assumed middle-class ("posh") accent.]

Other School B pupils also voiced their opinions of university students. For example:

Stuart, Year 11 pupil (white boy): I imagine they always talk like this, they go,"Yeah, chapter 9, yah."

Some of the African Caribbean pupils showed concern about the ethnic composition of the student body in higher education:

Hazel: Is the vast majority white at university?

Sherice: What colour are your room-mates?

Therefore, it can be seen that the pupils at School B perceived university students to be different from them in terms of social class, and in the case of the black pupils, also in terms of ethnicity.

As pupils at School B appeared to be uninformed with respect to higher education, I decided that I would attempt to arrange a trip to Birmingham

University for pupils at School B who were interested. I spoke to (the aforementioned) Mr Jones (white), the teacher responsible for careers to see how the trip could be organised. When I told Mr Jones what I wanted to do, his reply was, 'I suggest you just grab them because they're leaving next week'. I had expected that he may have co-operated with me to organise the trip formally within the school. Also I did not know whether I should take schoolchildren anywhere without permission from either the school or their guardians. I was left, therefore, to collect telephone numbers or addresses of pupils whom I could find in the corridors or playground.

At School C teachers appeared to differentiate between pupils in the 'upper' and 'lower' bands. That is, some pupils were seen as suitable for A level courses and others were not. For example, whilst I was observing a geography lesson, the teacher (white female) said that GNVQ (General National Vocational Qualification) was more appropriate for some pupils than A level. She did however say that universities now accept GNVQ.

Pupils at School C did seem to be encouraged to undertake A level courses and appeared to be expected to progress into higher education. For example, a Year 11 pupil (African Caribbean girl) told me, whilst I was carrying out observation, that when she told the Deputy Headteacher (white female) that she wanted to study hairdressing, the Deputy Headteacher tried to encourage her to stay on at school and take A levels instead. Pupils from this school were sent to Birmingham University for work experience. Also all Year 12 pupils attended the annual open day at Birmingham University.

At School D some efforts were made to educate pupils about higher education, however the teachers generally did still have low expectations of the pupils. One Year 13 pupil had this to say:

> Kamaljit (Asian, Sikh girl): When I decided to apply for law, Mr Boyle [Head of Sixth Form] shoved this article under my nose saying how qualified barristers and solicitors, they don't get jobs...and he shoved this other article under Jasbinder's [Asian, Sikh girl] nose and he said,"there aren't many jobs in the media"...And what really got to me was when he said, "Don't bother applying to Birmingham University because you aren't going to get in anyway."

At this school it seemed that certain universities, that is, those which had previously been polytechnics were seen as appropriate for the pupils to apply to, whilst others were not.

Preparation for examinations

The way in which pupils are prepared for their examinations is probably the most important factor in determining their level of achievement. To some extent it may be possible to resist teacher expectations, however if pupils are not properly prepared for their examinations this will no doubt greatly impede their performance. I found marked differences between the study schools with respect to this factor. At School A, even on the day when I began observing lessons, during the week after the February half term, pupils had already finished some syllabuses and had begun to revise during lessons. At School C syllabuses tended to be completed by the Easter holiday. At School B, in contrast, pupils were still being given new topics in some subjects at the beginning of May, when I finished my observation in this school.

Another major difference in the way that pupils were prepared for examinations was in how familiar or not they were with past examination papers. At School A pupils tended to have had a great deal of practice in working on past examination papers; whilst at School B pupils appeared not to be at all familiar with the format of their approaching examinations. At School C pupils appeared to have had some practice in completing past examination papers. At School D I did not observe classes but according to the Year 13 pupils whom I interviewed, pupils seemed to have finished some syllabuses by the Easter holiday, but not others. Pupils seemed to have had some practice in answering past examination questions.

The questionnaire data revealed differences between how well prepared pupils at School A felt in comparison to pupils at Schools B, C and D. For example, 96 per cent of Year 11 pupils at School A felt that they had covered 'all' or 'most' of the necessary topics for their GCSE examinations. However at Schools B, C and D the figures were 78, 80 and 74 per cent respectively. Conversely, only 3 per cent of pupils at School A felt that they had only covered 'some' of the necessary topics for their examinations. This applied to 22, 20 and 26 per cent of pupils at Schools B, C and D respectively. Similarly 93 per cent of pupils at School A felt that they were familiar with the format of their forthcoming examinations in 'all' or 'most' subjects. The percentages for Schools B, C and D were 84, 82 and 69. At School A just 4 per cent of pupils felt that they were only familiar with the format of their forthcoming examinations in 'some' subjects. At Schools B, C and D, the proportions were 16, 17 and 26 per cent respectively.[7]

Pupils' responses during interviews also indicated differences between the four schools.

The following excerpt is from an interview with a pupil at School A:

CG: Have you finished all the syllabuses?

Hannah, Year 11 pupil (white girl): Yeah, yeah, we've started revision in everything really.

CG: Are you familiar with the format of your exams?

Hannah: Yeah, I think so. Pretty much.

CG: Have you seen past papers?

Hannah: Yeah in most subjects we've looked at quite a few.

The next extract is from an interview with a group of Year 11 pupils at School B:

CG: Are you feeling well prepared for your GCSEs?

Answer: No. [All together: Jenny, Clare and Stuart, two white girls and a white boy.]

CG: Why not?

Stuart: Because they've [the teachers] given us too much revision in the last couple of weeks...Giving us subjects we've never done before.

Jenny: Yeah it's all stuff we should have done a couple of years ago. They're cramming it all in now, at the last minute.

Stuart: There's no time to revise.

The following excerpt is from an interview which I conducted with an African Caribbean boy in Year 11 at School B:

CG: Have you finished all your syllabuses?

Lyndon: Some.

CG: Have you seen any past papers for any subjects?

Lyndon: No.

The next extract is from an interview with two Asian, Sikh girls who were Year 11 pupils at School C:

CG: Have you finished your syllabuses?

Amritpal: Yes we've finished all of them now.

CG: Have you seen past papers?

Amritpal: We've been given GCSE questions. The teachers go over them so we know what type of things we're going to get in the exams.

The following extract is from an interview which I conducted with three Asian, Sikh boys who were Year 13 pupils studying for A levels at School D. Two of the pupils had taken A levels already the previous year, but were now retaking A levels because they did not achieve the grades which were required, in order for them to be accepted onto the higher education courses which they had chosen.

CG: Are you familiar with the format of the exam [mathematics]?

Daljit: Yes 'cause we'd done it last year. So we're very familiar with it this year. But if we were familiar with it last year, I reckon I would have done a lot better.

The interviews with pupils at each school were all carried out at the same time in the academic year.

Reasons for differences between schools

The social class composition of the schools appeared to be a major factor in contributing to the differential expectations of the teachers within the different schools. At School A where the pupils were predominantly (if not exclusively) middle class, they were viewed by the teachers as being within the same social category as themselves. For example, once when I was observing a chemistry lesson, the teacher (white male) mentioned that he had been to school with the father of one of the pupils in the class. The teacher and the pupil's father had both attended a very similar boys' independent school. On another occasion, a teacher (white female) informed me (whilst I was speaking informally with her in the staff room) that she had worked for one year in a 'very rough school - the sort of school where I had to stop pupils jumping out of the window'. She went on to tell me that it was 'very different here'. These statements demonstrate the way in which teachers compare schools, viewing them as very different from each other, and as having different kinds of pupils. This teacher also told me that her daughter had attended School A. A theme of 'us' and 'them' can be seen. That is, the pupils at School A were like the teachers and their families. Pupils at the other types of schools were different from the pupils at School A and different from the teachers.

At School B, in contrast to School A, the pupils came predominantly (if not solely) from working-class backgrounds (with a substantial proportion of their parents/guardians actually being unemployed). At School B the pupils were viewed as being within a different social category to the teachers with regard to social class. At School B, whilst I was observing a design class, the teacher (white male) spoke about how the parents of the pupils at School B were 'poorly educated'. He went on to inform me that 'poorly educated parents tend to have poorly educated children'. He also spoke about the way in which the 'white working-class children' in the school spoke. For example he said, 'they say likkle instead of little, not like you and me'. Once again the theme of 'us' and 'them' can be clearly seen. In this school however, the pupils are 'them', regardless of their ethnicity. That is, the teachers saw the white pupils within the school as being different from them, on the basis of social class.

Later, when I interviewed the aforementioned design teacher at School B he went on to speak at length about the pupils in terms of their social class backgrounds, relating this to their ability in the subject which he taught.

Design Teacher (white male): The socio-economic situation is horrendous, in fact I would say the weakest home backgrounds are the whites. You're talking the bottom of the barrel...developing your own ideas as a designer. That takes a lot of intellect up there. You're talking aesthetic skills, colours, layouts...And for this type of child...If you're coming from a house and not a home, where you haven't got nice carpets, nice furnishings. The ability to appreciate aesthetic things, some of it will be innate maybe, I don't know. Most of it will be through your environment. If your environment is not nice or pleasant, how are you going to appreciate other people's environment? Now I can't prove that, but I'm sure that people who have nice things around them will appreciate nice things. I can only take my own children who will look at something and say, 'Oh that's nice, can I have that in my bedroom?' 'Why?' 'Cause it goes with the curtains'. Now I get that off of my children who are fairly young. Now I suspect that these children here wouldn't.

[I had not mentioned either social class or ethnicity to this teacher.]

School D, like School B, was comprised predominantly of working-class pupils. School C was more mixed than Schools A, B or D in terms of its social class composition. Perhaps it was due to School C being mixed in terms of its social class composition that the expectations of the teachers lay somewhere between those at School A and those at Schools B and D.

It may be the case that the expectations which the teachers held of the pupils in terms of their future careers, and whether or not they were likely to progress into higher education, influenced how important the teachers then saw the pupils' public examination results to be. That is, if teachers have low expectations of the pupils in terms of their future careers, then they may not think that the pupils' public examination results are very important. A consequence of this could be that there is then no great emphasis on obtaining good examination results and therefore on preparing pupils for their examinations. It may follow then that the expectations which teachers have in terms of pupils' examination results are also low. In contrast, if teachers have high expectations of pupils in terms of their future careers, good examination results may then be seen as a priority and it is more likely that there will be an emphasis on the preparation of pupils for public examinations. As a consequence of this teachers may have higher expectations of how pupils will then perform in these examinations.

Conclusion

The findings of this study show that there are stark differences between schools in how effectively they prepare pupils for their public examinations. The findings show that schools may range from those that finish syllabuses well in advance of examinations and allow pupils to become familiar with the type of questions which they will be expected to answer in their examinations; to those which finish syllabuses just before the examinations, or not at all, and which do not allow pupils the chance to become familiar with the type of questions with which they will be presented in their examinations. The findings also suggest a relationship between the expectations which teachers have of pupils and how effectively pupils are prepared for examinations. It appears that teacher expectations

97

and the emphasis upon preparations for examinations are part of a general school ethos, which may be related to the social class composition of the school. These two factors, of teacher expectation and how pupils are prepared for public examinations, also appear to be related to the public examination results which a school achieves.

How then does this study contribute to the debate which is concerned with the achievement of pupils of different ethnic origins? Although I have not yet statistically analysed the data that I have collected, which pertains to the distribution of pupils of different ethnic origins among schools in Birmingham; the trend appears to be that pupils of African Caribbean, Bangladeshi and Pakistani origins (those ethnic groups which are deemed to be underachieving) tend to be over-represented in the schools which have low average levels of achievement. (Pupils of these ethnic origins are conversely under-represented in the more effective schools.)

I have similarly not as yet analysed the data which I have collected on the achievements of pupils of different ethnic origins within schools. In the cases of the schools in which I carried out my qualitative research there did not appear to be any difference in achievement of pupils of different ethnic origins *within* schools. Teachers did not on the whole differentiate between pupils of different ethnic origins when giving their views on how they expected pupils to perform in public examinations. (Although teachers may, of course, have been wary about distinguishing between pupils of different ethnic origins.)

It therefore appears, that in terms of achievement in GCSE and A level examinations, the school attended is a major determinant of a pupil's achievement. The findings of a study by Smith and Tomlinson implied 'dramatic differences between the schools in our sample in terms of the exam results they achieve with children whose attainment was at a given level three years before' (1989, p. 268). They go on to say, 'the academic level at which a child is expected to compete is more a function of school policies and practices than of the individual qualities of the child' (Ibid., p. 302).

This study however goes further than that of Smith and Tomlinson, in that it examines the distribution of pupils of different ethnic origins among schools of varying degrees of effectiveness and compares the achievements of pupils of different ethnic origins within each school in Birmingham under the auspices of the LEA. In addition, this study proffers some explanations for the differences between schools in levels of achievement.

So what then are the implications of the findings of this study in terms of possible interventions which could be made in education policy and practice? Teachers and careers officers could be made aware of the ways in which they may categorise pupils in terms of both ethnicity and social class; and of the ensuing expectations associated with such forms of categorisation. That is, teachers and careers officers have been found to have low expectations of working-class and black pupils with respect to both examination results and their future careers. Awareness of this problem should be incorporated into teacher training and into the training of careers officers. Teachers and careers officers who are already qualified should also receive some form of training which encompasses these issues. Pupils and teachers could be interviewed to monitor the expectations which teachers have of pupils.

Inspections of schools should be carried out to ensure that pupils are adequately prepared for GCSE and A level examinations. That is, schools should be inspected to ensure that GCSE and A level syllabuses and coursework have been completed at an appropriate stage in the academic year; and that pupils are familiar with past examination papers. Interviews with pupils could also be conducted to aid in the evaluation of how well prepared pupils are for their examinations.

In addition, pupils in all schools should be educated about further and higher education; by both teachers and careers officers. This should be made a compulsory part of careers education within secondary schools. This education should include visits to further and higher education institutions and the chance to speak to students within further and higher education who come from a similar background to the pupils concerned.

If such changes were implemented the standard of education in less effective schools could be greatly improved and the inequalities which currently persist within the education system would be significantly diminished. As Smith and Tomlinson (1989, p. 307) write, 'action is needed to improve standards for all children in the poorer schools'.

Notes

1   The term 'black' is used throughout this chapter in its political sense, to include everybody except those who are solely of European descent.

2   1992 was the first year in which league tables were published.

3   The categories employed here are those used in the Policy Studies Institute report. It is likely that finer divisions of categories may reveal differences between different groups. For example, the 'Indian' category could be broken down into 'Sikh' and 'Hindu'.

4   The use of male employees for classification is, of course, somewhat

problematic, in that this form of categorisation is based upon an assumption of people living within nuclear family groupings with the male adult having a job which is within a 'higher' socio-economic category, than the job (if any) of his female partner. Obviously such a living/economic arrangement is not a reality for a substantial number of people, and tends to be less the case for certain ethnic groups than for others. However, I feel that the figures quoted do represent a real difference in the socio-economic composition of different black ethnic groups.

5   The Muslim pupils in the study were predominantly of Pakistani origin. The Muslim pupils quoted in this chapter: 'Tariq' and 'Zahid', were of Pakistani and Bangladeshi origins respectively.

6   The pupils of Indian origin within the study were predominantly Sikh.

7   It may not be accurate to compare School C with the other schools, with respect to the statistics relating to questions about how well prepared pupils perceived that they were for their examinations, as my research in School C was conducted a year later than in the other schools, and in this particular year GCSE Technology was made compulsory for all pupils (attending state schools) for the first time. Many pupils at School C indicated that they did not feel well prepared in this one particular subject.

References

Department of Education and Science (1985), *Education For All: A brief guide to the main issues of the Report*, The Report of the Committee for Inquiry into the Education of Children from Ethnic Minority Groups, 'The Swann Report', HMSO: London.

Drew, D. and Gray, J. (1991), 'The Black-White Gap in Examination Results: A Statistical Critique of a Decade's Research', *New Community*, 17, 2, pp. 159-72.

Eggleston, S.J., Dunn, D.K. and Anjali, M., with Wright, C. (1986), *Education For Some: The Educational and Vocational Experiences of 15-18 Year Old Members of Minority Ethnic Groups*, Trentham Books: Stoke on Trent.

Jones, T. (1993), *Britain's Ethnic Minorities*, Policy Studies Institute: London.

Nuttall, D. and Goldstein, H. et al. (1989), 'Differential School Effectiveness', *International Journal of Educational Research*, 13, pp.

769-76.

Rattansi, A. (1992), '"Changing the Subject?" Racism, Culture and Education', in Donald, J. and Rattansi, A. (eds), *'Race', Culture and Difference*, Sage Publications Ltd: London.

Reeves, F. and Chevannes, M. (1981), 'The Underachievement of Rampton', *Multiracial Education*, 12, 1, pp. 35-42.

Rutter, M., Maughan, B., Mortimore, P., Ouston, J. and Smith, A. (1979), *Fifteen Thousand Hours*, Open Books Publishing Ltd: Somerset.

Smith, D.J. and Tomlinson, S. (1989), *The School Effect*, Policy Studies Institute: London.

5 The Experiences of Asian Pharmacy Professionals

Karen Hassell

Introduction

A recurring theme in the literature on ethnic minority groups' participation in the labour market is their relative concentration in the lower level and more poorly paid jobs compared to the white labour force, and in particular their concentration in self-employment (Brown, 1984). However, there is growing evidence to suggest that some groups are increasingly represented in the managerial and professional classes such that the proportion of African Asian and Indian male employees in the top category is as high as for white males (Jones, 1993, Modood, 1991).

Despite the recognition that an increasing proportion of ethnic minorities are represented in the managerial and professional classes, empirical work to ascertain which professional occupations are represented has so far been limited to just a few professions (Smith, 1980, Smith, 1989, Ranger, 1988, Anwar and Ali, 1987). These studies have consistently demonstrated that discrimination against ethnic minority employees is widespread and even where they have penetrated into the higher status occupations, (e.g. medicine), they tend to be confined to the less popular specialties of the profession. This suggests that equality is limited to statistical representation only, while equal treatment in relation to recruitment, opportunity or promotion is far less common.

A previous small-scale study by the author was the first empirical study to draw attention to the large presence of Asians in the pharmacy profession (Hassell, 1996a). Findings indicated that racial discrimination may also be taking place in this profession.

This paper reports results from a recent, larger scale study, which offers, for the first time, some detailed insights into the experiences of Asian

103

pharmacy professionals. The paper presents a preliminary view on the nature and extent of ethnic minority participation in pharmacy, drawing on information from a variety of sources: some secondary data analysis, and some primary data collected by means of focus groups with first year pharmacy students, interviews with pharmacy proprietors, and a postal survey of over 1300 pharmacists. In an attempt to illustrate the trends in Asian participation in pharmacy, and to ensure that the experiences of the Asian pharmacists could be set firmly within the context of the experiences of pharmacists in general, the survey drew on a comparative analysis of three cohorts of white and ethnic minority pharmacists from three separate registration years: 1975, 1985 and 1991.

Data on which 'specialty' they work in and job position is presented. Differences between the different cohorts of qualifiers, in particular, differences regarding motivations for entry into the profession and class origins are discussed; information on career opportunities and any barriers such as racial discrimination, and data on career preferences, are also presented. The paper finishes by drawing on existing explanations for the development of ethnic minority business in an attempt to explain Asian entry into the profession, in particular into pharmacy ownership. Despite pharmacy being considered a profession, it is also characterised by its very distinct entrepreneurial and business role, so the frameworks may be useful for understanding how and why Asian pharmacists choose to work in retail pharmacy.

First though, in order to place the new developments in context, the paper begins with some background on the pharmacy profession.

Some background information on the pharmacy profession

The (Royal) Pharmaceutical Society of Great Britain (RPSGB) was incorporated by Royal Charter in 1843, conferring on the Society at the time a moral responsibility for supervising the activities of all 'chemists and druggists'. Up until 1949 when the Society was responsible for the education of its members, qualification was via a 3 to 5 year articled apprenticeship followed by a mandatory 1 year academic course. The college component increased throughout the 1950s and 1960s and the apprenticeship was replaced by a single year of post-graduate training. From 1967 pharmacy became a degree course requiring science 'A' levels for entry. Today students of pharmacy must undertake and pass not only a four year degree course (recently changed from a three year course) but also a year's supervised preregistration experience in practice. There are

16 schools of pharmacy and annual intakes total around 1300 (1994 data). Most graduates work in one of two branches: community and hospital. Others work in industry and some work for Health Authorities or in academia.

Apart from the changes mentioned above, the profession has recently undergone other 'restructuring'. While overall the number of pharmacies has fallen, from 15,000 in 1955 to 9,771 today, chain store pharmacies (and supermarket pharmacies) are more prominent and have gained in importance at the expense of independent pharmacies. In 1958 large chain pharmacies accounted for 14% of all pharmacies, today they account for 34%; the remainder are either independent pharmacies or small chains (DoH, 1995). As a result, the employment status of the workforce has altered such that there are an increasing number of employees and a decreasing number of self-employed contractors (Smith, 1992, Magirr and Ottewill, 1995). Part-time work has increased, particularly in the retail sector, and there has also been a steady increase in the number and proportion of women entering pharmacy (Brown et al., 1992). This process of 'feminisation' has lead to some interesting sociological debates about whether women's entry into pharmacy should be viewed as an indication of the declining status of the profession (Crompton and Sanderson, 1986, 1990, Muzzin et al., 1994), or whether, as others argue, it should be seem more as a sign of the real progress women have made in employment and educational achievements (Bottero, 1992).

There are just over 34,500 pharmacists on the Register, but 15% practice in a field other than pharmacy or are not in paid employment (Table 5.1). Pharmacy, probably more than any other profession, is the most conspicuously connected with entrepreneurialism and retailing; this is reflected in the numbers of those in pharmacy employment who practice in the community (i.e. retail) sector of the profession (72%). The other main sector of employment is the NHS, but industry, wholesaling, academia, and Health Authorities also employ pharmacists. In community practice men are in the majority (55%), while women predominate in hospital pharmacy (68%). Among the younger pharmacists (20-39 years) women are by far in the majority (60%).

Ethnic minority pharmacists

So what evidence is there for the popularity of pharmacy for ethnic minority groups? In the absence of any ethnic monitoring undertaken by the RPSGB precise figures on the number and ethnic origins of members are not available. Previously, anecdotal evidence has estimated the proportion of Asian pharmacy practitioners to be anywhere between 7% and 11%, and likely to be higher for some sectors of the profession (Anon., 1987, Anon., 1992, Anon., 1993). A partial picture emerges from the various secondary sources of data, described below.

Table 5.1
Age group and principal occupation estimates of 1994 membership by gender

Principal Occupation *	Male (n/col %)	Female (n/col %)	Total (n/col %)
Community	11,648 (63)	9,527 (59)	21,175 (61)
Hospital	1,767 (10)	3,759 (23)	5,526 (16)
Industry	993 (5)	665 (4)	1,658 (5)
Wholesale	61 (-)	16 (-)	77 (-)
Teaching	271(1)	121 (1)	392 (1)
Other pharmacy	353 (2)	337 (2)	690 (2)
Non-pharmacy	442 (2)	347 (2)	789 (2)
No paid employment	2,894 (16)	1,455 (9)	4,349 (13)

Age Group	Male	Female	All
under 39 years	6,540 (35%)	9,697 (60%)	16,237 (30%)
40 to 59 years	6,854 (37%)	4,927 (30%)	11,781 (34%)
60 yrs and over	5,034 (27%)	1,605 (10%)	6,639 (19%)
TOTAL	18,428	16,229	34,657

* based on estimates. *Source*: Survey of pharmacists, 1993 and 1994. *Pharmaceutical Journal* (1996), 256, 784-86.

From a review of names in the Annual Registers of Pharmaceutical Chemists it is clear that 'Asian' involvement in the pharmacy profession began in the late 1960s and early 1970s. Addresses alongside the names indicate that many of the first 'Asian' pharmacists came from countries such as Kenya, Uganda and Tanzania. The rate of entry was rapid. The sharpest increase occurred during the mid to late 1970s, but the last two decades witnessed a steady increase in the number of South Asian names on the Pharmaceutical Register. Two names in particular predominate: Patel and Shah.

The data provided by the RPSGB for graduates qualifying as pharmacists in 1975, 1985 and 1991 provide another indication of the trends in the number of qualifiers from an ethnic minority (Table 5.2). While the precise ethnic origin of the pharmacists is not known with any certainty from these administrative records, by reference to family name pharmacists could be identified as being from an ethnic minority or not (Nicoll et al., 1986). Using this method ethnic minority pharmacists accounted for 21% of all 2716 pharmacists who qualified during these three years. Overall, there was a 34% increase in the number of qualifiers from 1975 to 1991. However, the number of white pharmacists increased by only 22%, while the number of ethnic minority pharmacists increased by 103%, such that in 1975 they represented 15% of all qualifiers that year, by 1991 they represented 23%.

Table 5.2
% of qualifiers and % change, by year of qualification, gender and ethnic origin

			(row percentages)		
Registrati-on Yr	Total (n)	White male	White female	Minority male	Minority female
1975	756	35%	49%	11%	4%
1985	945	29%	49%	14%	9%
1991	1015	22%	55%	12%	11%
All years	2716	28%	51%	12.4%	8.4%
% change	+34%	-16%	+49%	+42%	+200%

Taking the three years of qualifiers together, most pharmacists are female (60%). However, the proportion of women registering as pharmacists compared to men increased from 53% in 1975 to 68% in 1991, representing an increase of 66%, while the number of men qualifying showed a drop of 2% over the same period. This drop however is mainly due to the large drop (16%) in the number of white men qualifying. As a proportion of all men, minority males on the other hand, increased their proportion from 24% in 1975 to 35% in 1991, an increase of 42%.

Among white pharmacists women dominate, such that 65% of all white pharmacists are female, while females account for 40% of all ethnic minority pharmacists. Although as a proportion of all women their share has only increased from 7% in 1975 to 17% in 1991, the number of ethnic minority women has nevertheless increased by over 200%, such that the number of ethnic minority women who registered as pharmacists in 1991 almost equalled the number of ethnic minority men.

An analysis of university applications and admissions data provide information regarding the ethnic origins of *recent* applicants to pharmacy courses, and confirm that most of the ethnic minority entrants to pharmacy are in fact Asian, and mostly Indian. Analysis of 1994 data from the Universities Central Admission Service (UCAS), comparing admissions to pharmacy with four other professional degree courses: medicine, law, accountancy and dentistry, shows quite clearly that people from the Asian ethnic group form a higher proportion of admissions for all five of the courses relative both to their proportion in the U.K. population and relative to their overall proportion of admissions to all university courses together. Of the five though, pharmacy has by far the highest proportion of Asian students relative to white students.

Results from the survey are presented next. Before presenting some of the differences between the pharmacists in relation to practice patterns and motivations for entering pharmacy, some basic demographic data are given first.

Survey results: Ethnic group and country of birth

Ethnic group categories used in the questionnaire were those used in the 1991 Census, but one extra category, 'African Asian' was added. This was because preliminary analysis of Annual Registers of Chemists indicated that many 'Asian' pharmacists were from East Africa. Their economic and class profile is known to be very different when compared with other Asian minorities so this addition was considered important.

Of the 823 respondents whose questionnaire could be used, 546 classified themselves as white. While the vast majority of these were born in the U.K, just over 1% were born in other European countries and 2.4% were born elsewhere (including New Zealand, Eire and USA). Of the 277 ethnic minority pharmacists the majority gave their ethnic group as African Asian (42%) or Indian (28%). Pakistani and Chinese pharmacists accounted for 8% and 9% respectively, and Black African pharmacists accounted for 5%. Only two pharmacists gave their ethnic group as Bangladeshi, and two were Black Caribbean. Seventeen (6%) classified themselves as other Asian (Table 5.3).

Just over three quarters of all minority pharmacists (77%) were born overseas. Among the African Asian pharmacists all except one were born overseas. Over half (63) were born in Kenya, 21% were born in Uganda

(24) and 16% were born in Tanzania (19). While these three East African countries accounted for the country of birth for just over 40% of all the minority pharmacists in this sample, the Indian sub-continent accounted for 17%, and Far Eastern countries (eg, China, Hong Kong, Vietnam and Malaysia) accounted for nearly 8%.

Most of the ethnic minority pharmacists who were born overseas arrived during the 1960s and 1970s (81%). Forty six per cent (n=94) arrived in the 1970s. Most of these (48) arrived in the first three years of that decade, and with the exception of 7, all were from East African countries. Most of those who were born overseas (41%) came to the UK because of family migration, but a substantial minority (16%) came because of political unrest in their home country, and again most of these pharmacists were from East African countries. Thirty-three % of ethnic minority pharmacists born overseas came for their primary or pharmacy education.

Table 5.3
Ethnic group of pharmacists

Ethnic Group	Frequency (column %)			% born overseas
	Male	Female	Total	
All White	167(31%)	379 (69%)	546	3.5
African Asian	70	47	117 (42.2%)	99
Indian	36	42	78 (28.2%)	53
Chinese	13	11	24 (8.7%)	83
Pakistani	17	6	23 (8.3%)	57
Asian other	12	5	17 (6.1%)	88
Black African	4	10	14 (5.1%)	50
Black Caribbean	0	2	2 (0.7%)	0
Bangladeshi	0	2	2 (0.7%)	0
Base: all minority pharmacists	152 (55%)	125 (45%)	277	77

Practice branch in which pharmacists employed

Where exactly do the ethnic minority pharmacists practice? Do they predominate in any one practice branch, are they concentrated in particular job positions? Table 5.4 shows that the majority work in community (retail) pharmacy. Over two thirds of all respondents (70%) work in community pharmacy, closely resembling the national picture. However, 89% of minority male pharmacists and 75% of minority women work in community pharmacy compared with 68% and 62% of white pharmacists (p = <0.05).

Table 5.4
Practice specialty in which pharmacists are working

	ALL	Registration Year 1975	1985	1991	White Male	Female	Minority Male	Female
Community	70.1	71	73	67	68	62	89	75
Hospital	19.6	19	17	22	16	28	6	17
Industry	5.5	3	6	7	9	6	2	3
Other pharmacy	4.9	7	4	4	8	4	3	5
Base: all working in pharmacy	762	199	260	303	157	348	145	112

p > 0.05   Chi^2 = 51.8, df = 9, p = 0.00000

Although the Chi^2 test is invalid due to low cell frequencies it is nevertheless interesting to note the distribution of practice specialty between the individual ethnic groups. Of the 111 pharmacists of African Asian origin employed in pharmacy, 93% work in the community sector and 6% in hospitals, higher than average and higher than all ethnic minority groups together. Chinese and Indian pharmacists are also predominantly found in community pharmacy (81% and 78%), while Black African pharmacists (64%) and other Asian pharmacists (62%) closely resemble the proportion of white pharmacists (64%) working in community pharmacy.

Job position

The category 'community pharmacy' masks quite different occupational types. It includes those working as employees, at different levels, for either large chain store pharmacies (such as Boots) or small chain and independently owned pharmacies. It also includes those owning their own pharmacy (ie, self-employed) and locum pharmacists. These are diverse employment positions with incumbents commanding very different salary and status levels. The majority of white pharmacists working in community pharmacy work as 'managers' (46%), with only 16% owning their own pharmacy (Table 5.5). The majority of ethnic minority pharmacists on the other hand, are owners, while just under a third are managers. The

110

proportion working as a locum or as an 'other employee' (ie, not managers) are similar for both groups.

Table 5.5
Position in community setting by sex/race cohort

		White		Minority		ALL	
	ALL	Male	Female	Male	Female	White	Minority
Locum	25	13	32	22	27	26	24
Manager	40	51	44	23	43	46	31
Other employee	10	2	17	4	12	12	7
Owner	25	34	7	52	18	16	38
Base (n)	534	106	215	129	84	321	213

column percentages

p=0.000

While self-employment levels in community pharmacy are a lot higher for all ethnic minority respondents than is typical for all pharmacists together, the African Asian pharmacists in particular, are significantly represented among proprietors. A quarter of all pharmacists working in retail pharmacy are owners, however among African Asian pharmacists the proportion of owners is 43%. This compares with 30% of 'South Asian' pharmacists and 29% of the small number of Chinese pharmacists. Among men the trend is even more pronounced, with more than twice the proportion of African Asian males owning their own pharmacy compared to white males (59% and 27% respectively).

As might be expected there is a significant difference between male and female pharmacists with regard to ownership, such that only 9% of females overall are pharmacy owners, compared with 38% of men. The fact that there are proportionately more white females than white males could account for the lower representation of whites as pharmacy owners. However, controlling for gender, ethnic minority males still have a higher self-employment profile, with 47% of them overall owning their own pharmacy compared to 27% of white males (p= <0.05). While fewer women are pharmacy owners, there is nevertheless a significant difference between white and minority females such that proportionately more ethnic minority females are also owners (18% compared with 7% of white females). However among the women pharmacists it is the 'South Asian' women who have a higher proportion of pharmacy owners - 22% compared with 14% of African Asian respondents and 6% of white female

111

pharmacists. Caution should be exercised here however, because numbers with regard in particular to the female respondents, are small when sub-samples are analysed separately.

Characteristics of owners

Respondents were asked what their original reasons were for going into business, and given a list of four to choose from along with an 'other reason' category. No statistically significant differences were found between both groups. Greater autonomy/independence was the reason cited by most respondents (82% and 76% white and ethnic minority respectively). Slightly more ethnic minority pharmacists than white went into business because of having a family background in business (24% against 18%) and slightly more white than ethnic minority pharmacists did it because their earning potential would be greater (50% against 42%).

Pharmacists are quite young when they become owners (average of 29.6 years). White pharmacists, however, are slightly older than the mean, (31 years), and minority pharmacists are younger (28.8), (Independent t-test, $p = 0.013$). African Asian pharmacists were the youngest (28.2 years).

Most pharmacists took over an established business (78%). While minority pharmacists had a slightly greater tendency to open a new business (25% compared with 14%) this difference did not reach statistical significance. Both white and minority pharmacists used, on average, two sources to raise capital for their business, while banks and personal loans were the most common sources of finance. Bank loans were used by 73% of the pharmacy owners (66% and 77% of white and minority pharmacists respectively), and personal savings were used by 59% (55% and 61% respectively), 42% used a loan from family (36% and 45% respectively), 31% raised finance through a wholesaler loan scheme, 9% loaned money from friends. Interestingly, no one reported using a rotating credit scheme to raise business finance.

Minority pharmacists differ significantly in relation to the location of the pharmacy in which they work. More than twice the proportion of minority pharmacists work in inner cities compared with white pharmacists (28% and 14% respectively), and more than three times the proportion of white pharmacists work in rural locations (25% and 8% respectively). This pattern held true regardless of job position held in the pharmacy.

Pharmacy ownership seems to provide a good living, such that in this sample more minority pharmacists than white are found in the highest income bracket, with just over twice the proportion earning over £42,500 when compared to white pharmacists (15% and 7% respectively). This difference is significant but only holds true for those pharmacists who work in retail practice. Nobody who works in hospital practice earns above £42,500, and while slightly more ethnic minority pharmacists are in the lowest income bracket (62% compared with 53%) this difference does not reach statistical significance. There are only 26 minority pharmacists working in hospital practice however, so once again caution should be exercised in interpreting these figures.

On the whole, the minority retail pharmacists work significantly longer hours than white pharmacists, even controlling for work extent. White pharmacists who work full-time work an average 43.1 hour week, while African Asians work an average of 49.5 hours, the South Asians work 45.1 hours and the Chinese work an average of 45.7 hours per week (p = 0.000, anova). Minority owner pharmacists work an even longer week - 52.4 hours compared with 47 hours for white pharmacy owners.

Differences between registration cohorts

Are there any differences between the pharmacists in the different qualification cohorts? While comparing the pharmacists between cohorts can provide useful insights into trends and changing patterns of ethnic minority participation in pharmacy, readers ought to be aware of the small sample sizes when the data is analysed in this way. While this is partly a reflection, in absolute terms, of the relatively small number of ethnic minority pharmacists in the three particular qualification years, it also reflects the lower response rate to the questionnaire from the ethnic minority pharmacists.

If the different qualification cohorts are analysed separately an interesting picture emerges with regard to the ethnic group breakdown of the minority respondents. While there are only 23 Pakistani pharmacists in the sample as a whole, 14 (61%) are 1991 qualifiers and both Bangladeshi pharmacists are also from the 1991 cohort. Of the 78 Indian pharmacists 45 (58%) are 1991 qualifiers, 3.5 times the number in the 1975 cohort. Among the minority pharmacists, African Asian pharmacists dominated the 1975 cohort, but the 1991 cohort was dominated instead by pharmacists of Indian origin. The majority of minority pharmacists from each of the cohorts are overseas born, but the proportion born overseas diminishes substantially from the 1975 to the 1991 cohort. All ethnic minority pharmacists who qualified in 1975 were born overseas, while in 1991 46% were UK born.

Class origins of respondents

In looking at stratification position the SOC schema was used to classify father's occupation at the time the respondent was at school (Table 6). Most respondents in each of the three cohorts had fathers whose jobs at the time placed them in the top two social classes (61%, 60% and 66% in the three cohorts respectively), indicating that on the whole pharmacy recruits from the non-manual rather than manual classes. However, minor changes have taken place in the class composition of the earlier and later cohorts. Overall, the proportion of white pharmacists in the top two classes has increased from 57% in 1975 to 72% in 1991, while almost the reverse has happened for the minority pharmacists - from 70% in 1975 to 58% in 1991. This may be a result of the changing nature of the ethnic group composition of the minority pharmacists, who in 1975 were predominantly East African Asian, compared with 1991 when they were predominantly Indian.

In 1975 57% of the white pharmacists were in social class I and II compared with 70% of the minority pharmacists. The latter however, compared with white pharmacists, were over represented in social class II (56% compared with 28%) and under represented in social class I (15% compared with 29%). The concentration in social class II is primarily because of the major presence of the African Asian pharmacists in the 1975 cohort whose fathers' were typically owners of small businesses in the East African countries where they lived prior to migration to the U.K.

Table 5.6
Social class (according to father's occupation) and ethnic group of pharmacists in all cohorts together

column percentages

SOCIAL CLASS	White	All Minority	South Asian	African Asian	Chinese	Black	Other	ALL
I	33	20	13	20	23	70	27	29
II	34	44	34	56	45	0	47	37
III (N)	12	7	9	5	14	10	7	11
III (M)	15	17	24	12	18	10	13	16
IV	4	9	15	7	0	10	7	6
V	1	2	4	0	0	0	0	1
B a s e (n)	519	243	91	105	22	10	15	762

114

The 1985 cohort saw an increase in the proportion of white pharmacists in the top two classes (65%) but a decrease in the proportion of minority pharmacists (52%) in the same categories. This may partly be due to the growing (but still small) number of Indian pharmacists in the 1985 cohort, the majority of whom (30%, n=7) were in social class IIIM. African Asian pharmacists were still concentrated and over represented in class II, (again because of the preponderance of fathers who were self-employed business owners), but compared with those in 1975 there were also more in social class IIIM.

Between the 1985 and 1991 cohorts, the proportion in social class I increased from 24% to 31%. Indian pharmacists were still under represented in class I and II compared to the cohort as a whole; African Asian pharmacists while increasing their proportion in class I from 16% in 1985 to 27% in 1991 still remain concentrated and over represented in social class II.

Career motivation

Interestingly, career intentions varied significantly between the ethnic groups, and any differences were exaggerated throughout subsequent qualification cohorts. The majority of both White and African Asian pharmacists in 1975 (84% and 80%) originally wanted to study pharmacy, while 6% and 18% wanted to study medicine. However, the opposite was true for the very small number of Indian pharmacists who qualified in 1975-8 (80%) originally wanted to study medicine and 20% wanted to study pharmacy. In 1985 the proportion who wanted to study medicine increased slightly compared with the previous decade - 17% against 13%. While medicine was still a firm favourite among the minority pharmacists (29% originally wanted to study medicine), a growing proportion (17%) chose other degree courses in preference to pharmacy. Overall, in 1985 significantly fewer minority respondents (54%) compared to white respondents (77%) had chosen pharmacy as their first choice. By 1991 19% wanted to study medicine, 12% of the white pharmacists and 29% of the minority pharmacists, and fewer had chosen other courses.

Just over 10% of the 1975 cohort reported having relatives who were pharmacists at the time they were choosing their course. African Asian pharmacists in the 1975 cohort were slightly more likely to have a pharmacist in the family than white pharmacists (15% compared with 10%), however the difference did not reach statistical significance. The proportion of pharmacists in the 1985 cohort who had a pharmacist relative increased to 20%, but unlike the 1975 cohort, there are significant differences between white and minority pharmacists in the 1985 cohort, such that proportionately more minority than white pharmacists had a pharmacist in the family (28% and 16% respectively). Compared with Indian pharmacists, African Asian pharmacists were even more likely to have a pharmacist relative (22% and 41% respectively), a reflection perhaps of their earlier representation in the profession. By 1991 fewer white respondents had pharmacist relatives (11%), while the proportion among Indian and African Asians was 16% and 53% respectively. Over the three years as a whole ethnic minority pharmacists were also more likely to have personal or family friends who were pharmacists (34% compared with 22%).

While by no means the main influence on career choice, wanting to own a business was a minor or major influence on choosing pharmacy for significantly more of the minority pharmacists than the white respondents throughout each of the qualification cohorts. In 1975 64% of the minority pharmacists thought it an important consideration (compared with 21% of whites); by 1991 the proportion had dropped to 52%. In 1975 the proportion of African Asians who thought it a minor or major consideration was 72%, in 1985 this had fallen to 54%, and the proportion fell again in 1991. Indian students in 1991 were actually more likely than the African Asian students to want their own business, 59% compared with 47%.

Branch intention

In their last year of pharmacy school most of the 1975 qualifiers knew which branch of pharmacy they wanted to work in - 42% wanted to work in retail practice, 22% wanted to work in hospital, and 4% wanted to work in another branch or go into research. Perhaps not surprisingly at this early stage in their career, a large proportion overall were undecided or had no clear idea about what they wanted to do (31%). There were clear differences between white and minority pharmacists with regard to career intention however. Significantly more minority pharmacists intended on going into community pharmacy (57% compared with 37%), while only 6%, compared with 28% of the white pharmacists, had decided on hospital practice. While on the whole the 1975 respondents reported no difficulties getting their first job immediately after their pre-registration post, some pharmacists, proportionately more minority respondents than white, reported having some or great difficulty getting their pre-registration post (22% and 6% respectively). The exact nature of this difficulty was explored in an open question. Preliminary perusal of the answers suggests a variety of factors were of concern to the minority pharmacists. Most comments from the 1975 cohort were about the general difficulty of getting an interview or a job in a fiercely competitive situation.

Among the 1985 cohort the proportions who intended to work in community and hospital pharmacy were similar to those of the 1975 qualifiers. However, in comparison with the earlier cohort more ethnic minority pharmacists expressed an intention to work in hospital practice (13% compared with 6%). Among the 1985 qualifiers, the South Asian pharmacists had a similar profile to the white pharmacists with regard to practice intentions, that is, that while most preferred community practice, some mentioned hospital practice, while African Asian pharmacists maintained their preference for community practice. As with the 1975 qualifiers, the majority of those in the 1985 cohort with firm intentions about the branch in which they intended to work succeeded with their intention and very few, white or minority, reported any difficulties (9% in both cases) getting their first job. However, like the 1975 qualifiers, a small proportion of the 1985 cohort did report difficulties getting a pre-registration position, and the proportion is larger among the later cohort (20% compared with 10%). Like the 1975 cohort, significantly more minority pharmacists from among the 1985 qualifiers reported difficulties securing their pre-registration post compared with the white pharmacists (30% and 15% respectively). As with the 1975 cohort, competition for places was viewed as a cause of difficulty for some. A very small number mentioned racial discrimination, and several talked about the difficulties securing a position in the geographical location of their choice.

Very similar trends were seen in the 1991 cohort regarding practice intentions, but it seems that an increasing proportion of minority pharmacists reported some or great difficulty getting their pre-registration position. The proportion was 22% in 1975, by 1991 it was 37%. This probably reflects the difficulties generally in the number of places available, but the higher proportion of minority students who report difficulties compared to white students (21%) raises some concerns.

Respondents were asked why they chose their preferred branch, and many of the ethnic minority pharmacists mentioned wanting their own business as a reason for wanting to go in to community pharmacy, as well as the status they perceived it held. Others commented on community pharmacy providing a good mix of professional and business activities, and for some the prospect of earning a good living was a motivator. These reasons seemed to be apparent throughout each of the registration cohorts.

Possible explanations for concentration of Asian pharmacists in pharmacy business

Why should the Asian respondents be concentrated so heavily in retail pharmacy? Do minority pharmacists start their career with the intention of going into business or does their career and daily work experience over a number of years affect their aspirations and progress such that they are 'pushed' into self-employment? At this point it is useful to look at some of the theoretical frameworks which have been developed to explain ethnic minority involvement in business.

The stereotypical image of Asians in business is one of an over-worked individual, surviving on low profit margins and managing only with the help of family support and long hours, often pushed into self-employment in order to minimise the effects of blocked mobility (Jones, 1982, Brooks, 1983, Robinson and Flintoff, 1982). Such 'structural' explanations for entry into business focus on the position of migrants within the social and economic structure, and explain minority business as a reaction to any disadvantage they experience. The nature of their entry into and role within the labour market is seen as a motivating factor in ethnic minority business development. Discriminatory employment practices and the type of industries in which minority groups work have a detrimental effect on their employment opportunities and self-employment is considered a way out of the cycle of disadvantage. High levels of unemployment, discriminatory employment practices, poor qualifications, and personal experiences of racial discrimination in the workplace, are all, according to this model, very strong pre-disposing factors pushing ethnic minorities towards self-employment. Can pharmacy business be typified in this way?

Clearly pharmacists are well-educated and if they are more likely to be found in self-employment compared with white pharmacists it would be difficult to argue that they are pushed into self-employment because of poor qualifications, or indeed because of unemployment, since in the pharmacy profession this is negligible (Anon., 1996). However, we could speculate that it is discrimination which pushes ethnic minority pharmacists into the self-employed sector of the profession. It is possible that Asian pharmacy business is a product of racial disadvantage, with Asian minorities using entry into retail pharmacy as a strategy for occupational mobility because their career paths in other branches of the profession are blocked.

There is some evidence to suggest that ethnic minority pharmacists may be discriminated against early on in their careers. The greater difficulty experienced by the ethnic minority pharmacy graduates obtaining pre-registration positions have already been noted. A few ethnic minority respondents, notably employees working for chain pharmacies and those working in industry, also mentioned their personal experience of racial discrimination, or their fear of it occurring later on in their career:

I have applied for many positions in the past where not only was I the only internal applicant and most suitably qualified..., I was turned down due to racism. I have spoken to colleagues in different hospitals who have encountered racism as a barrier in career progression *(male, aged 29, Indian, born in Malawi, works in hospital pharmacy)*.

I work for a large company and come from an ethnic minority; when I look at all the top jobs they are occupied by non-blacks. Pharmacy is a profession with a high black percentage compared to other professions, so the distribution should show this *(male, aged 26, Indian, born in U.K., works in industry)*.

This *fear* of being on the receiving end of racial discrimination could be enough to prevent some from choosing a career outside retail pharmacy. Accounts of racism which came out during the face to face interviews with owner pharmacists, suggest that the experience of colleagues or friends working for multiples may have had an impact on their own career intentions:

Yes, progression up the career ladder [is difficult], because most of the chaps who come out of [company X], you ask them and they say there weren't many prospects, or that somebody newly qualified went up the ladder faster than me *(male, owner, aged 54, East African Asian, born in Tanzania)*.

Some of the problems that Asian pharmacists face is that some day their face won't fit, in employment. This was my fear. My uncle who set up his own business in 1980 was told there was only so far he could go into Boots. That level and no more. Doesn't matter how many years service and how brilliant you are, you rise to that level and then that's it, you don't go any further *(male, owner, aged 33, born in Kenya)*.

Findings from another part of the study (Hassell, 1996b) also suggest that minority pharmacists may be discriminated against through their experiences of the disciplinary procedures in the profession - that is, more minority pharmacists than white appear before the Statutory Committee. This committee however, deals primarily with offences committed by community practitioners. Since most minority pharmacists work in this sector of the profession anyway, it could be that their apparent over representation before the disciplinary body is simply a reflection of the number practising in this branch.

The other main model put forward to explain ethnic minority business development is referred to as the 'cultural' model. This model argues that the cultural and class resources of some ethnic minority groups are more important in motivating individuals to go into self-employment (Waldinger et al., 1990, Robinson and Flintoff, 1982, Baker, 1981/82). So, for example, a distinction is drawn between Asian sub-groups, some of whom have previous business experience, and a strong entrepreneurial ethic or long-standing tradition of involvement in trade. Attitudes and cultural heritage or attributes such as diligence, hard work, family and kinship ties, are all said to equip individual members of an ethnic group for business, by offering important sources of recruitment and networking. This cultural heritage, attributes and ethnic resources, are thus said to act as strong 'pull' factors, pre-disposing many towards self-employment, and are seen as more important than 'push' factors such as unemployment. In addition to these 'ethnic resources' other writers have argued that entrepreneurs will also draw on class resources (Modood, 1991, Rafiq, 1992, Ram and Holliday, 1993). Access to money to invest in business, educational and technical skills, all determined by social class life experiences, will help determine the type of business that is set up. This model assumes that self-employment is an option freely chosen by individuals who then build up from their ethnic and class resources.

There is some evidence from the survey to support this model. There are many Asian pharmacists in this sample from East Africa. Most, if not all come from a trading background. Their class position, by virtue of having fathers who owned their own businesses, is predominantly middle class, unlike the Indian and Pakistani pharmacists whose class origins are more mixed, with a greater proportion coming from the manual classes.

Many left the East African countries in which they lived because of the 'Africanisation' policies, and sought in this country a professional occupation which would improve their own class status but which would at the same time offer some scope to pursue business opportunities. Wanting to work in a well respected profession and wanting their own business were both seen as important factors in choosing to do pharmacy. Many specifically intended to work in the retail sector of the profession because of the opportunity it provided for business ownership. Many of the ethnic minority pharmacists, especially the East African Asians, were also more likely to have family and or friends in pharmacy, suggesting that occupational inheritance in ownership is also important.

One other model, which combines elements of both the models discussed so far, is the 'opportunity' model (Waldinger et al., 1990, Yoon, 1995). It takes a more interactive approach, arguing that it is important to take account of the economic environment in which business operates as well as the resources different ethnic groups bring (or do not, as the case may be) to business development. This model suggests that the market conditions, access to ownership, any predisposing factors such as blocked mobility or aspiration levels of the ethnic group members *and* their ability to mobilise resources should all be considered together in looking for explanations about ethnic business development. This model may help to explain the differences between the different ethnic groups, most particularly the two largest groups, the Indians and the African Asians. For instance, the Indian pharmacists, whose entry into the profession occurred later than the East African Asians, and many of whom are British born, are more likely to have more diverse career intentions, with a greater proportion aiming to work in hospital pharmacy rather than in a retail setting. They are less likely to be attracted to pharmacy because of the business opportunities, are more likely to come from manual class backgrounds compared with the African Asian pharmacists, and less likely to have friends or family in business or in the pharmacy profession. Class resources such as these are an important explanatory factor in the 'opportunity' model, since without them, the model maintains, it is more difficult to set up in business. The owner pharmacists who were interviewed often talked about the resources they called upon throughout the course of developing their pharmacy business, including advice from family about setting up a business; advice and physical help in running the pharmacy, as well as financial support. The survey results demonstrate that these type of resources are not available to all ethnic groups equally, suggesting that this model may be have more power in explaining the differences in pharmacy business ownership among the different groups in the study. It could be for example, that the more recent entry of Indians to pharmacy, has more parallels with the feminisation process which has, and still is, taking place in the profession.

Conclusion

It is clear from the analysis of the names of pharmacists who qualified in 1975, 1985 and 1991, provided by the RPSGB, that the pharmacy profession is becoming increasingly 'Asianised'. Not just because of the increased participation of Asians themselves however, but also because of the decline in the number of white men joining the profession. The feminisation process noted by previous researcher continues, but ethnic minority women are playing an increasingly important part in this process.

The findings from this study indicate that previous figures have under estimated the extent of ethnic minority participation in the pharmacy profession. Compared to their proportion in the population as a whole, all the ethnic minority groups are over represented in pharmacy.

With negligible to low unemployment, and with lower pre-entry qualification requirements compared to, say, medicine, the pharmacy profession provides easier access to a professional occupation and excellent employment prospects for those who choose a career in it. With the same basic qualification and skill level on graduation all groups of pharmacists potentially have equal opportunities to enter any sector of the profession they prefer. Nevertheless, some ethnic minority groups are over represented as owners in the retail sector. Compared to the white pharmacists all minority ethnic groups except the Black African and Other Asian pharmacists are disproportionately found in retail practice and all except the Black Africans are over represented as self-employed owners. In particular, the East African Asians, the Indian and Pakistani pharmacists are over-represented as owners, while white and Black African pharmacists are under represented.

That most of the minority ethnic groups possess a cultural preference for self-employment has been demonstrated. Compared to the average and to white pharmacists as a group, all the ethnic minority groups except the Other Asians were more heavily influenced by the opportunities for business in choosing a pharmacy career and a greater percentage of the Indian, Pakistani and East African Asian pharmacists always intended to work in retail pharmacy after qualification. Of all the ethnic groups though, the East African Asians have by far the highest actual presence as self-employed owner pharmacists, suggesting that factors other than cultural predisposition are important in determining pharmacy self-employment.

The results suggest support for the interactive model of entrepreneurship as an explanation for ethnic minority group participation in pharmacy business since, as Mars and Ward argue, a predisposition to business, while a bonus, is only one resource needed for commercial success (Mars and Ward, 1984). While access to finance is one such major resource, with ethnic groups often having a preferential access to informal sources of finance, the pharmacists do not appear to be any different regarding access to capital, with most owner pharmacists, irrespective of ethnic status, using banks for capital loans. This is probably not too surprising given that pharmacy is a high status occupation, seen as a lucrative and safe, fairly stable, investment for banks (Dhalla, 1993). As such the pharmacists would have less need to turn to informal sources for help. Furthermore, the sort of money which is necessary to open a pharmacy business may be outwith the resources of even the most successful business oriented ethnic minority family.

Some ethnic groups however, do appear to have certain advantages with regard to other key resources. With the highest self-employment rate the East African Asian pharmacists appear to have particular privileges over other groups which may facilitate their entry into retail pharmacy. They are more likely to come from a business oriented family, and they are more likely to have a relative who is also a pharmacist, thus are more likely to have better access to business or financial advice.

The findings have several implications for the profession itself. The very young and teenagers make up a larger proportion of ethnic minority populations and since higher education is encouraged among some ethnic minority groups, (reflected in their greater propensity to stay in full-time education), their presence may well increase over the next few years. Certainly the UCAS data confirm this. Discussions between the Commission for Racial Equality and the RPSGB indicate a reluctance on the part of the professional body to recognise the ethnic diversity in the profession (Editorial, 1996). One effect of this 'colour blind' approach is that accusations of racial prejudice, which the profession is becoming increasingly alert to, cannot be countered. Another is that workforce planning cannot take account of changing practice patterns, and the different motivations and aspirations of all pharmacists.

If the prospect of owning a business is what is attracting some ethnic minority students to enter pharmacy then the changing organisational structure in terms of the growing prominence of chain pharmacies, contract limitations preventing new businesses opening, and the increased employee status highlighted earlier on, will have the greatest impact on ethnic minority pharmacists. If, on the other hand, a growing proportion of the younger ethnic minority pharmacists are broadening their career aspirations to include sectors of the profession other than retail, there is a danger that stereotyping all 'Asian' pharmacists as wanting to become entrepreneurs, or discriminating against those who choose specialties other than business ownership, will reduce the career opportunities available to them. This could cause high levels of dissatisfaction among practitioners, unemployment even, and may ultimately have wider implications for future workforce planning, especially in those sectors of the profession in which there is expected to be a shortfall of practitioners.

References

Anon. (1987), 'Report of BPSA 1987 Conference Proceedings', *Pharmaceutical Journal*, 238, 529.

Anon. (1992), 'Oswhal Pharmacists', *Pharmaceutical Journal*, October 17, 512.

Anon. (1993), '50% of independent pharmacies Asian owned', *Pharmaceutical Journal*, December 4, 781.

Anon. (1996), 'Survey suggests hospital manpower shortage', *Pharmaceutical Journal*, 256, 853.

Anwar, M. and Ali, A. (1987), *Overseas Doctors. Experience and Expectations: A research Study*, CRE: London.

Baker, A.M. (1981/2), 'Ethnic enterprise and modern capitalism: Asian small business', *New Community*, Vol. 9, pp. 478-86.

Bottero, W. (1992), 'The changing face of the Professions? Gender and explanations of women's entry to pharmacy', *Work, Employment and Society*, Vol. 6, No. 3, pp. 329-346.

Brooks, A. (1983), 'Black businesses in Lambeth: obstacles to expansion', *New Community*, Vol. 11, No. 1, pp. 42-54.

Brown, C. (1984), *Black and White Britain: the third PSI Survey*, Heinemann: London.

Brown, M.E., Ellis, S., Linley, P.A., and Booth, T.G. (1992), 'Professional values and pharmacy practice: implications of a predominantly female Register of Pharmaceutical Chemists', *The International Journal of Pharmacy Practice*, Vol. 1, pp. 178-83.

Crompton, R. and Sanderson, K. (1986), 'Credentials and careers: some implications of the increase in professional qualifications amongst women', *Sociology*, Vol. 20, No. 1, pp. 25-42.

Crompton, R. and Sanderson, K. (1990), 'Qualifications and occupations: the example of pharmacy', in *Gendered Jobs and Social Change*, Unwin Hyman: London, pp. 65-88.

Dhalla, M. (1993), 'Banking on pharmacy', *Pharmaceutical Journal*, Vol. 251.

DoH (1995), *Statistical Bulletin: General Pharmaceutical Services in England 1994-95*, Government Statistical Service: London.

Editorial (1996), 'Pharmacists and ethnicity', *Pharmaceutical Journal*, Vol. 256.

Hassell, K. (1996a), 'White and ethnic minority pharmacists' professional practice patterns and reasons for choosing pharmacy', *The International Journal of Pharmacy Practice*, Vol. 4, pp. 43-51.

Hassell, K. (1996b), 'A Study of Statutory Committee Charges and Ethnic Origin', *Pharmaceutical Journal*, Vol. 257, R43.

Jones, T. (1982), 'Small business development and the Asian community in Britain', *New Community*, Vol. 9, pp. 467-77.

Jones, T. (1993), *Britain's Ethnic Minorities*, Policy Studies Institute: London.

Magirr, P. and Ottewill, R. (1995), 'Measuring employee/contractor balance', *Pharmaceutical Journal*, Vol. 254, pp. 876-879.

Mars, G. and Ward, R. (1984), 'Ethnic business development in Britain: opportunities and resources', in *Ethnic Communities in Business*, R. Ward and R. Jenkins (eds), Cambridge University Press: Cambridge, pp. 1-19.

Modood, T. (1991), 'The Indian Economic Success: A challenge to some race relations assumptions', *Policy and Politics*, Vol. 19, No. 3, pp. 177-189.

Muzzin, L., Brown, G.P., and Hornosty, R.W. (1994), 'Consequences of feminisation of a profession: The case of Canadian Pharmacy', *Women and Health*, Vol. 21, Nos 2/3, pp. 39-56.

Nicoll, A., Bassett, K., Ulijaszek, S.J. (1986), 'What's in a name? Accuracy of using surnames and forenames in ascribing Asian ethnic identity in English populations', *Journal of Epidemiology and Community Health*, Vol. 40, pp. 364-8.

Rafiq, M. (1992), 'Ethnicity and Enterprise: A comparison of Muslim and non-Muslim owned Asian business in Britain', *New Community*, Vol. 19, pp. 43-60.

Ram, M. and Holliday, J. (1993), 'Relative merits: family culture and kinship in small firms', *Sociology*, Vol. 27, pp. 629-48.

Ranger, C. (1988), *Ethnic Minority School Teachers: A survey in eight local education authorities*, CRE: London.

Robinson, V. and Flintoff, I. (1982), 'Asian retailing in Coventry', *New Community*, Vol. 10, No. 2, pp. 251-8.

Smith, A. (1992), 'Pharmacy - moving towards an employee profession', *Chemist and Druggist*, 29 August, pp. 364-365.

Smith, D. J. (1980), *Overseas Doctors in the National Health Service*, PSI: London.

Smith, P. (1989), *The Bar Council Race Relations Survey*, SCPR: London.

Waldinger, R., Aldrich, H. and Ward, R. (1990), 'Opportunities, Group Characteristics and Strategies', in Waldinger, R., Aldrich, H., Ward, R. (eds), *Ethnic Entrepreneurs*, Sage: London.

Yoon, I.J. (1995), 'The growth of Korean immigrant entrepreneurship in Chicago', *Ethnic and Racial Studies*, Vol. 18, No. 2, pp. 315-335.

6 Poverty, Race and Partnership: A Study of the Third European Anti-Poverty Programme in Liverpool

Gideon Ben-Tovim, Manneh Brown, Paul Kyprianou and Barney Rooney

Introduction

A project to combat poverty targeted particularly at Liverpool's Black community, and based around a partnership methodology, is of particular relevance to the current period, when 'social exclusion' and partnership working are two of the key issues on the current national social policy agenda.

Liverpool was one of the sites of the Third European Anti-Poverty programme and the University of Liverpool was contracted to act as the local evaluator of this strand of the programme. This paper attempts to draw out some of the key issues that emerged from this programme, in the hope that lessons may be learnt for future anti-poverty, race specific and partnership projects.

Liverpool is a city with a tradition of strong Black community organisation, multiple social policy experimentation, with key national and now European regeneration developments. There is also a growing recognition of the value of partnerships and community participation, with the latest approach to partnerships, the 'Pathways to Integration' programme funded under the European Objective One programme, considered to be at the leading edge of community based regeneration.

The Liverpool case-study then, of the Poverty Three programme, is of significance for any contemporary over-view of urban inequality and any future development of European social initiatives. Racism, poverty, social exclusion are all inextricably linked in the Granby/Toxteth area, where Britain's longest established Black community and Britain's poorest region have intertwined to produce a situation of profound social disadvantage that may be a sign-post for other cities in the context of continued poverty, racism and xenophobia.

The third European anti-poverty programme

The European Community Programme for the Social and Economic Integration of the Least Privileged Groups, or Poverty 3 as it became more commonly known, followed two previous Community Programmes to combat poverty (1975-1980 and 1984-1989). The duration of Poverty 3 was to be 5 years, 1989-1994, though it actually began on the 1st March 1990. The Programme was seen as making a qualitative and quantitative step forward in the support given to innovation in respect of anti-poverty policy and practice. Poverty 3 was to be 'a coherent multi-dimensional approach to poverty and social exclusion based on partnership with public and private institutions and with the participation of the least privileged groups'.[1]

As well as having to be multi-dimensional, participative and based on a partnership, the model projects had other principles to which they were to adhere. These were additionality - the attracting of extra resources; exchange - the sharing of good practices; subsidiarity -being operated at the appropriate, lowest organisational level i.e. informed by the experience of excluded groups themselves; transferability - that activities of the project should be capable of being used elsewhere; and visibility - that activities should be open to public scrutiny.

The context

Poverty 3 was launched against a background of increasing poverty, unemployment and homelessness in the European Community. The impact of poverty on an increasingly large scale threatened political and social stability as well as being damaging to the economies and welfare systems of member States.

Nowhere in Europe was poverty growing faster than in the UK. The final report of the Second European Poverty Programme identified Britain as having the sharpest increase in poverty between 1980 and 1985. The CPAG produced evidence to show that nearly a fifth of the population was in poverty which had increased from 4.9 million in 1979 to over 10 million in 1987. Follow up work published by the Joseph Rowntree Foundation confirmed the trend in economic inequality, noting that between 1979 and 1992 the poorest 20 to 30 percent of the population failed to benefit from economic growth and that only one country in the world had a greater growth in income inequality than Britain between 1979 and 1990.

The Granby/Toxteth Community Project was the only 'model action' established in England, i.e. an initiative that was intended to provide an example of how member states could tackle social exclusion in their own countries. Liverpool's inclusion was based on its long tern economic decline, the impact of continued population loss and the growth of poverty and deprivation in the city. Liverpool's unique economic position as one of the poorest parts of Europe was subsequently confirmed in its identification as an Objective One Region. Research undertaken on behalf of the City Council in 1989 had shown that 40 per-cent of the population could be described as living in poverty, with a further 16 per-cent in intense poverty.[2]

One of the groups identified as most subject to poverty was Liverpool's Black population. The wards of Granby and Abercromby which have the highest percentage of the Black population were ranked amongst the most deprived wards of the city, with 63 per-cent of households in this area living in poverty, and with a black male unemployment rate of 56 per-cent.[3]

A crucial early turning-point in the life of the Project in Liverpool was the decision by the Management Committee to accept, on the recommendation of the evaluation team, the centrality of 'race' as the defining factor in the experience of social exclusion within the Granby/Toxteth area. The original Partner Agencies were the City Council, the University of Liverpool, the Health Authority, and a few representatives of several central government and local voluntary organisations including Merseyside Race Equality Council, Granby Toxteth Task Force, and Merseyside Task Force (later Government Office on Merseyside). They were then joined on the Management Committee by representatives of three umbrella bodies that had emerged from different elements within the Black community. The members of the staff team that were ultimately recruited were themselves predominantly recruited from the local Black community.

The Liverpool project raises issues, then of particular interest concerning the development of partnership where the issue of social exclusion is compounded with the issue of race. How successful, was the attempt in Liverpool to give a particularly significant profile to the race factor, including seeking representation within the Partnership of voices from the local black community, and also deliberately seeking staff with particular awareness of the problem of racism and knowledge of Liverpool's local black community?

The central issue of partnership

Liverpool has witnessed virtually all the social policy initiatives that have been directed towards arresting urban decline, promoting economic regeneration, tackling poverty and wider social exclusion. Previous initiatives had called for a 'total approach' to tackling poverty, a theme echoed in Poverty 3's call for 'multi-dimensionality' of approach. Experience of these earlier projects (Shelter Neighbourhood Action Project, Community Development Project, Inner Area Study) pointed to the need to be realistic about what a relatively small project could achieve, so that energies were not dissipated, or false expectations raised.[4]

The extent of organisational resistance to change was evidenced in previous local initiatives. This has important implications for Poverty 3, and its efforts to bring about significant changes within the Partner Agencies themselves and the way in which they related to the target area and dealt with issues of racism and poverty. It was intended that the Partnership members would be taking leading role themselves in focusing on the problems to be addressed.

Thus a crucial lesson of earlier urban policy experiments had been the reality that organisations had consistently failed to co-operate or give up power, and that even achieving co-ordination and co-operation between organisations was problematic. If this trend were repeated in Poverty 3, the notion of partnership would be seriously undermined.

As we shall see, these crucial lessons were not adequately learnt in the Poverty 3 partnership. The Management Committee never really 'gelled' into a coherent, body; relationships with the Project staff were unclear and uneasy; power was not given up or shared; community participation was not seriously addressed. The key principles of multi-dimensionality, partnership and participation were never satisfactorily adopted, and although some useful specific projects were delivered, these were not ultimately developed within a self-sustaining strategic framework.

The fundamental problem was the failure to develop a clear and open partnership, both in terms of the relationships between the Partners themselves, and in terms of their relationship with the staff group. The relative weakness of the Partnership and the tensions within it were reflected in the ultimate lack of a clear overall strategy for the programme (the 'multi-dimensionality' issue) and in the absence of on-going mechanisms for community accountability and involvement (the 'participation' principle).

What is partnership?

For the European Commission, in framing Poverty 3, 'Partnership is viable only if all the key players share a common approach. Partnership involves collective responsibility for the success of the entire Project and assumes the players are in a position to define a joint strategy based on a consensus which transcends their respective interests or differences'.[5]

At a practical level, an effective partnership would see a co-ordinated use of resources to maximise their benefit. Partnership also has the potential for changing individual and organisational attitudes. The Commission suggested that by 'giving informal or voluntary elements in the local mix the opportunity and confidence to confront more powerful interests; giving official agencies greater credibility with alienated groups; Partnerships have the potential to achieve all these effects'.[6]

Thus partnership was not viewed simply as a process of bringing together the various key players, with the term itself implying that there should be equality of influence. Partnership also had to involve those groups experiencing social exclusion. To what extent did the Granby Toxteth Community Project (GTCP) achieve these objectives contained in the general aim of achieving partnership?

The Commission's conditions of 'common approach', 'collective responsibility' and 'consensus which transcends their respective interests or differences' set conditions on the nature of the expected partnership which promised interesting dynamics given that the activity to counter 'exclusion' would attempt to draw together parties who, on the ground could clearly be seen to have opposed social and economic interests, though these may not have been acted out in my coherent structural way at the time.

The social exclusion of the Black community in Granby/Toxteth was understood by all parties to lie somewhere within the interaction of ideological, social and economic representations of racism, though different members would have had different interpretations of the balance in the mix. All subscribed to the idea that this exclusion was not simply a historical legacy but about contemporary dynamics in the social and economic life of the city, within which their agencies played a part. Their policy commitment was to take action to counter the influence of a living racism within their own practices and services, and their participation in Poverty 3 was one expression of that commitment.

But the 'model' for establishing partnership across the divide of exclusion proved to be elusive. The primary partnership of mainstream agencies (University, City Council, Health Authority) had the task of defining who would be drawn into the Partnership to represent the socially excluded and then had to find some way of working which established partnership across this division.

Having decided that race was central there was a range of options available, options which are well rehearsed in the history of race relations. They could carefully manage the selection of Black representation around compliant individuals; or they could take a developmental approach to support a process leading to some sort of democratic representation; or they could just put out the feelers and hope that they would get a constructive response. In the end they tried elements of all except the developmental approach.

As they moved to extend the partnership the reality of the divide came in to play and their approach were greeted by an ambivalent response from Black organisations. There were complaints that the Project had only been successful in attracting funding because it had invoked the issue of race and poverty, but that, having got the money, it had lost interest and was only attempting to engage the community belatedly because of EC scrutiny of evident incompetence in getting the project up and running (an accurate perception). A number of community based meetings considered the politics of joining the partnership, debating between abstention or making a strategic bid for ownership through participation, and they decided on the latter.

So, far from drawing ageants with different interests into a forum where they might find common ground, the Partnership Board was established as a theatre of division; the Management Committee became a forum for race politics at crude level, politics which were fundamentally oppositional and often directed to undermine the legitmacy of mainstream organisations and their confidence in dealing with Black community issues.

The mainstream maintained their formal authority but they were unable to translate it into influence within the Management Committee, unable to find the common ground and common cause which the programme required. They were more successful in expressing their authority through the contractual relationship with the employed staff of the project team but in the rough and tumble of the management group they were awkward and de-skilled. They therefore vested no authority in the Committee; some withdrew, others retained a formal presence but they did their business elsewhere. The partnership was fundamentally undermined.

While Black community representation could, and did, cause discomfort in the Committee, and could exert some influence over the allocation of some resources, they failed to translate their ability to discomfort into any constructive agenda which was in line with the objectives of Poverty 3 and which they could either carry on their own or share with the mainstream.

132

The Background Report had pointed out that there would be real difficulties in drawing people from the excluded community into effective partnerships.

'It is naive to presume that (project) activities which attempt to find an effective way of relating the experiences of people (in the target community) to the roles, responsibilities and day to day practices of the partner agenceis will not cause friction.' The Report proposed that to establish a partnership based on *equality* of contribution the Board had to consider adopting a structure which would allow both 'cooperative or oppositional action, and it recommended that the project should try to manage the potential for friction by institutionalising its divisions in an adversarial model which would: 'acknowledge that there is a shared interest in contesting poverty in the area but that the definition of issues (for action) requires a recognition that organisations and poor communities have different experiences, interests and constraints'. The mainstream Management Committee would have none of it.

The purpose of partnership working, that there is some collective dynamic that can transcend sectoral interest and give added value to individual contributions, was threatened from the day that the primary partners attempted to incorporate the 'excluded' in the structure of partnership. They managed the engagement without skill, foresight or courage and the partnership succumbed to the very divisions it was set up to bridge.

The crucial, defining feature of a successful partnership is a clear understanding by the partners, from the outset, of what the partnership would entail. The concept of partnership needed to be clearly defined and transparent guidelines were required that addressed such issues as who should represent Partners, what their roles and responsibilities were, what commitment to the Partnership actually meant and what mechanisms were required to translate this into action.

Throughout the life of the Project these issues were never satisfactorily resolved. Thus the issue of whether a Partnership member was there as an individual, or as an organisational representative, has significant implications for the strategic impact of the Project as a whole. It became clear, as the Project developed, that representatives did not seem to feed-back to their organisations what was happening within the Project, and so had limited impact on the mainstream activities of their institutions as they might relate to the race equality/anti-poverty agenda that the Project as a whole was seeking to address. There is little indication that the mainstream institutions gave recognition to their members' involvement in the Poverty 3 initiative, in terms of adequate time for meetings and follow-up work,

133

and indeed significant personnel and structural changes affected all the major Partner Agencies during the life-time of the Project.

A crucial issue with respect to the composition of the Partnership concerned the nature of the representation of local community groups or organisations on the Partnership itself. There was only one local organisation linked to the Black community involved at the outset, the Merseyside Race Equality Council. Unfortunately, this organisation was itself going through a difficult period during the life of the Project, and it was ultimately dissolved by the Commission for Racial Equality because of its internal organisational difficulties and its lack of external impact.

In seeking to strengthen its membership from within the Black community, the Management Committee sought to broaden its base by including representatives of three other umbrella organisations seeking to represent Black groups within the area. There are of course, many organisations operating within the Black community, which is not a homogeneous entity, but is made up of a range of different groupings and interests, none of which individually can be seen as representing the interests of the whole of the Black community. The Black community can be defined as such by the consolidating experience of racism, whilst this can be manifested in a range of different contexts that influence the development of a number of differing organisations, with varying degrees of credibility, durability or effectiveness.

With each of the organisations that became represented on the Partnership, there were questions about how effectively they were able to, or did, represent significant parts of the Black community. We have seen that the Merseyside Racial Equality Council effectively ceased to operate during the life of the Project; and as it transpired, all of the other three organisations involved had little significant base of active membership which could act as a conduit between the Management Committee and the Black Community whom they were supposed to represent. Thus the Afro-Asian-Caribbean Standing Committee was essentially a long-standing, traditional network rather than an active membership based organisation. The Confederation of Black Organisations had come into existence as a pressure group to intervene in a local regeneration initiative which had little community involvement. But like many issue based organisations, once the particular concern comes to some form of resolution, the organisation declines, and this has been the case with the CBO which largely ceased to exist as a viable organisation. The final group, Federation of Liverpool Black Organisations, had emerged as a political organisation to stand independent Black councillors, in local elections, but after the failure of two annual attempts, involving a declining number of participants, the organisation ceased to exist in any meaningful way as a representative body.

Thus all four organisations that were represented on the Management Committee were fundamentally flawed in terms of meaningful, active membership based groupings and yet the individuals involved continued until the end of the Project, and were never replaced. For a Project concerned to combat racism, this raised significant problems of legitimacy. The issue of Black community representation within the Partnership was an important issue that was never satisfactorily resolved. The question was clearly fudged by the Management Committee as a whole, who allowed the continuation of what was effectively only token community involvement in the management of the Project. No attempt was made to help develop organisations capable of providing a strong local residential perspective; and there was no initiative to formally involve some of the many active local projects, initiatives and interest groups.

There are several possible explanations for the failure to address this issue. There is the vested interest of existing representatives in maintaining the status quo, rather than acquiescing in their own lack of representative authority. Some of the existing Partner Agencies might have had anxieties in extending community participation, particularly by Black organisations, and perhaps therefore had their own interest in not challenging what they might have felt was simply too difficult a problem. Certainly if the membership of the Management Committee had been extended, it might have increased demands made on Partner Agencies. The Management Committee might have become more the forum of competing community interests and a less predictable body.

While it may have been easier not to tackle this issue, it meant that a wider community perspective was not developed. There was for instance, no involvement of community organisations representing women, or specifically black women, though these existed in the area. It was known that women as a group are over-represented in poverty and the socio-economic position of Black women is particularly disadvantaged. In fact the Management Committee was almost exclusively a male preserve.

Clearly, a partnership along the lines of the European Commission's intentions, was not established. The failure to include locally elected City Councillors was a further strand of the 'democratic deficit' of this initiative, which reflected perhaps the agenda of the central government of that time to by-pass local Councils in order to achieve a more direct though less accountable relationship with local communities. This dovetailed with the European Commission's aspiration to achieve the direct participation of the excluded.

The GTCP Management Committee was, then, insulated both from active community groups and from elected representatives. This meant that the 'Partnership' was in effect not 'owned' by any accountable organisation, a feature that perhaps contributed to the relative lack of public concern when the Project came to an end and to the failure to develop any consistent exit strategy.

The weakness of the Partnership, and its lack of a community involvement strategy, contrasts significantly with other initiatives established during the life-time of the GTCP such as City Challenge, where a systematic attempt was made to establish a broader organisational forum to link the voluntary and community sectors into the partnership board. The question must arise as to what extent did the issue of race encourage Partner Agencies to short-circuit procedures and issues that they would pursue more openly and consistently in other networks and institutional settings?

Participation and the black community

The European Commission saw the participation of the groups most affected by social exclusion to be essential for the action taken by local projects to be effective in achieving economic and social integration. 'The active involvement of the groups concerned in the integration process is a prerequisite for and a symbol of its success. It forms part of an approach which promotes citizenship and democracy, and wants the groups involved to be active partners in the policies being conducted'.

Historically, Liverpool's Black community has not enjoyed a good track-record of involvement with statutory and mainstream agencies. Lord Gifford's Inquiry suggested that 'Black organisations have been slighted and alienated by the local authority over many years'.[7] The experience of the Militant controlled Labour Council was still fresh in people's memory. It was recalled as a time when there had been manipulation of the community, attempts to fragment it, to co-opt parts of it and to question the legitimacy and representativeness of its organisations and structures.[8] The local community had not forgotten the attempts by the Liberal administration in an earlier period to shut down the Charles Wootton Centre for allowing the Liverpool 8 Defence Committee to have its head-quarters in its basement during the period of the 'riots' of 1981. The widespread and long-standing exclusion of the local black population from mainstream employment opportunities, and from access to key services (e.g. good quality council housing or high-achieving local schools) was a further cause for suspicion of the local establishment.[9]

To break through these barriers in terms of the workings of a local partnership body was likely, then, to be particularly challenging. We have already seen that the organisations that were brought on to the Management Committee to represent the Black community were not in a position to do this effectively. It was even more important then, that other ways of achieving participation were developed.

The original proposal put forward by the evaluation team was that representative structures and processes had to be established if participation was to be achieved in the terms called for by the Commission; in the first instance this would need to be based on existing community organisations and with their assistance, the participation and representation of 'target groups' would be developed. The formula proposed was for the creation of a number of forums based on target groups, which would elect or nominate a representative to be on the Management Committee.

In the end, the Project team developed some consultative forums, but these became issue based, e.g. over welfare rights or health, and had no impact on the overall management of the Project, where the forums were not represented. The Project team argued that the original participation methodology was 'arduous and unworkable' and attempts to involve the community 'met with apathy and disinterest'.[10] These are the natural experience of individuals and groups who lack power and influence and whose views are either not sought or are disregarded. By definition, these are central characteristics of social exclusion. It was virtually inevitable that the Project would encounter such attitudes and feelings, given the long history of marginalisation and alienation experienced by Liverpool's Black community.

Countering these and developing mechanisms to involve the community in the project needed to be viewed as a priority by the Management Committee and by Project staff. But community participation was never given a high enough priority by the Project, and it appears that both Management Committee members and Staff found it more congenial, in terms of their own respective interests and convenience, to accept a very limited formal community input to the initiative.

Clearly, then, the Commission's vision of participation by groups experiencing social exclusion with respect to management and policy development was not achieved within the Project. The involvement of a few individuals who appeared or claimed to represent the community was used as a short-cut to establishing deeper mechanisms of community participation. A key lesson here is that it requires time, imagination, resources and good-will, to systematically draw the energy of disadvantaged communities into the new initiatives and structures of regeneration partnerships.

The limits of multi-dimensionality

The third major principle lying behind Poverty 3, apart from partnership and participation was the issue of multi-dimensionality, which reflects the recognition that poverty and exclusion are multi-faceted phenomena. Income poverty is only one facet, others include access to, and quality of, basic services-education, housing, health, social welfare, as well as issues such as the quality of people's environment and employment opportunities. Over-riding these strands of exclusion lies the experience of racism, affecting all of these facets in the lives of the Black community. Hence there was a need to develop generalised strategies that were both coherent and co-ordinated. According to the Commission, then, what is needed is a strategic approach, not just a 'simple juxtaposition of isolated activities which have nothing in common or which are jumbled together in random groupings'.[11]

The lack of mutual confidence that emerged within the Management Committee, both amongst themselves and between Management and Staff, meant that the Partnership was too weak to develop a focused, strategic approach to dealing with poverty and racism. Thus the potentially broad base of the Project was not exploited to widen the impact and profile of the initiative. Likewise, the 'clout' represented on the Management Committee was not utilised to achieve high level policy, or structural, changes.

A specific example of the ad hoc, rather than strategic method of work can be seen in the approach to Welfare Benefits. Valuable work was done at a local level on this, an important issue given the high number of people in the area in receipt of state benefits; but the lack of strategic focus was manifest in the failure to seek to bring representatives of the Benefits Agency, or representatives of the Department of Social Security, onto the Management Committee, which would have developed their involvement in the Project and might have fostered joint policy initiatives.

Again, while some equal opportunities and positive action work was undertaken with local employers, the Project's initiatives were relatively under-developed in this area, and did not amount to a strategic approach. There was, for example, no private sector involvement on the Management Committee, which inevitably limited the focus of the Project. Even though the issue of equal opportunities was raised with respect to the Partner

Agencies' own employment profiles, this issue was not pursued systematically by Project Staff.

Indeed the historic ambivalence towards the mainstream institutions was reflected in the essential lack of willingness by the Project team to engage regularly with the public sector Partner Agencies. Achieving policy development with statutory bodies was not seen as a key task. Hence though the Project engaged in a range of activities, these did not amount to a strategic approach that engaged the Partner Agencies in a coherent and collaborative way. This clearly represented a lost opportunity, given the formal commitment of the Partners to contributing through their own organisations to policies and practices to reduce racism and poverty.

The most telling indicator of the absence of multi-dimensional approach came at the end of the Project. Given its pre-determined duration, there was a need to have a clear vision of what was to be achieved over this period and how the work was to be progressed once the GTCP had gone. As we have seen, there was a lack of structures and mechanisms tying Partner Agencies into a collaborative process of tackling racism and poverty during the life-time of the Project. This meant that there was no strategic, or operational pressure on the Management Committee to identify how such work was to be carried forward at the end of the project. The GTCP was simply allowed to wither away.

This contrasts with the elaborate and protracted efforts to provide an exit strategy for the locally based, government led Granby Toxteth Task Force, involving both the prolongation of the life of the Task Force, and the establishment of a successor body. Significantly it was some of the same Partner Agencies that were involved in the GTCP Management Committee that were able to find the means to simultaneously collaborate strategically in a different organisational context. This could suggest that the Partner Agencies were ultimately lacking in commitment to the partnership represented by the GTCP, with its clear formal race specific brief and its predominantly Black Staff; or if not lacking commitment, they were nonetheless disabled by the race issue to deal appropriately and professionally with the organisational and strategic demands of the initiative. It was perhaps this lack of commitment, or lack of appropriate responsiveness, that ultimately undermined the potential of the Project for multi-dimensionality.

The implementation of the project and its impact

The lack of a coherent and collaborative strategy involving the Partners, the Staff and the community, had the effect of limiting the effectiveness of the initiatives undertaken by the Staff of the project, whose responsibilities included welfare rights, training, health development, policy development and resources.

Thus one of the specific aims of the Project ultimately agreed by the Management Committee was to highlight the effects of poverty and racism in the Granby Toxteth community, and as a result two useful pieces of work were produced, one on employment policies of partner agencies, and another an in-depth survey of the needs of the Somali community with the active involvement of the Somali community itself.

The lack of strategic focus of the Project as a whole, and the lack of clarity over responsibilities, meant that these pieces of work were not followed up by sustained lobbying, or policy development. Likewise a local Skills Audit was commissioned, but not built into any practical follow-up action. It appeared that the Staff group felt it was the responsibility of the Partner Agencies to follow up the work of policy development; and on the other hand, the Management Committee did not pursue the development of milestones and performance indicators against which progress could have been measured and which might have generated a degree of pressure to ensure strategic targets were met.

A second aim was concerned with the active participation of the local community. Here, although the idea of linking community participation to the management of the Project was ultimately shelved, a degree of community participation was achieved in relation to some 'issue based' initiatives. Thus a local Health Forum was established by the Health Development Officer, which has become a useful network for members of the community and professional workers with health interests, and it has sought to intervene on policy and practice issues of Health and Social Services Agencies. Community involvement was also sustained for a period around the establishment of a pressure group to oppose the Child Support Act and to influence the Child Support Agency.

A further way of involving the community was through the establishment of a small grants scheme for start-up costs on innovative, self-help projects where other funds were not available. In total, over 50 different groups received financial help, including Luncheon Clubs, Arts projects, and advisory agencies. Although useful work was supported there seems to have been no clear strategic focus again - thus, it is not clear on what basis grants were given to the range of organisations and projects involved, and

140

there was little systematic follow-up or evaluation as to the impact of the grants.

Community training was also provided to individuals, including assertiveness training for the long-term unemployed and single parents; capacity-building courses for individuals working in local voluntary organisations; and popular pre-interview training. Training was also provided on equal opportunities issues to employers. While the training provided by the Project was beneficial in itself, there was no overall plan and no systematic monitoring of the effects. It is difficult, therefore to judge the impact of the training programme, as with the small grant programme, as once again there was no clear strategy and little systematic monitoring and review of the take up of training, which again was not systematically linked into the employment policies and practices of the Partner Agencies.

It is also difficult to judge the impact of the involvement of individual Staff in many external bodies during the life of the project, though this might well have had a cumulative impact on the outlook and activities of the organisations involved, such as the local City Challenge initiative and the Objective One Monitoring Committee. In some cases, however, clear successor organisations were established through the activities of the GTCP, such as the Toxteth Health Forum discussed above and the Granby Advice and Information Project which grew out of the information and training activities of the Project in the field of Welfare Benefits and Rights. The focus of this initiative is on empowering and informing the community by ensuring more local advice and training is available.

Again, though, this valuable development of work of the GTCP has not involved a focus on the on-going transformation of mainstream institutions policies, and practices, which should have been the other complementary approach to the community-based and representational activity. The lack of an integrated, multi-dimensional Partnership approach meant that the Project became more of a conventional community-based project, meeting some immediate or identified community or advocacy need rather than working collaboratively with key agencies to address the underlying causes and issues that created the need in the first place.

This unevenness of strategic approach to community participation was echoed by a parallel lack of coherence in the implementation of the third aim of the Project, i.e. the active participation of Partner Agencies in the development of policies and programmes aimed at the alleviation of poverty and racism in the Granby Toxteth area. Here the potential for developing the robust and targeted training and employment action highlighted at the beginning of the Project as a crucial mechanism for tackling racism and

141

poverty was never fully realised. Ad hoc steps were taken during the life of the Project, and since, to improve the track-record of mainstream employers with respect to training and employment opportunities of the local Black community, and to meeting some of the key service needs of Black and other minority ethnic groups. But the outcomes have been limited and still marginal to the massive exclusion of Liverpool's Black community from the labour market, and their significant under-achievement in key indicators such as education or health.

The scale of the task continues to require determined partnership and proactive links being established and maintained with the Black community. There is still a need for systematic and coherent training, employment and business creation measures, and a consistent measuring of outcomes and performance. The Granby Toxteth Community Project could have been at the forefront of developing these linkages and steps, through its community base and establishment contacts.

Perhaps the relatively short life-span of the project (little more than three years effectively, through staffing problems in the initial period and inevitable individual exit moves by people on short-term contracts), and the considerable turn-over and structural changes within Partner Agencies, provided too brief and unstable a base with which to accomplish this task, which involves trying to find sustainable mechanisms with which to overcome generations of racist exclusion. Also the relatively small resource contained within the Project, as measured against the complexity and size of the public and private sector agencies with a potential impact on the Granby community, and the proliferation of fragmented and frequently competitive initiatives, projects, and employment and training institutional players, makes for a difficult terrain within which to have a sustained impact even in the best of partnership circumstances.

The fourth aim of the Project, to build up community resources to highlight the inter-relationship between poverty and racism in the locality, indicated, again, the strengths and limits of the Project; on the one hand a locally disseminated quality newsletter, and useful materials resource base. and some valuable individual initiatives, such as the development of photography and journalism courses; but on the other, limited lasting or strategic developments, so that for example the issue of a satisfactory, locally produced and managed community newspaper has still not been resolved, a gap filled only by the Merseyside Police's local newsletter.

The final aim, to ensure that racism was seen as a key element in the explanation of poverty in the Poverty 3 programme and in future anti-poverty initiatives at European, national and local levels had the effect of ensuring that the needs of the Black community were at the forefront of the work of the Project. Some useful international links were forged, including with the Danish government which used the Liverpool experience to explore ways of accommodating the significant increase of the settlement of visible minorities in their country. Locally, most mainstream institutions do make reference to the particular needs of Liverpool's Black community, whilst equal opportunity policies are widespread, and feature in many Mission Statements. Arguably, the GTCP has been one of the influences that helped sustain the ideological climate to legitimise the specific focus on racism and on targeting the needs of the Black community.

But, as we have seen, the general acknowledgement of the issue of race has not necessarily been translated into sustained and monitored action. Both the local and the national agendas have moved on in the recent period towards a broad focus on social disadvantage, in Liverpool's case with an attempt to reach all the 'pathways' areas where there is a concentration on poverty and unemployment,[12] which subsequently brought addition Single Regeneration Budget resources to three pathways areas but not Granby Toxteth (despite it being the only area with a significant Black population) and in the Government's case with a broad approach to 'social exclusion' with so far limited reference to the particular connections between poverty and racism.

The contradictions of partnership

We have suggested that the overall principles lying behind the establishment of the Granby Toxteth Community Project, i.e. partnership, participation and multi-dimensionality in an attempt to tackle the linked issues of racism and poverty were not fully realised. Given the ambitious nature of the aims, and the relatively limited nature of the Project, this is not altogether surprising. But there were specific issues with respect to the relationship between Management Committee and Staff that proved fundamental in the ability of the Project to achieve its overall, far-reaching aims, and which are perhaps of wider relevance to the process of construction of partnerships.

Conflicts and tensions with respect to full-time professional staff and voluntary committee membership are endemic; and partnerships between powerful institutional agencies and relatively disadvantaged community organisations have an inbuilt danger of token collaboration, with the organisations not yielding power or individual freedom of competitive action whatever the rhetoric of co-operation. Thus to create meaningful and effective partnerships, including participation and multi-dimensionality, is full of potential pitfalls and contradictions, even without the added complexity of race factor.

This Partnership seems to have lost its way as a strategic initiative, and ended more as an issue based, community project, with few organic links being forged between the work of Project staff and the activities of Partner Agencies, which were meant to be brought together through the reinforcing linkages of the Management Committee.

Underlying tensions were never properly resolved. Thus Partner Agencies felt that staff had a 'hands off approach' to what was a 'community-owned' project, and were unwilling to engage with the public sector institutions; instead they found it easier to criticise a racist system from an outsider position, rather than get involved (or be seen to get involved) in the process of changing it. This tactical self-preservation by Project Staff had the effect of letting Partner Agencies 'off the hook', so that they were not subject to the sustained, dialogue and collaborative effort necessary to challenge and ameliorate entrenched racial exclusion.

On the other hand the suspicion and mistrust of the Staff was not entirely misplaced. After all, the Partners were representatives of agencies that had at best an uneven track-record on 'race'. Staff appeared to lack confidence in the commitment, legitimacy and competence of the Partners to wish them to have a more substantial role in the project; which in its turn made some Partners reluctant to get involved. Staff were also aware of the lack of representativeness and the fluctuation in membership of individuals on the Committee, and their apparent failure to 'put their own houses in order'; there were also evidence of the unwillingness of Partners to openly share the separate agendas, interests and power of their own organisations.

The limitations in the relationship between Management Committee and Staff had significant consequences. Partner Agencies were not the subject of rigorous scrutiny in respect to their policies and practices, Staff were not challenged as to the extent to which strategic objectives were being met. While there was valuable work undertaken by the GTCP, overall it lacked a strategic focus, as seen for example in the absence of a clear strategy on training and employment and the exclusion of the Black community from the workforce.

The clearest indication of the lack of a coherent overall approach by the Project was the absence of an agreed or implemented exit strategy. This was particularly significant given the development of new economic and social regeneration initiatives that were occurring as the Project ended. Thus there was no community preparedness for the new local partnership initiatives established under the European Objective One and 'Urban' frameworks, which have been constructed almost from scratch with little reference to the GTCP structures or experience.

Participation and partnership are at the forefront of a whole spectrum of current policy initiatives, but as we have seen they can run the danger of being little more than rhetoric. The developing and the sustaining of community participation in any policy initiatives will almost certainly require the deployment of significant resources if it is not to be tokenistic. Agencies need to be prepared to deal with issues of representation and be willing to accept the pressures, demands and changes that may be made upon them through meaningful community participation.

This Project demonstrates the complexity and difficulty of constructing purposive alliances that bring together players with potentially different interests such as public sector agencies and 'community' groups, voluntary management committees and full-time professional staff, central government representatives and local councils; private industry and the voluntary sector.

Large public sector agencies are themselves complex, diverse, bureaucratic, containing multiple sources of interest and power. Having a 'representative' sit on a management committee may give the illusion of involvement of that agency as a whole (a City Council, a University, a Government Office, a Health Authority, as in the case of the GTCP) but the representative may not in fact be able to easily influence, mobilise or change that agency, making the 'partnership' little more than a liaison 'Community' representatives may appear or claim to speak on behalf of a larger constituency, but again may actually have limited ability to act as a conduit for broader local forces, again making the 'partnership' little more than a collection of more or less vociferous or effective individuals.

Surface activity may be generated, to fit in with externally imposed funding criteria, but this may have only a tenuous strategic basis in really redistributing power and resources to the most disadvantaged and excluded members of the community; employed staff may resent the intrusion or involvement of enthusiastic volunteers or management committee members, and develop their own professional interests as a higher priority than the broader objectives of the partnership as a whole; agencies with power and influence may be willing to engage in partnerships if they do not jeopardise their interests, but they may not be willing or able to share their power with local, possibly short term and weaker players.

The experience of the GTCP shows the need for all those involved in partnership arrangements to be clear what is meant by this in terms of roles, responsibilities and powers as well as what the implications may be in respect of their time and commitment. They need to ensure that formal mechanisms are in place to enable their representatives to be in the position to genuinely commit their own organisations as a whole to the particular aims and needs of the partnership. Partner Agencies should consider the question of whether they are prepared to accept community organisations having an equality of influence. This will make it even more important to establish mechanisms that ensure community representation is secured through open and accountable processes.

The underlying issue of 'race'

Apart from the broader contradictions of establishing effective and equitable strategic partnerships involving big institutional players and representatives from the voluntary and community sector. The issue of 'race' can throw up the sort of additional tensions which were not fully resolved in the case of the Project under discussion. The lack of strategic assertiveness and clarity on behalf of the Management Committee may be located in the context of how the issue of 'race' has frequently been dealt with by some major local agencies. On Merseyside, as elsewhere in the country, there has frequently been a lack of confidence within agencies in how to address racism and equal opportunities. This in part stems from the historic existence of institutional racism within many mainstream organisations.

This lack of confidence has meant that on occasion inappropriate responses have resulted where for example bad practice, or lack of accountability, has not been challenged by funding agencies, because a project is viewed as being a Black project, and the funding agency is concerned at being accused of being 'racist'. In situations such as this, mainstream institutions may be satisfied with token gestures or marginal responses, which indicate that the issue has been addressed. This may be through the appointment of a Black member of staff, or support for a project that involves Black people at some level.

In this Project, the funding bodies did take the important step of agreeing for the Project to open itself up to the Black community and to employ predominantly Black staff. They did not however have the capacity or the confidence (or perhaps the self-interest) to challenge the limited form of community representation that did emerge; nor did they appear really willing and able to steer the staff towards adhering to the strategic goals of the Project as a whole. This enabled their own institutions to remain fundamentally untouched by the Project, whilst having some of the benefits of supporting a significant European initiative. It is as if the work of the

Project and the Management Committee was a world of its own, sealed off from the on-going life of the major institutions, rather than providing a catalyst for the strategic orientation of the Agencies as envisaged by the Commission in establishing the initiative.

The issue of racial exclusion, and its links with poverty, is still a fundamental problem in Liverpool,[13] in Britain and across Europe, which needs to be seen as a uniquely impermeable and divisive form of social exclusion, requiring specific anti-racist as well as general anti-poverty measures. Partnership principles are a significant development away from authoritarian or paternalistic approaches to social policy. We hope that this paper can be used to help ensure that evolving and future partnerships developed to seek to eliminate racial exclusion are built on the strongest possible foundation of previous efforts, experiences and lessons from the continuing and complex struggle for racial equality and justice.

Notes

1   European Commission, Report on the Implementation of the Community Programme for the Social and Economic Integration of the Least Privileged Groups, 'Poverty 3', 1989-94; 89/457/EEC of 18 July 1989.

2   See Liverpool Quality of Life Survey, Liverpool City Council 1991.

3   See the 1991 Census.

4   See Interim Background Report Poverty 3, University of Liverpool, Race and Social Policy Unit, 1991.

5   European Commission, op cit.

6   Ibid.

7   See Gifford, Lord, Brown, W. and Bundey, R. (1989), *Loosen the Shackles*, Karia Press.

8   Ben-Tovim, G. (ed.) (1986), *The Racial Politics of Militant Liverpool Black Caucus*, Runnymede Trust.

9   See Ben-Tovim, G., Gabriel, J., Law, I. and Stredder, K. (1986), *The Local Politics of Race*, Macmillan.

10   See Granby Toxteth Community Project, Report on Third Contractual Period 1994.

11   Europe Commission op cit.

12   See Merseyside 2000, Programming Document for Objective One, European Commission, 1994.

13   See Ben-Tovim, G., Kyprianou, P., King, L. and Rooney, B. (1996), *Racial Harassment on Merseyside*, EOLAS and University

of Liverpool; Rooney, B. and Brown, M. (1996), *Locked Out - Housing and Young Black People on Merseyside*, Shelter and FBHO; EOLAS (1995), *Health Needs Assessment of Black and Ethnic Minority Communities in Liverpool*, Liverpool Health Authority.

7 Racism, Immigration Policy and Welfare Policing: The Case of the Asylum and Immigration Act

Dr Dee Cook

Introduction

The conference paper upon which this Chapter is based was first presented in April 1996, at a time when the Asylum and Immigration Bill (AIB) was passing through parliament. Since then the provisions of the subsequent 1996 Asylum and Immigration Act (AIA) have been fully implemented (in January 1997) and a New Labour government has been elected - and yet this draconian legislation remains intact. Its far-reaching effects are clearly evident, in terms of the criminalization and impoverishment of asylum-seekers and their families, and the realities of welfare policing for those deemed 'suspected immigration offenders'.

As the AIA began its parliamentary passage, political commentators had located its origins in 'scroungerphobia', xenophobia and the electoral imperative:

> The race card usually lands face down on the table. Its potency is surreptitious, and its playing, by otherwise respectable politicians, is always deniable... But a party in desperate political trouble has persuaded itself that this card...is one of the few trumps with which it can be sure of taking a trick (Hugo Young, The *Guardian*, 12th December 95).

With hindsight, it is clear that not even the 'race card' could ensure a Conservative electoral victory in 1997. But it is significant that, in failing to repeal the AIA, New Labour has not disassociated itself from this insidious 'trick'.

The central argument of the Chapter is that the AIA marked the fusion of a cluster of populist and distinctly racialised concerns around:

immigration policy
'suspicious' citizenship
welfare 'scrounging' and
(social) policing.

The Chapter will develop this argument by, firstly, tracing the origins of this legislation by examining the historical, political and ideological context within which it was set. Secondly, it will look at the provisions of the Act itself and its potentially damaging effects on the lives of all black and Asian families (and visible minority ethnic communities) in Britain. Thirdly, it will examine the AIA in the context of a broader trend over the past decade towards the criminalization of key marginalized social groups. Fourthly, it will briefly address the notion of a contemporary political 'convergence' on immigration and asylum issues - between the political Right and Left, and across Europe.

The background: continuities and changes

An analysis of British post-war immigration policy reveals several key themes which continue to permeate discourses around 'race' and immigration in the late 1990s. Briefly, these themes include:

1 *racialisation* as in the post-war era the issue of 'immigration' became synonymous with 'race' in both popular and political discourses;
2 *the 'numbers game'*, as calls for reductions in the 'tide' of black immigration grew;
3 the *language of fear, 'swamping' and social disorder* within which 'black' immigration and settlement was constituted as, by definition, a 'problem';
4 the theme of *'no recourse to public funds'*, in response to the charge that immigrants were drawn to Britain by the *'honeypot'* of the Welfare State (Cook, 1993).

To take the first two themes together, it could be argued that the primary objective of post-war immigration policy has been to 'keep as many black people as possible, whether Asians or Afro-Caribbeans, out of the country' (Gordon, 1991, p. 77). The *numbers game* which was a defining feature

150

of the 1960s and 1970s vocabulary of immigration became subsumed in the 1980s within a lexis of street crime, fear, riot and social disorder: the very names of locations such as Brixton, Toxteth and Moss Side assumed symbolic resonance, as the 'enemy without' was transformed into the 'enemy within', in both political and popular discourses.

In the 1990s we are witnessing a further conjunction: the earlier language of fear, swamping, crime and disorder have not disappeared, but have been incorporated into a broader theme, that of *suspect citizenship* (Cook, 1993). This discourse marks a contestation not only of a subject's legal citizenship, but of definitions of their identity and assumptions about their personal desert. Moreover, formal legal citizenship is no longer a sufficient condition of 'belonging', 'deserving' or of Britishness. The 'Cricket Test' put forward by Norman Tebbit in 1990 suggested we ask of 'immigrant groups' (sic), 'Which side do they cheer for?' at cricket matches.
To this question, Tariq Modood responded that

> Many young Asian people...know how thoroughly they are a product of British society, outside of which they would be lost. Yet they cannot glory in their Britishness for what, after all, is their status here? (Modood, 1992, p. 23).

The citizenship of black and Asian Britons is therefore rendered suspect, always liable to challenge, proof and re-approval. The boundaries of what actually constitutes citizenship are also blurred by a conflation of the issues of nationality and immigration control at the level of policy-making. Increasingly, issues of Nationality (and legal citizenship) have become inseparable from those of Immigration control (and illegal or suspect citizenship), as the 'tail' of immigration control, 'is wagging the dog' of Nationality Law (Nicol, 1993).

Moral panics over 'bogus asylum seekers' and 'illegal immigrants' have served to stereotype all visible minorities as, by definition, not only suspicious citizens, but potential 'scroungers' too (a theme to be more fully explored in section 3 below).

The racialisation of the 'scrounger' mythology has, in part, been possible because the connection between immigration and welfare provision has long been seen as a direct, instrumental one: advocates of tougher immigration policies have, for half a century, argued that generous welfare benefits act as a *'honeypot'*, attracting immigrants who then live happily off the state. This view displays ignorance of Social Security rules which are based on the principle that immigrants should have 'no recourse to public funds', a principle which has progressively justified withdrawing the rights to a variety of benefits from immigrants and their dependants (see JCWI, 1995). In addition, the honeypot view is further contradicted by evidence of deeply held cultural traditions within some minority ethnic communities, which consider 'living off the state' as shameful (Law et.al., 1994). Nevertheless, the connections between immigration, 'race' and welfare scrounging remain ideologically potent.

The link between citizenship and welfare rights has never been clearer than in the case of the 1996 AIA. It is most significant that when the Bill was announced at the Conservative party conference in 1995, its proposals were central not only to the speech of the Home Secretary, Michael Howard, but also to that of the Secretary of State for Social Security Peter Lilley too. Echoing the 'honeypot view', Peter Lilley lamented that

> The trouble is our system almost invites people to claim asylum to claim British benefits.

In a similar vein Michael Howard stated that

> We are seen as a very attractive destination because of the ease with which people can gain access to jobs and benefits... Only a tiny proportion (of asylum seekers) are genuine refugees (*The Guardian*, 26th October 1995).

By contrast, the United Nations High Commissioner for Refugees (UNHCR) issued a Ministerial briefing which refuted the view that most claims were bogus and that Britain was a 'soft touch'. Rather, they argued,

> the rise in asylum claims may be more rationally seen as a consequence of the unprecedented scale of global conflict which produces refugee flows (*The Guardian*, 13th January, 1996).

Immigration policy and the Asylum and Immigration Act 1996

Broadly, most immigration into the UK currently derives from two sources, a) *asylum*; b) *family formation;* both of which have been the target of control policies designed to slow down its flow 'to a trickle' (Menski, 1994).

The dual aims of cost-cutting, while at the same time demonstrating the 'something is being done', lie at the heart of both immigration and social security policies - the fusion of these two policy areas is particularly evident in the case of the Asylum and Immigration Act (1996).

The 1993 Asylum and Immigration Appeals Act had already curtailed the grounds for asylum appeals, speeded up judgements and effectively provided a deterrent to potential asylum seekers. But the provisions of the 1996 AIA went much further: they included withdrawing asylum seekers' rights to income support, child benefits and public housing which, the Treasury estimated, would 'save' £200 million. However, Local Authorities are, in practice, footing the bill because of their statutory duties under the Children Act to feed, clothe and shelter the children of asylum seekers (*Poverty*, Spring 1997). Arguably, therefore, the AIA was always more about deterrence and racial politics than about cash savings.

The implementation of the 1996 Act therefore put into practice the following principles:

1 the *'fast tracking'* of appeals, to effectively 'slam the door closed' quicker;
2 the judgement of asylum cases not on their individual merits, but on general criteria, including the notorious *'White List'*[1] which notes the countries from which *all* asylum applications will be presumed to be bogus;
3 the *withdrawal of social security*, housing rights from asylum seekers;
4 anyone who does not satisfy entry clearance requirements is liable to *detention* (the decision on detention and bail being taken by Home Office Immigration and Nationality Department - IND - officials);
5 applicants may suffer *detention without limit of time* if it is considered that they 'would not meet the conditions attached to remaining at liberty' - although there is no official definition of what this phrase means!
6 restrictions on asylum applications, effected under the *Carriers Liability Act* (whereby airlines and shipping companies are liable to fines if they fail to ensure passengers have visas before embarking).

(*NACRO Race Policies into Action*, Spring 1997)

According to NACRO, the result of the AIA provisions is that

The Immigration and Nationality Department [IND] possesses and exercises powers which are much more familiar to the criminal justice system and are not found elsewhere within the civil jurisdiction (ibid, 3).

Moreover, due to pressure of numbers on limited accommodation, asylum detainees and *suspected immigration 'offenders'* may be held in police cells, prison establishments or in Immigration Service accommodation which the National Audit Office acknowledged was 'of a poor standard' (NAO, 1995, p. 71). These material conditions themselves mirror the blurring of boundaries between *the suspect citizen* and *the criminal*: the pejorative use of the terms 'suspect' and 'offender' in itself enables and reinforces the criminalization of immigration and asylum issues.

The United Nations High Commission for Refugees states that:

only in exceptional circumstances should any asylum seeker be detained at all and that they should never be held in prison (*Race Policies into Action*, Issue 12, Summer 1997).

But, in the UK, incarceration for asylum seekers is the 'first resort rather than a last': latest figures indicate 400 detainees held in prisons and a further 400 in detention centres (ibid).

According to research by Amnesty International, detainees have no reliable information about the nature of their detention or likely date of release. Moreover, the decision to detain was usually taken by personnel of low rank and was not subject to independent scrutiny (Amnesty, 1997). Unsurprisingly, Amnesty concluded that detention authorised by the AIA 1996 was arbitrary - and this disturbing picture continues.

The UNHCR also notes that asylum seekers suffer considerable physical and emotional stress, a view supported by earlier Home Office research acknowledging that they endure

a high rate of physical and psychological suffering largely consequent upon the past experiences that led individuals to seek asylum, and because of separation from their families.

Separation from family and the detention of 'suspect' applicants compounds this stress, as do the material conditions referred to by the NAO. The rising suicide rate among datainees since the Act's implementation is a matter of serious concern (CARF, 1997a).

Nonetheless, both Michael Howard and Peter Lilley had emphasised that *'deserving'* asylum and immigration applicants had 'nothing to fear' from this legislation, a reassurance which has been rendered hollow - not only because of the deterrent character of the regulations themselves, and the appalling physical conditions that these civil prisoners suffer - but because of the suspicion, fear and stress which *all* visible minorities are increasingly likely to suffer as a result of this legislation. Nonetheless, these provisions remain intact under New Labour.

The Commission for Racial Equality had described the Asylum and Immigration Bill as having an 'anti-black and xenophobic message', a message which will permeate the lives of all 'visible' ethnic minorities in Britain, regardless of their formal citizenship status. The level of policing which is both *encouraged and enabled* by the provisions of the AIA will particularly affect families as they interact with a variety of social, legal and welfare agencies. The dubious practice of passport checking where individuals 'appear to be foreign' has long rendered the citizenship rights of Black people in Britain *questionable* (Cook, 1993). But under the AIA this practice will be developed as school's Head Teachers, hospital administrators, housing and social security staff are trained and encouraged to identify and report suspected illegal immigrants.

Similarly, employers are required to confirm workers' immigration status and may be fined up to £5,000 for hiring illegal immigrant labour, despite the protests of employers groups that this proposal could lead to discrimination. In response, the Commission for Racial Equality has issued guidelines for employers to help them avoid breaching the Race Relations Act (1976) while complying with section 8 of the AIA 1996.

The role of employers and social welfare agencies in 'snooping' adds another dimension to the existing policing (official and unofficial) of visible minorities: for example, 1993 around 60% of cases of 'suspected immigration offenders' were referred to the Home Office by the police and by anonymous 'tip-offs' from the public (although, significantly, three quarters of these were found to be groundless - NAO, 1995). The AIA, dubbed a 'snoopers charter', can only add to this climate of fear and suspicion surrounding all minority ethnic groups, which will find expression in the routine policing of families in schools, hospitals, housing and social security offices and at work.

There have been early indications of the effects of such policing on minority ethnic groups at work and in public places: according to national press reports, the University College London Hospitals Trust issued letters to 'domestics and porters...the two groups with largest proportions of black and Asian staff' warning them that under the AIA it was a criminal offence to employ illegal immigrants. The North Middlesex Hospital was investigated by the Commission for Racial Equality after a GP alleged that the hospital was screening patients whose first language was not English (Fekete, 1997, p. 13). At the same time, the Conservative government's reply to the Social Security Advisory Committee (SSAC), to address their concerns that the Act would prove damaging to race relations, was illuminating:

> of course, the proposals, by their very nature mean that the Benefits Agency and Local Authorities must identify claimants by their immigration status.

This was precisely the fear of the SSAC!

It is worth emphasising the fundamental change which the AIA has signalled towards 'social policing' has been supported by an official move towards 'data matching' and *inter-departmental co-operation* (Cook, 1996). Routine practice on information disclosure *between* departments has been radically changed to accommodate the objectives of the AIA: a Memorandum of Understanding between the BA and the IND was signed in October 1995 in anticipation of the implementation of the Act. It allows for an unprecedented level of information to pass between the two departments - notably, information can be shared if the individual is a *'known or suspected immigration offender'* (ibid).

The AIA thus enables a new and covert form of 'SUS' law which signals a worrying blurring of the boundaries between the jurisdictions of the civil and criminal law. Asylum applicants who have broken no criminal law may nonetheless be incarcerated in penal institutions - a fact emphasised by the protests and hunger strikes of detainees in Rochester Prison. But more generally, this fusion of immigration, welfare and criminal law has wider social implications. There is much evidence that minority ethnic communities are liable to disproportionate *formal policing,* immigration legislation has added another dimension - by enabling the intensified *social policing* of visible minority ethnic families, groups and communities in Britain.

So, has anything changed under New Labour? In July 1997 the High Court ruled that the policy of barring asylum seekers from employment while their requests were being considered was 'unlawful and irrational' as it aimed to discourage bogus refugees, but in practice adversely affected genuine applicants (*Poverty*, No. 98, Autumn 1997, p. 7). According to the campaigning group *Justice*, nothing has changed in real terms, although they recently indicated a 'softer' political tone in relation to asylum seekers' appeals. Nonetheless, the legislation passed by the last government remains on the statute book and significantly, the Liberal Democrats were the only major political party to state a commitment to repeal the AIA in their 1997 manifesto. It is difficult to see how policies based on AIA legislation accord with New Labour's commitment to social justice and to 'attack discrimination in all its forms' (Blair, 2.6.97).

Immigration and family formation

Despite the immigration and asylum 'panic', which is both signified and engendered by the AIA, official statistics show that between 1993 and 1994, 'a fall of 3,000 in acceptances of recognised refugees and exceptional leave cases more than offset rises in UK ancestry and employment cases, children and wives' (Social Policy Digest, *Journal of Social Policy* April 1996).

Although applications for asylum increased by 50% over this period, only 4% of decisions resulted in asylum being granted. Moreover, taken together these figures demonstrate the ideologies of *'swamping'* and the *numbers game* are still evident in the ways in which immigration is perceived and constructed as 'a problem', despite a net fall in those entering the UK. Such perceptions are bound to shape the experiences of all Black and Asian families living in Britain.

At a time when the family is extolled as the cornerstone of the 'civilised' (and law-abiding) society, and the institutions of marriage and family are valorised both by the political right and centre left, it is deeply ironic that the families of those seeking entry into the UK will find themselves at best, policed by a variety of state agencies, at worst, separated from loved ones and so excluded from a full family life.

According to political commentators from the New Right and Christian Left alike, an enduring marriage and fatherhood is crucial to family life not only in establishing emotional security for spouses and children alike, but also in providing a broader framework of duties and responsibilities which enhance economic and social stability. So, not only is the 'two parent family a superior environment for the nurturing of children' but is an essential component of civilised society and 'free institutions' (Murray, 1994). Illegitimacy and lone parenthood are, in such perspectives, coterminous with social 'deterioration', 'degeneration' of the lower classes and the expansion of the underclass or 'New Rabble' (ibid). Alternatively, they are seen as profoundly disadvantageous for the economic and moral health of the families involved (Blair, 1997).

Paradoxically, the allegedly pivotal role of the family in ensuring social cohesion and developing 'dutiful citizens' is totally disregarded where Black and Asian family formation is concerned. Hence, although

> The marriage bond not only creates the 'husband and wife', it creates 'uncles' and 'aunts' and 'grandmothers' and 'grandfathers' with a long-term relationship to the child (Dennis and Erdos, 1993, p. 70),

immigration policy actively deters the establishment of precisely these relationships. Immigration rules passed in recent years - such as the Habitual Residence Test, Primary Purpose Rule (PPR), as well as maintenance, accommodation and 'exclusivity' rules - have combined to undermine family and social solidarity among ethnic minorities. As argued above, such policies derive from the need to cut welfare expenditure. But, as Menski comments,

> family migration should not be allowed to become a matter of calculating sums: in its very nature it is an area of law in which financial factors should take a back seat in comparison with individual rights to family and private life (Menski, 1994, p. 113).

It seems that what could be regarded as 'traditional' family values are turned on their head where 'family' and 'race' intersect, and more particularly where women are concerned. For example, Fiona Williams has argued that whereas the state has typically served to reinforce women's mothering role,

> for Black women the emphasis has not been so much on the endowment of motherhood, and the maintenance of dependants, but on the restriction of motherhood and limitation and control of dependants (Williams, 1989, p. 186, emphasis in original).

These restrictions and controls are illustrated by both immigration and reproductive policies, the latter echoing the racist assumptions about black sexuality which underlie the 'numbers game' (ibid, p. 187).

The notorious Primary Purpose Rule in practice regulates family formation and affects Asian women in particular (JCWI, 1995). The rule states that the spouse of a man or woman settled in the UK who wishes to enter must prove that the primary purpose of the marriage was not to obtain entry into the UK. The burden of proof required by immigration officials inevitably leads to separation, stress and deterrence. It is worth noting that there are no documented PPR cases involving two white spouses, and that the effects of the rule are not only racialised, but gendered. Such rules

> not only structurally marginalise all ethnic minorities in Britain, (but) also wilfully disregard the legitimate expectations and socio-psychological needs of Asian women in Britain (Menski, 1996).

Similarly, campaigning groups have argued that the 1988 Immigration Act's 'one year rule', (under which women who leave violent husbands within one year of marriage may find themselves liable to deportation), may force women to stay with abusive partners to prevent deportation... though, at the same time, it may well save the state paying income support!

Taken together, the AIA, and immigration rules which accompany it, serve to deter immigration and to cut welfare spending by ever-tighter welfare policing of the lives of those who seek refuge and citizenship. At the same time, its provisions are bound to affect *all* individuals form visible minority ethnic groups who are liable to find themselves subject to official scrutiny. The basis for this scrutiny is, at its crudest, the assumption that non-white citizens are by definition 'suspect citizens' and so are more prone to corrupt practices and fraud in pursuit of the 'honeypot' benefits offered by the welfare state.

'Bogus' citizens and the criminalization of marginal groups

Politicians continue to forge a link in the public mind between the issues of immigration control, asylum and benefit fraud as they attempt to justify what are (in the eyes of critics) draconian immigration rules. For example, when (in February 1996) the Court of Appeal upheld the legality of the AIB regulations, the judges nonetheless expressed concern that withdrawal of benefits from asylum seekers would have 'disastrous and unwelcome consequences' as legitimate refugees could be placed in 'a penurious and perilous condition' while seeking to assert their rights in this country (*The Guardian*, 27th March 1996). But, perhaps unsurprisingly, the Secretary of State for Social Security Peter Lilley interpreted their judgement very differently. He said it gave 'a clear message to those who are abusing the system to claim benefits' (ibid). Issues of poverty were subsumed in the scrounger mythology. In January 1997, as the provisions of the AIA came into force, the Red Cross distributed food parcels in the UK - to London

Refugee Shelters, for asylum seekers (Social Policy Digest in *Journal of Social Policy,* Vol. 26, 1997, p. 384).

The theme of abuse continues to permeate political discourses around the AIA: in supporting the AIA through parliament, the then Conservative Minister Anne Widdicombe propounded the need for 'firm but fair' immigration regulations. Her Labour successor, Mike O'Brien, has been equally eager to confirm the Labour 'Government's commitment to firm and fair immigration control' (Home Office Press Release, 6.8.97). When inspecting new equipment at Dover, designed to detect illegal immigrants he continued:

> We support genuine asylum seekers, but intend to stop those who abuse the system.

But it can be argued that this legislation has itself generated illegality, firstly by denying many refugees a legal means of entry, but, crucially, by means of a procedural vicious circle. To explain the latter, the AIA is based on the twin assumptions that asylum claims from certain (listed 'safe') countries, and claims not made within 3 days of arrival, can be treated as bogus. The issue of the 'white list' has already been addressed, but where the 3 day rule is concerned Amnesty International argues that 71% of all those who *were* eventually granted asylum in the UK between 1992-5 applied more than three days after entry, and so would now be regarded as 'bogus'. It therefore seems clear that the provisions of the AIA, (running entirely counter to principles of natural justice), result in *procedural* stipulations governing the assessment of the *validity* of asylum claims.

In a recent analysis of Local Authority responses to the AIA, the Campaign Against Racism and Fascism (CARF) points out another aspect of the self-fulfilling connection between AIA rules and allegedly fraudulent applications for asylum:

> Without the money to attend [Home Office] Lunar House, in Croydon, or the immigration office at Heathrow for interview, or Feltham for their appeal hearing, many will find their claims deemed 'withdrawn' or summarily rejected. As the refusal statistics are swollen, and the government can point to even more 'bogus' claims, the vicious circle is complete (CARF, 1997b, 6).

Not only does this process construct the 'bogus' asylum seeker of media mythology, but, in addition, more direct official processes serve to criminalise those seeking refuge. The fingerprinting of all asylum applicants (including unaccompanied refugee children) has been common practice since 1993. As Webber (1996) points out, this measure, which affects 40,000 people a year, is justified by the need to detect fraud by multiple claimants - of whom precisely 11 have been convicted.

More tellingly, notorious cases of the forcible restraint and deportation of asylum applicants beg crucial questions about the ways in which the boundaries between welfare and immigration policing and formal policing have been blurred beyond clear recognition:

> When people are subjected to routine fingerprinting, when they are locked up, when they are restrained by body belts and leg shackles and thirteen feet of tape, or forcibly injected with sedatives to keep them quiet as they are bundled onto airacraft, it seems reasonable to ask what have they done? The answer is that they have tried to come to Western Europe to seek asylum, or to live here with their families... (Webber, 1996, p. 1).

People and groups at the margins of society and law: links between welfare, marginalization and criminalization

I have argued, so far, that the criminalization of immigration and asylum issues is effected in a variety of ways:

1 through the ideological linking (forged and reinforced by politicians and media alike) of the perceived problems of immigration, race and social security fraud;
2 through a particular pejorative lexis - dominated by the word 'bogus', which is invariably associated with asylum seeking - used in both political and popular discourse;
3 through the AIAs use of generic (not individually-based) procedures for assessing asylum applications, which generate a self-fulfilling prophecy of rejected and/or by definition 'bogus' claims;
4 by means of AIA legislative provisions which enable and promote formal and informal welfare policing of visible minority ethnic families and groups;
5 through the operation of (welfare and immigration) policing practices which signify a collapse of boundaries between civil and criminal jurisdictions where 'suspected immigration offenders' and asylum seekers are concerned;

6 by the inappropriate use of penal establishments (and penal regimes) for the incarceration of asylum detainees.

But these modes of criminalization need to be set within a broader political, social and ideological context, a context within which (other) key marginalized groups have also been effectively criminalized over the past decade.

Diagram 1 offers a simple visual representation of a complex series of relationships between a range of social groups who are located at various points on the margins of society and/or the margins of the law. Over the past decade, the lives, values and activities of these groups have been variously constituted as problematic, morally questionable, deviant or criminal. Although the boundaries between such categorisations are far from clear, the (literally) grey area in the diagram represents the area within which these individuals may be criminalised without having necessarily broken the criminal law.

To give some examples, it can be argued that, in certain locations in the UK the homeless and beggars are currently subjected to a 'zero tolerance' policing which criminalised their very existence (and the same may be said of travellers); some aspects of the leisure and behaviour of young people are seen as threatening and delinquent, irrespective of whether they break the criminal law; single mothers have long been blamed for a variety of social problems including poor family discipline and educational performance, and are often the scapegoats for crime, delinquency and the 'underclass' which allegedly breeds it (Cook, 1997); and, as already argued, the mythology of the social security 'scrounger' stigmatises welfare claimants (particularly the unemployed and lone parents) as, by definition, undeserving and as potential fraudsters.

The nature and cause of any drift from the grey area of criminalization to the commission of crime (signified in the lower third of the diagram) is beyond the scope of this Chapter (but see Cook, 1997). But where issues of asylum and immigration are concerned, the themes described in part 2 above provide a rich vein which may be tapped by racialised discourses linking (and converge around) the issues of 'race', welfare and crime. The provisions of the AIA (described in part 3) make it more likely that individuals from visible minority ethnic groups may 'drift' towards the margins of society and the law - because they are more likely to be regarded as by definition 'suspect' citizens; more likely to be the object of official surveillance by a variety of state agencies; and more liable to formal criminalization.

Concluding comments

Asylum, immigration policy and political convergence

I have already argued, in the context of the UK, that the New Labour government has yet to make a demonstrable break with the past in terms of asylum and immigration policy: as CARF recently noted, there have been rumours of fairer rules and a more sympathetic approach but, so far, 'they are only rumours' (CARF, 1997, p. 10). But what of the broader European context? With states driving for greater economic convergence (post-Maastricht), the need to cut welfare expenditure has increasingly become a European-wide political imperative. As Liz Fekete points out, this has profound implications for asylum and immigration policies:

> The easiest place to cut public expenditure is in welfare. But this is also the least popular, as European governments are finding out to their cost. Hence, not wishing to risk social dislocation or lose potential power, governments are responding to public protest by providing thinner but continued protection for the more privileged sections of society, while attacking the welfare rights of more vulnerable constituencies, increasingly portrayed as unwilling to work and dependent on welfare. The most vulnerable of these are the former guestworkers and seasonal workers, the asylum seekers and de-facto refugees whom Europe is already in the process of excluding. Without nationality and citizenship rights they have no social rights either. And popular racism - which has already defined them as 'illegals' and 'scroungers' - gives European governments the mandate to exclude them from social provision altogether (Fekete, 1997, p. 12).

This analysis clearly reflects the central argument of this Chapter and chimes with its discussion of the processes whereby marginal groups are criminalized, particularly through the mechanisms put in place to police both welfare and immigration policy. In summary, both Fekete's European perspective and the argument presented here support the disturbing contention that

> Racism today is not so much and ideological project as an instrument of policy (Sivanandan, 1997).

Nowhere is the work of this instrument more evident than in the case of the Asylum and Immigration Act 1996.

Note

1 The 'White List named countries which, according to the then Home Secretary, Michael Howard have 'no serious risk of persecution' as they possess:

'functioning institutions, stability and pluralism in sufficient measure to support an assessment that in general people living there are not at risk'.

At the time of the AIB's drafting, the white list included Zaire and Nigeria, both countries under oppressive military rule. The execution of Ken SaroWiwa and fellow environmental activists by the Nigerian military government (within weeks of the announcement of the list) and subsequent political turmoil in Zaire, are testimony to the failure of Home Office's judgement on what constitutes 'stability and pluralism' and lack of personal risk. It also evidences the problems inherent in moving away from an individually based assessment of asylum applications towards one based on generic political (and, given substantial British investment in Nigeria, many would argue, economic) criteria (Webber, 1997).

References

Amnesty International (1996), *Cell Culture*, Amnesty: London.

Blair, Tony (1997), Speech at the Aylesbury Estate, Southwark, June 2nd 1997.

Campaign Against Racism and Fascism (1997), CARF, No.39, August/September, 1997.

Cook, D. (1997), *Poverty, Crime and Punishment*, Child Poverty Action Group: London.

Cook, D. (1996), 'Official Secrecy and Social Policy Research: the case of the Asylum and Immigration Bill' in H. Dean (ed.), *Ethics and Social Policy Research*, Social Policy Association and University of Luton Press.

Cook, D. (1993), 'Racism, Citizenship and Exclusion' in D. Cook and B. Hudson (eds) *Racism and Criminology*, Sage Publications: London.

Dennis, N. and Erdos, G. (1993), *Families Without Fatherhood*, IEA Health and Welfare Unit: London.

Fekete, L. (1997), 'Blackening the Economy: the path to Convergence' in

Race and Class, Vol. 39, No. 1.

Gordon, P. (1991), 'Forms of Exclusion: citizenship, race and poverty' in S. Becker (ed.), *Windows of Opportunity*, CPAG: London.

Joint Council for the Welfare of Immigrants (1995), *Immigration and Nationality Handbook*, JCWI: London.

Law, I. Hylton, C., Karmani, A. and Deacon, A. (1994), 'Perceptions of Social Security among black minority ethnic groups: evidence from field work in Leeds', paper to the SPA Conference, The University of Liverpool.

Menski, W. (1994), 'Family Migration and the new Immigration Rules' in *Immigration and Nationality Law and Practice*, Vol. 8, No. 4, 1994.

Menski, W. (1996), 'The Primary Purpose Rule and Asian Women' in S. Fenton (ed.), *The Family, Economic and Social Change in Europe*, Edward Mellin Press: London.

Modood, T. (1992), *Not Easy Being British*, Runnymeade Trust and Trentham Books: Stoke-on-Trent.

Murray, C. (1994), *Underclass: the Crisis Deepens*, IEA, London.

National Audit Office (1995), *Entry into the Kingdom: HC 204*, HMSO: London.

Nicol, A. (1993), 'Nationality and Immigration' in R. Blackburn (ed.) *Rights of Citizenship*, Mansell Publishing: London.

Sivanandan, A. (1997), 'Europe - the Wages of Racism: Introduction' in *Race and Class*, Vol. 39, No. 1.

Webber, F. (1996), *Crimes of Arrival: immigrants and asylum seekers in the new Europe*, Statewatch: London.

Williams, F. (1989), *Social Policy: a Critical Introduction*, Polity Press: Cambridge.

8 One Who Teaches From Experience: Social Action and the Development of Anti-racist Research and Practice

Jennie Fleming and Rhonda Wattley

Introduction

This chapter is about a specific period in the development of a community based project for black families in Nottingham. It outlines the community consultation phase and early development of the project. Since this period the project has been relocated from the community into the NSPCC's (National Society for the Prevention of Cruelty to Children) child protection office. This chapter has been written by a black woman and a white woman. Rhonda Wattley is a community social worker at the NSPCC and Jennie Fleming works as a research fellow at De Montfort University. Both are directors of the Centre for Social Action.

The Centre for Social Action has always been concerned, and put in the central position, the experience of the users of welfare services. The Centre's work includes direct work with community members, research consultancy, training and project development. All our work is rooted in putting people first. Our research work is based on a process by which people can consider and voice their views and experiences. As a result of this we have, time and time again, heard from minority ethnic groups in Britain about the experience of racism in the delivery of welfare services.

The quotes in this chapter are all taken from discussions we have had with black people in the course of our work. They have been attributed to speakers as they were recorded at the time, unfortunately there is no consistency in how people's race has been recorded and so attributed. In this paper we use the term black to include all people who are seen, or see themselves, as non-white (Cress Welsing, 1991, p. ii). We do not intend to imply that black people are a homogeneous group, however black people do all experience racism, discrimination and inequality as a result of white peoples' negative attitudes towards races, cultures, religions or languages other than their own.

Black people experience racism in the education system:

> They tell you how to think, what to think, and when to think it. As a black person your real experience doesn't fit into their world. *African Carribbean woman.*

> Black children need to know that knowledge can also come from people who look like them and that people who look like them have done things that are worth every body knowing about. Black children can grow up and not ever see a black adult in a position of power. This gives them the message 'You will not grow up, you will not be successful, there is no point in trying and that you are unimportant.' *Black woman.*

Racism effects social services:

> They are a lot of do-gooders and a very middle class white organisation. *Black parent* (Thompson and Fleming, 1993).

> As a child protection agency we often *pretend* to provide a service for black children and families in the context of a 'helping' relationship, without first identifying and acknowledging what the history and experiences of black people have been. *Black social worker* (Thompson and Fleming, 1993).

Health services are also pervaded by racism:

> If you can communicate in English you are much better off... The better you can communicate in English the better treatment you get. *Asian man* (Fleming and Harrison, 1994).

> Places have signs saying, 'If you need help with language, ask.' But how can I ask? No one understands me. *Asian woman* (Fleming and Harrison, 1994, p. 53).

Racism is an every day experience for black people:

> Racial harassment is a common feature of our lives. *Black woman* (Fleming and Harrison, 1994).

They think we're stupid. People think Asian woman can't do anything. *Asian woman* (Fleming and Harrison, 1994).

Having to go always go to white people in white agencies. They make us feel like we are begging; we lose our respect and dignity. *Asian woman* (Fleming and Harrison, 1994).

There is a wealth of evidence from other writers that the delivery of welfare services to minority ethnic groups in Britain is all the time tempered by the effects of racism, intentional or unintentional. Paulette Haughton (1997) writes of how many black youth, especially African-Caribbean males, are out-of-school or excluded from London schools, as school does not respond to their needs. Kanchan Jadeja comments, 'Community care consultation practices, however, have left black people and voluntary groups cynical about the attitudes and approaches of local authorities and health authorities to black communities' (Jadeja, 1997). Dominelli (1989) outlines the twin discriminatory processes that black families experience in social work, exclusion from valuable resources but inclusion in measures that effect social control. In 'Black Girls Speak Out', (Rouf, 1991) two young black women talk of their experience of being sexually abused and one of them says, 'I couldn't tell about my Dad because...I thought white people would make racist comments.' (p. 3).

There are many different analyses of racism, its causes, its manifestations and the ways forward, which have been widely discussed elsewhere (see, for example, Angela Davis, 1982, bell hooks, 1991, 1992, Tizard and Phoenix, 1993, Ahmad, 1990, Cress Wesling, 1991 and Akbar, 1985). Davis places race strongly within the context of capitalism. She writes that people should 'link our grass-roots organizing, our essential involvement in electoral politics, and our involvement as activities in mass struggles to the long range goal of fundamentally transforming the socioeconomic conditions that generate and persistently nourish the forms of oppression we suffer' (Davis, 1984, p. 14). hooks comes from a feminist perspective which leads her to challenge the simplistic assumption of common experience for black people. Bringing a feminist analysis to her analysis of racism she shows that black women are not just likely to be marginalised by white men and women, but to see black women as often marginalised by black men too. She writes, 'I became increasingly aware that I could arrive at a thorough understanding of the black female experience and our relationship to society as a whole only by examining both the politics of racism and sexism from a feminist perspective' (hooks, 1981, p. 13). Ahmad on the other hand writes specifically of how racism effects the practice of social work and provides an invaluable series of questions to challenge social workers in their work with black families and encourage them to develop anti-racist practice (Ahmad, 1990, p. 26). This notion of linking analysis with the context of good practice is continued in 'All Equal Under the Act' (Macdonald, 1991) which calls itself a 'practical guide to the Children Act 1989 for social workers'. In it the authors explore and analyse the past oppressive nature of social work with black children and disabled children and begins to explore how to develop anti-discriminatory practice.

Dominelli writes, 'It is important that white social work practitioners and educators create a theory of racism contextualising social work within the state apparatus, understand the dynamics of racism in both its covert and overt forms, recognise its legitimation through social processes and institutions and institutions outside social work structures - in what they do and what they don't do' (Dominelli, 1988, p. 17). These macro level theories of racism manifest themselves in the face-to-face, every day experience of black people. Whatever the preferred analysis, we believe that services to black children and families need to clearly identify racism as a common and pervasive factor in their lives.

A paper presented to the NSPCC's Black Workers Group (NSPCC Special Projects) in 1993, suggests that most mainstream services (and white practitioners) adopt a number of strategies that seek to ignore the impact of racism in black people's lives, for example:

1 Assumption that either racism does not exist or is irrelevant in most situations.
2 Fail to acknowledge own racism.
3 Placing responsibility for getting rid of racism on black people through 'dumping'. In practice this often means referring black clients to black workers.
4 Acceptance of racism in wider society but denial that it pervades day to day practice.
5 Adoption of a 'colour blind' approach which seeks to treat black people as white, but asserting that 'everyone is the same' - this approach denies and negates black people's experience of black people.
6 Adoption of a patronising approach in which superficial acknowledgement of specific experience and a veneer of equality is underpinned by the assumption that white lifestyles are really superior.

170

It was to try and break out of these modes and models that the NSPCC in 1993 commissioned the Centre for Social Action to undertake a study within the black communities in inner city Nottingham to assess the feasibility of establishing a Black Families Centre. The Centre for Social Action has a philosophical base and has developed methods of work that enable the voice of people to be heard. The above examples of bad practice outlined by the NSPCC black workers group could be turned around and used to devise strategies for good practice. For example, white workers acknowledging their own racism, using a truly egalitarian approach, recognising the differences between people and working appropriately with all people would be the basis of practice that is relevant to black people. Such principles are the integral to the work of the Centre for Social Action and are encompassed in our principles that are set out later in the paper.

The social action approach developed out of a dissatisfaction with conventional approaches to social and community work. In these areas people were being subjected to a range of interventions by various agencies, but these interventions were not seen as tackling the very real issues of poverty, unemployment and racism. Building on the doctrine of Pualo Freire, 'Pedagogy of the Oppressed' (1972), the Centre for Social Action aims to change the way in which professional agencies view communities by helping them vocalise their own needs and desires. The social action approach has been developed over many years by practitioners, educators and policy makers to address the problems and aspirations of the people and communities with whom health and welfare practitioners work. Social action practice now covers research, consultancy, training and most importantly direct practice with people and communities.

In an article in 'Shabab - Celebrating Black young people's community action', a black worker says, 'social action's promise of reaffirmation and empowerment is important to Black workers, communities and organisations... The 'each one teach one' type of community development which the Centre for Social Action is involved in, aims to provide the community with the tools to do their own research and analysis and thus putting them in charge of their own development' (Gould, 1997).

The Centre's approach is committed to addressing participants lives and experience in their own terms, to creating understanding grounded in their actual experience and language, to seeing what is there, not what we have been taught is there, not even what we might wish to find, but what is (adapted from Du Bois, 1983, p. 108-10).

The Centre acknowledges that, for a long time, services to black people have been inappropriate to the needs and experience of black people. Therefore, research was needed with black communities to find these views, opinions and needs, if services are ever going to develop that meet their needs. The aim of the Centre's study was to talk with people in two specific areas in Nottingham, to find out what families with black children considered their own needs to be, why they thought these needs exist and how they could be best met.

The work of the Centre for Social Action is based on a set of principles which need to underpin our work for it to be relevant to the people with whom we work and to actively address their concerns and needs. The principles are not static but are a starting point for workers who wish to contribute to enabling people to find solutions to their own problem.

1 All people have skills and understanding which they can draw on to tackle the problems they face. Professionals should not attach negative labels to service users.
2 All people have rights, including the right to be heard, the right to define the issues facing them and the right to take action on their own behalf.
3 People acting collectively can be powerful. People who lack power can gain it through working together with others.
4 Individuals in difficulty are often confronted by complex issues rooted in social policies, the environment and economy. Responses to these problems should reflect this understanding.
5 Methods of working must reflect non-elitist principles. Workers do not 'lead' the group but facilitate members in making decisions for themselves and controlling whatever outcome ensues. Though special skills are employed, these do not accord privilege and are not solely the province of workers.
6 Workers should strive to challenge inequality and discrimination in relation to race, gender, sexual orientation, age, class, disability or any other form of social differentiation maintained by the inequitable exercise of power.

The approach to research at the Centre is based on a commitment to empowering service users to define their own needs and to facilitate them to shape their own services. We see the role of a researcher as being to set in motion a process whereby people can set their own agendas and goals and develop ways of achieving them. We look to develop collaborative approach which builds on participants' own experiences and understandings and will offer concepts which people can engage with.

The Centre employed a black woman with considerable community work experience, on a six month contract, to undertake the study. She was supervised and supported by the authors of this paper. Punjabi/English

172

translation was available. However, it was not needed; all interviews were conducted in English.

We recognised the complex ethical and power issues, (for a predominately white organisation) of conducting such a research project within black communities: the researcher's relationship to the communities under review, questions of sponsorship and confidentiality, the ways in which research may help to popularise myths about communities and the potential for the misuse of any findings of the research. We understood our responsibility to address these issues, to anticipate and counter-act the possibility of misuse. Our aim was not to focus on the black communities and their cultural and family networks, but rather to focus on their experiences and the problems they face, and examine the personal and institutional ways through which white racism operates.

The study fell into 3 main phases: orientation and initial information gathering; making contact with local parents and collecting their views and opinions; writing the report and presenting it to the NSPCC. Using the information and continuing the community involvement in developing the plans for the family centre was the responsibility of the NSPCC, after the research contract was finished.

The orientation phase involved reading and talking with professionals, community leaders and community members to establish what were the issues and concerns that needed investigating further. From these conversations a schedule for 'guided conversation' was drawn up. This included areas such as: what people's views of the NSPCC and social services were, where they got support from at present, if a black family centre were set up, what would they like to see there and what sort of environment and service would make it possible for them to use it.

The views of many local black parents were sought. After some discussion it was decided that white parents with black children would be included in the research. At the time the definition of a black family did not usually include white parents with black children. Contact was made through community groups, schools, social services, parents groups and using the 'snowballing' sampling technique. Snowballing is a useful technique for making contact with people when there is no formal sampling frame, as was the case in this situation. There was no 'list' of families with black children in the areas to use as a sampling frame. In snowballing the researcher asks one person with the characteristics they are interested in, in this case parents or carers of black children, to put them in contact with other people with those characteristics. This is done with each contact and so quite a big sample can be built up (see Rehman and Walker, 1995). It also has the advantage of enabling people who do *not* go to groups to have their opinions included, and allowing people to define themselves as fitting the criteria, not relying on definition by the professional.

Local professionals were also contacted, for example from social services, community organisations, the Women's Centre and schools. It was felt important to include the views of people who offer services to black people to see if their perspective was similar to that of the black community members who are actual or potential users of services. This way a range of views and opinions on the issues investigated was obtained, though the loudest voice is that of the black families.

Summarising the results briefly, people knew very little of the NSPCC and social services; they were identified as white agencies that many people would be reluctant to contact. All the following quotes are from 'Nottingham Black Families Project, Background Study'.

> After my experiences as a child in care these are the last places I would want my children connected with. *Mixed race woman.*

> When my child was young, the blue spot on her back was very prominent, at the time not many people were aware that is a prominent characteristic in black children, I was questioned in detail about it. *White woman.*

> It is not an organisation people like me have contact with. *Asian woman.*

> My husband would not let me contact them. *Asian woman.*

Many people knew very little about the NSPCC. Where people did know of social services or the NSPCC they were seen as predominantly organisations involved with child abuse and who had the power to take children away.

> I know it is for children, but I don't know what it does. *Asian man.*

> I look at them as being there to take your children away at the slightest incident. *White woman.*

Some people involved in the study had had contact with social services and revealed varying opinions:

They said, 'Sorry, there are no resources available, you're coping well enough on your own'. *White woman.*

They were very helpful. *African Caribbean woman.*

Once they get their teeth in, they never let go. *African Caribbean woman.*

Most of the parents spoken to got their support from their family, with their, or their partner's mothers, playing a significant role:

Help for me is my family. *Asian woman.*

Help or support would be family first. People from outside the family would not be considered. *Asian man.*

If there were problems with my children I would talk to my parents or in laws. *Asian woman.*

A few people had contact with supportive community organisations.

The local community centre is very supportive and concerned with black children and the problems they may have at school, especially exclusion. *African Caribbean woman.*

The parents and professionals who contributed to the research felt that services in the area were average in quantity. However, the biggest problem was seen as the lack of services that could be used by the many people of different cultural, racial, religious and language backgrounds to the dominant 'norm' of white and English speaking.

Developing services that are culturally appropriate to black communities is not a straight forward task. At present our complex society is organised around the values of the dominant majority. Movement towards making services appropriate to black communities does not lie in creating leaflets in different languages informing about the services but making no other alterations, nor does it lie in encroaching on the black communities and being seen as colonising and intruding on communities. Services must not take the place of existing support networks but must compliment existing ways of dealing with issues and be responsive to and informed by the issues raised by black people. Services should develop from the bottom up, not the top down.

There was considerable support for the idea of a Black Families Project from the people spoken to. However, there was some disquiet about it being an NSPCC project, as the NSPCC was seen to be involved in child abuse and so there was stigma attached to using their services. The need was felt to be for a supportive and preventative project offering services like:

A family support group, cultural awareness for parents of mixed race children, support for the child, a drop-in. It must be staffed by black workers. *Black woman.*

Somewhere to go and not feel guilty. *Black woman.*

It sounds like something that should have happened years ago. *Black man.*

People were also asked about who should be able to use any project that might come out of the research. Considerable discussion was given to white parents of mixed race children. This was discussed by both white and black parents. Many of the white mothers of black children were single parents.

White parents can never teach a black child, so a white mother's needs are bigger than those of a black mother. *African Caribbean woman.*

Personally, I welcome white mums who are interested in black culture and knowledge for their children's benefit. *African Caribbean woman.*

They need support when their child starts to identify with being black. Black children with black parents have that link automatically, but a black child with a white parent is going to have problems. *African Caribbean woman.*

I wasn't aware that I might have any special needs in bringing up my child because she is mixed race. *White woman.*

It would be nice to have a group of our own, so we can compare how we are bringing our children up. *White woman.*

People also felt it was important that the project was *not* at the existing NSPCC building, partly because of the image of the service offered there and partly because it was not seen as local and identified as a black building.

Black families project

The NSPCC is an independent charity set up to prevent child abuse and protect children. In a recent policy document they say,

> The abuse of children is a universal problem, affecting children of all classes, cultures and racial groups. Child abuse is a socially defined phenomenon, in that those actions which are seen to constitute abuse are dependent upon prevalent values and practices and such attitudes have varied over time. Internationally attitudes towards children are becoming more consistent, reflecting the beliefs that children have inalienable rights to be protected from harm, which must be respected and promoted by parents, the community, political and social institutions. The basis rights of children cannot always be met by their parents or carers and often children are harmed by the actions of others. These unmet rights and the risk of consequent harm create a range of 'needs', the fulfilling of which would ensure the safety and well being of all children.
> ...The term *prevention* is used by the NSPCC to describe those activities which, as their prime objective, seek to deter child abuse from happening in the first place, whilst *protection* describes those activities undertaken following abuse, which seek to mitigate the impact of abuse and to prevent its reoccurrence. Neither of these terms is discrete nor mutually exclusive. Often work in this field involves both sorts of activity and both terms appear in the title of the strategy to emphasise their parallel importance within our work.

Taking the findings from the research and translating those findings into meaningful practice presented fresh challenges for the NSPCC organisation. A brief examination of the findings illustrated a deep dissatisfaction amongst services users and research participants regarding their relationship with general provision for families with Black children.

> There is a lack of availability of social workers when you need to discuss problems. *Black woman.*

> I think there should be a strong body of black workers within social services who can offer support when you are at your wits end. So far

I have only had white workers who do not really understand Black children. *Black woman.*

By the end of 1993 NSPCC were ready to recruit a small skilled staff team to develop the proposed project's services in consultation with the participants of the research. The project was called Camara. The naming of the project had to span both the African and Asian communities in both language and philosophy. Much consultation with community leaders workers and individuals led the worker team to choose a name which has this meaning: 'Camara - one who teaches from experience'. The name was to define the future role for the the project. The following quotation from Camara's leaflet for parents/carers gives some insight into the aims of philosophy (NSPCC East, 1996).

WHY THE CAMARA PROJECT WAS ESTABLISHED FOR BLACK CHILDREN

We know from the figures for the area that while Black children make up under 7% of the population of Nottinghamshire, they account for over 15% of the total number of children in care.

We know that as Black people we all have unique needs and different cultures which the services currently provided often do not take into account.

We know your need for help may be immediate, and you do not want to be told to come back later when there is a worker who can see you.

We know you may not have the confidence to go to other services outside the area to find help.

THE PROJECT EXISTS TO:

1 Contribute towards a reduction in the number of Black children in care.

2 Work in partnership with parents/carers of Black children, to provide activities which meet the relevant needs as identified by families.

3 Provide an open door, self referral service for Black families.

4 Develop ways of working with Black families against discrimination.

5 Provide training and consultation for child care practitioners.

WHAT WE AIM TO DO:

To support parents and carers within the community to meet the needs of their children in an effective way.

To promote practice which helps to prevent all types of abuse of Black children.

To promote positive Black images.

To share in enhancing parenting skills.

To provide counselling for parents/carers of Black children and their families.

To have an outreach approach offering accessible help within the community.

To address issues which contribute to the stress of being a parent or carer.

WHO WE ARE:

Friendly professional Black workers are on hand who are experienced in assisting with a whole range of parenting and child care issues.

The Project - Camara

The Camara project was set up in 1993. There were 4 workers from Asian and African Caribbean backgrounds. Initially, the project was located in the NSPCC child protection office, but it moved for a period to a house within the neighbourhood that the project was working, which was specially converted for the project.

The pivotal subject of race was passionately explored through discussion by all involved in the project. The need to do this was also recognised by the NSPCC Black Workers Group. In these discussions negative views were challenged continuously and there developed and evolved a black

179

professional perspective which took as its starting point real day-to-day experiences of racism. Only when this has been done can the aim to empower black children and families to deal with their experiences begin. The workers were not only developing a prevention approach in practice, but were simultaneously developing the theories and arguments for the project's approach.

Intrinsic to the black perspective the project was using, were the following:

1 the need to promote the articulation of black people and to seek to replace the white distortion of black reality with black writing and black experience.
2 to develop an approach which not only addresses, but seeks to transform the unequal power relations which dominate the social and professional inter-action between black and white people into egalitarian ones.

Various writers (e.g. Bond, 1996) have noted how little has been written about the strengths of black families in Britain despite the acknowledgement that these families on the whole, are the main protectors of children. In their report on race and child protection, Dutt and Phillips (1996) conclude most communities have ways of protecting the children in their community, and go on to say, 'The long term effects of the care system on black children is negative and can result in black children developing a negative sense of self. In the face of racism black families and black communities provide the main source of support to black individuals and it is in the interests of black children therefore to remain part of their family and/or community' (1996, p. 187). Camara shared this view and its practice was based on it.

The team, the manager, the project users and supporters allocated time specifically to develop a more fundamental understanding of the impact of racism which interrupts the delivery of a required service. This lengthy work resulted in a 'empowerment practice strategy' which is outlined below. This was based on:

1 *Recognition of life experience*, which also takes into account the survival skills used by the person.
2 *Understanding of what the black experience is to the user*, providing them with opportunities to explore how much, or how little, race was a factor in their experiences.
3 *Sensitivity to racial and cultural pride.*

4 *Promotion of positive self image*, done in a variety of ways including, recognising and validating the strengths of the individual and their community, using and informing people of positive images of black people.
5 *Knowledge of family support systems* that people are already gaining strength from.
6 *Provision of positive role models*, through pictures, books, media and personal interaction.
7 *Enable a redress of the power imbalances*, as far as is possible, by helping people understand the existing power structures, their place in them and why this is so.
8 *Work actively against racism* in every situation.

This well developed strategy was to set the foundation for the areas of work, which had been identified by the research.

The philosophy of practice for the project was also based on social action. This model turns the role of the professional on its head (see Mullender and Ward, 1991). Instead of being the 'experts' and the holder of skills, knowledge and services, the professional becomes a facilitator where people are encouraged to:

1 Set their own agenda - they choose *what* issues of concerns they want to work on
2 Analyse critically their situation, look at *why* these situations exist
3 Devise ways of tackling these issues or concerns, *how* can they begin to be solved
4 Taken *action* for themselves
5 *Reflect* on their experiences, consolidate their learning and begin the process again.

The people themselves control the content, the analysis, the action and reflection. The professional provides the framework on process.

This practice approach is based on the same set of values of the research. This value base which underpins, the practise of both the research and the direct practise, draws heavily on the work of Paulo Freire, the women's movements challenge of authority, the disability rights movement (Oliver, 1992) and the work and struggles of black activists.

Work with fathers

Where did fathers fit into the project's ideology of preventing abuse to black children and promoting positive parenting? The issue of gender in relation to services delivered was approached directly from the user critique.

Camara set about exploring why fathers in general, but more specifically black fathers in particular, did not have access to services and support that enabled and encouraged them to have an active part in child care and an involvement in child protection.

The workers believed that fathers as a group had valuable, but generally unexplored, lessons to inform the practice of effective parenting.

The project established weekly group for fathers by successfully creating a safe environment. The process was not easy. At the time the workers in the team were all women, therefore a black man who shared the concerns had to be found to be a co-worker. Eventually contact was made with a student working on placement at a project concerned with domestic violence. After many planning meetings it was agreed to offer an opportunity to work with black men on the issues of race and the welfare of self and children. The student was already in contact with some men looking at relationship issues, family breakdown and domestic violence. Through these men and Camara's contacts a number of men who wanted to take part were contacted.

Although attendance was erratic, there was a core of 6 men, their ages ranged from 23-33 years. The age range was felt to be an advantage because it carried good learning and sharing potential. The members were from many racial backgrounds including bi-racial backgrounds. Two of the men were employed the remaining 4 were unemployed. On some occasions the participants involved friends.

The men did not previously know each other, so the first few weeks were largely spent enabling the group to bond. The workers provided a framework for the men to share common issues and experiences. The primary issues were racism, and their experiences of being fathered, or not as many of the men had been raised in a home without fathers.

You don't know what it is like to be a black man, they don't want to give you a job. No money usually means you can't see your kids. After all, they don't want a sob story. *Black man.*

Racism is at the root of all these situations. Nobody says it, but we all know the truth. *Black man.*

Many delicate issues were explored during the group's life. The key areas of concern for the group were: relationships within families, childhood experiences that have never been addressed, racism and its effect on their self image and future expectations, relationships with partners past and present, parenting in general and isolation.

The discussions which took place were very personal and emotional. The group of men were not used to sharing personal experiences and this meant that initially the group process was viewed as threatening by some of them. Issues regarding trust, support, respect, and interdependency were regular topics in the group and needed to be established for the discussions to be able to be developed.

The following quotes give some insights in to the discussions in the group.

> Nobody ever asks you about what it feels like to be male and black. *Black man.*

> I cannot believe I've repeated my father's pattern. I thought I was trying to be different from him. *Black man.*

> I am the common denominator in the break-ups I've had with my children's mothers. *Black man.*

The group ran for twelve weeks in 1995. The members believed the experience of being fathered profoundly influences how they themselves father. The experience in the group ranged from having very positive experience of being fathered to have no fathering at all. Through sharing these experiences the men began to critically analyse themselves as fathers, and began to develop support relevant to themselves as black fathers. Through this process they looked at images of fatherhood, the effects of racism on self image and expectations. One outcome of this group was that the fathers planned a regular picnic for themselves and their children to spend positive time with their children and to put into practice some of the things they had discussed about fathering in a supportive environment.

White women with black children

In the first weeks of the project the staff spent some time considering what a black family was. Does it include white parents with a black child? After lengthy discussions it was decided that the service would be based on a child centred approach and any family with a black child could use the project.

There was much evidence that this was an important area of work ro develop. Based on figures available, from Nottingham County Council Social Services Department (1993) the research stage illustrated what many public services had experienced, but had not at that time acknowledged, that the highest proportion of children in care in Nottinghamshire were institutionally classified as black. In the majority of cases the mother of the black child was white. A further examination of the figures highlighted a 'crisis' in which the child's race and gender (male) were identified by the mother as the reason for not being able to cope. More recent research confirms that this is still an issue. A recent report (Barn, Sinclair and Ferdinand, 1997) says that a significant number of mixed race children are referred to social services, mostly by their white mothers.

Whilst looking through the referrals made to Camara from the child protection team it was found that there was one reoccurring feature, which was white women with black children. They had come to the attention of the NSPCC because of their isolation and difficulties in parenting.

Unlike the development of the men's group, the project was already regularly in contact with white women with black children. Other professionals, for example teachers, educational psychologists, probation officers and Family Centre workers would frequently contact Camara either asking for support to develop work or for information about direct services with these families. As the following referral conversation shows,

> I'm not sure if you can help. I've got a client - she is white - she has got 2 children from a black partner. But you know, he is not around, I think the children need identity work. *White woman.*

All this information led to the development a group for white women with black children. The aim was for them to have access to a service which would address the experiences which lead to their isolation and their feelings of powerlessness. The first few women Camara worked with did not have a clear idea of what they wanted for their children or even for themselves. The workers helped them identify their issues.

> When my child tells me people don't like him 'cos he is black, I tell him I want him to be black. But it doesn't help. *White woman.*

> My son is suffering from racism and I want to stop it. *White woman.*

The project had a lot of experience of white women expressing an inability to maintain a relationship with their black child, which they perceived as being a consequence of their colour.

I just give up, he is just like his Dad. *White woman.*

This situation appeared to be more relevant when the father is no longer in contact. Bond also writes of this in her article about working with black families: 'Often when she looks at her child she is overwhelmed by her feelings of bitterness towards his father. Her son is coming home from school saying he is being bullied by white boys who taunt him with racist comments, and he wishes he were white. His mother knows she must help him but how can she when she too has some of those same racist feelings?' (Bond, 1996).

To meet the needs of this particular group of women, the project aimed, in partnership with the women, to develop positive strategies, keeping as a focus the identities of the women and their children. The group looked at their child's experiences and their own. These included, for example, their children's experiences at school. Initially the women voiced their feelings and the group gave them a place to express their concerns and worries, for example:

My child is suffering from racism at school and I am not having it. *White woman.*

I live in an all white area and I need to hear about other parents' issues. We need to be in a situation where our children are valued. *White woman.*

I want to be with other parents of black children to interrupt the isolation. *white woman*

Her nursery is really mono-cultural, there is one black doll and just white books. *White woman.*

My children haven't got any problems because they are black, you shouldn't draw attention to it, it's not their fault. *White woman.*

Through exploring and discussing what was happening with others, the women were able to move on from their anger and confusion. Discussions then ranged widely on such issues of standards of beauty and who decides them? Where do black people fit in to this? Can you make people like your child? Relationships with their children's fathers and how to keep the needs of your child central were also addressed. The women then moved on to look at strategies they could develop to cope with their experiences and feelings and how to support their children.

> My child is a constant reminder of racism. As long as he is in the school they have to think about racism. The minute he disappears they may not think about it. *White woman.*

> I recognised that racism is a taboo subject, to challenge it feels dangerous, but it can have positive effects. *White woman.*

> We have to teach our children to respect each other, both black and white. *White woman.*

At the end of the group the women did an evaluation and some of the things they said they had valued or gained from the group were: talking with black women (the workers) and being listened to, sharing experiences with other people and realising you are not alone, help with dealing with partners, acknowledging my children are black and the whole issue with family who are white.

Location

The research highlighted the need for the project to have a building separate to the NSPCC, with its own identity. In partnership with the City Challenge Initiative and the Nottingham City Housing department, a small residential premises was allocated to the NSPCC which met with the specifications set out in the research. Its location would bridge both the African/Asian communities. Unfortunately, due to harassment and vandalism the project had to move out of this building and has since been based at the NSPCC child protection team office.

The project itself is not immune to the racism it is attempting to deal with in its work. The same ignorance and prejudice that the black children face is the same one that drove the project out of its neighbourhood base.

186

Conclusion

For a long time services towards the black communities have been inappropriate to their needs. In this paper we have outlined how an attempt to make a service directly relevant to people's needs was developed. It represents an intermediate stage in a continuing process of development. The process is dynamic. There are always ways to learn and improve both research and practice. However, the research successfully engaged with local families with black children and involved them in looking critically at what they felt their support needs were and how these could best be met, by the NSPCC. The development of Camara is the result of that process.

The authors would like to acknowledge and thank Frances Thompson who undertook the original community consultation.

References

Ahmad, B. (1990), *Black Perspectives in Social Work Placements*, Venture Press: Birmingham.

Akbar, Na'im (1985), *The Community and Self*, Mind Productions and Associates: Florida.

Akbar, Na'im (1991), *Visions for Black Men*, Winston Derek Inc: Nashville.

Barn, R., Sinclair, R. and Ferdinand, D. (1997), *Acting on Principle: An examination of race and ethnicity in social services provision for children and families*, BAAF: London.

Bond, H. (1996), 'Mixed Blessings', *Community Care*, 31 Oct-6 Nov, pp. 26-29.

Cloke, C. and Davies, M. (ed.) (1995), *Participation and Empowerment in Child Protection*, Pitman: London.

Cress Welsing, F. (1991), *The ISIS Papers, The key to the colours*, Third World Press: Chicago.

Davis, A. (1982), *Woman, Race and Class*, Women's Press: London.

Davis, A. (1984), *Women, Culture and Politics*, Women's Press: London.

Dominelli, L. (1988), *Anti-racist Social Work*, Macmillan: Basingstoke.

Dominelli, L. (1989), 'An uncaring profession? An examination of racism and social work', *New Community*, Vol. 15, No. 3.

Du Bois, B. (1983), 'Passionate Scholarship: notes on values, knowing and method in feminist social science' in Bowles, G. and Duelli, A., *Theories of Women's Studies*, Routledge and Kegan Paul: London.

Dutt and Philips (1991), *Towards a Black Perspective in Child Protection*, Race Equality Unit: London.

Fleming, J. and Harrison, M. (1994), *Derby PRIDE Health Needs Study*, Derby Pride Ltd: Derby.

Fleming, J. and Ward, D. (1992), *For the children to be alright their mothers need to be alright*, NCH Action for Children and Centre for Social Action, University of Nottingham: Nottingham.

Freire, P. (1972), *Pedagogy of the Oppressed*, Penguin: Harmondsworth.

Gould, G. (1997), 'Action Janet, Black Social Action', *Shabab*, No. 20, May, pp. 14-16.

Haughton, P. (1997), 'Positive Opinions, Positive Outcomes', *Social Action Today*, No. 4, pp. 11-13.

hooks, b. (1992), *Ain't I a woman: black woman and feminism*, Pluto Press: London.

hooks, b. (1992), *Black Looks, Race and Representation*, Turnaround: London.

hooks, b. (1991), *Yearning: race, gender and cultural politics*, Turnaround: London.

Jadeja, K. (1997), 'Relationship Problems', *Community Care*, 29th May-4th June, p. 5.

Macdonald, S. (1991), *All Equal Under the Act?*, Race Equality Unit: London.

Mathias, B. and French, M. (1996), *Forty Ways to Raise a Non-Racist Child*, Harper perennial: New York.

Mullender, M. and Ward, D. (1991), *Self-Directed Group work - Users Taking Action for Empowerment*, Whiting and Birch: London.

NSPCC (1991), *"NSPCC Special Projects"* (unpublished).

NSPCC East (1996), *Child Abuse: A Prevention and Protection Strategy*, (unpublished).

Oliver, M. (1992), 'Changing the social relations of research production', *Disability Handicap and Society*, 7 (2), pp. 101-104.

Owen, M. and Farmer, E. (1996), 'Child Protection in a Multi-racial Context', *Policy and Politics*, Vol. 24, No. 3, pp. 299-313.

Rehman, H. and Walker (1995), 'Research black and minority ethnic groups', *Health Education Journal*, Vol. 54, No. 4, pp. 489-500.

Rejtman, R. (1997), 'Meeting the needs of Ethnic Minority Children and Young People in Care', *Childright*, No. 137, June, pp. 4-7.

Rouf, K. (1991), *Black Girls Speak Out*, Children's Society: London.

Thompson, F. and Fleming (1993), *Nottingham Black Families Project - A Background Study*, (Report to the NSPCC), Centre for Social Action, University of Nottingham: Nottingham.

Tizard, B. and Phoenix, A. (1993), *Black White and Mixed Race*, Routledge: London.

Varma, V. (1993), *How and Why Children Hate*, Jessica Kingsley Publishers Ltd: London.

9 Black Community Members as Researchers: Two Projects Compared

Simon Dyson and Mark Harrison

Introduction

This chapter will compare the experiences of two sets of research projects involving members of black and minority ethnic communities in the role of researchers. The first involved two parallel surveys of community awareness of sickle cell anaemia and beta-thalassaemia in Leicester (Dyson and Goyder, 1994a, 1994b). These two inherited blood disorders (collectively, the haemoglobinopathies) particularly affect peoples of African-Caribbean and South Asian descent respectively, although both conditions are found to some extent in many other ethnic groups. The research interviews were conducted by members of the local self-help groups (The Organization for Sickle Cell Anaemia Research and the Thalassaemia Society) and generated several potential learning points for future research involving community members in the research process.

These points were taken up in the second set of projects which involved work alongside the refugee Somali community in Tower Hamlets in East London. This community is thought to number around 30,000 people, principally displaced by the civil wars in Somalia. Building on contacts made in the course of a research project identifying housing needs of refugees (Harrison, 1993) the Centre for Social Action was commissioned by the Tower Hamlets Race Equality Council (THREC) to look at the take up of welfare services by the Somali community in the Bethnal Green City Challenge Area (Harrison et al, 1995). This THREC project tried to apply learning points from the haemoglobinopathy surveys in using members of the Somali community in the research. The collection of data was preceded by a workshop based around ten issues that had arisen in the Leicester surveys (Dyson, 1995).

There are clearly important and defining reasons why working in these ways should be considered appropriate, politically as well as professionally. Firstly, whether of African-Caribbean, South Asian or Somali descent, the interviewers share a common experience of racism. Involving communities in the interview process, recognizes that people have skills and understanding which they can bring to bear on their own circumstances and permits at least the possibility that white workers may share their skills and not keep what Bourdieu characterizes as cultural capital to themselves (Bourdieu and Passeron, 1977).

Secondly, in not proceeding to the other extreme in turning projects over to black community members wholesale, leaving people unsupported in circumstances made challenging by economic, policy and environment issues, such research approaches try to avoid the problem of setting up black projects to fail. To develop Bourne (1980), funding black community projects may be a strategy of socially controlling previously autonomous initiatives. But that control may be effected through monitoring requirements (e.g. in research terms does data pass tests of validity and reliability?) not because they are inappropriate (as Reed and Proctor, 1995, seem to imply) but because they are set against over-idealized versions of how they are applied in statutory organizations.

Thirdly, and specifically in connection with the processes of research, there are the issues of what may be termed research scepticism and research fatigue in the black communities. The former refers to the feeling that researchers take information from communities but those communities do not see the benefits of changes. The latter alludes to the degree of monitoring that can take place where marginal groups become the continued targets of researchers. Only by black and white workers successfully working together, it may be argued, can a situation be avoided whereby research participants are not themselves estranged from the research process (Oliver, 1992). Only by conducting research which effects change and provides community feedback can the conditions for changing the social relations of research production (Oliver, 1992) begin to be established.

This chapter will attempt to outline the theoretical background to the Social Action research method, describe the key differences between the social contexts of the two sets of projects; describe the issues involved in working on research projects with communities; and seek to identify what lessons seem to have potential for applicability across different situations.

Background

The starting point is to address the various critiques of conventional research and to offer an alternative approach. The model which we will elaborate is grounded in practice. This practice, Social Action has been developed over the last nineteen years. It emerged when a number of youth, community and social work practitioners and educators came together because they were dissatisfied with and critical of social and urban policy as it was affecting communities.

Out of this dialogue emerged a practice (which became known as Social Action) which rejected the value base and methods being employed by the mainstream professions and institutions responsible for social work, welfare and education. It became clear to us that the problems did not just lie in practice and practitioners but were principally rooted in the education and training of professionals and the research models and methods that informed and shaped policy and practice.

For our theoretical and practical inspiration we turned to Paulo Freire and Saul Alinsky. In practice we learnt lessons from community work and the experience of Community Development Projects (CDP's) and social education. We were influenced by the work and struggles of black writers and activists notably George Jackson and Steve Biko. We were inspired by the movement in youth culture and music particularly Reggae, Punk and Two Tone and drew strength and encouragement from the Women's Movement's challenge of (male) authority and professionalism over their lives. More recently the emergence of the disability rights movement, the Direct Action Network and the writing of Mike Oliver (1992) and others has reaffirmed and deepened our commitment to challenging current orthodoxies in social and urban policy.

From this critique, analysis and theoretical base we began to develop the framework for revolutionising practice.

This was a new model which turns the professional's role on its head (see Mullender and Ward, 1991). Instead of being the provider and giver of all knowledge, wisdom, skills and services - which we cannot deliver anyway, the professionals become facilitators or social educators where communities are encouraged to:

1   set the agenda
2   analyse critically their situation
3   devise ways of tackling issues, problems and concerns
4   take action for themselves

5   reflect on their experiences, consolidate the learning and begin the process again on a higher level.

Community members control the (subject) content, analysis, action and reflection. The professional provides the framework or process.

This approach which has been developed and refined is based on a set of values/principles.

These are:

1   All people have skills and understanding which they can draw on to tackle the problems they face.
2   All people have rights, including the right to be heard, the right to define issues facing them and the right to take action on their own behalf.
3   People acting collectively can be powerful. People who lack power and influence can gain it through working together in groups. Practice should reflect this understanding.
4   Individuals in difficulty are often confronted by complex issues rooted in social policy, the environment and the economy. Responses to them should reflect this understanding.
5   Methods of working must reflect non-elitist principles. Workers do not 'lead' the group but facilitate members in making decisions for themselves and controlling whatever outcome ensures. Though special skills and knowledge are employed, these do not accord privilege and are not solely the province of the workers.
6   We will strive through our work to challenge inequality and discrimination in relation to race, gender, sexual orientation, age, class, disability or any other form of social differentiation.

Having established the principles and parameters of this new groupwork method and having begun to test it out in practice, it became clear that the approach we were taking had wider implications for training and research. The existing training agencies were training people in the old methods, values and practices so in looking for appropriate training it became clear to us that we would have to train ourselves. The training and research processes and methods we have developed mirrored the Social Action process we carried out in the groupwork method.

This process is based on Freire's philosophy which has three elements, *Praxis* - critical reflection and human action. It incorporates the notion that Praxis is dialogue which consists of both action and reflection, or active reflection and reflective action, in an equal or balanced relationship. This dialogue breaks down the traditional relationship between teacher - student and the 'banking' concept of education and replaces it with a partnership where roles interchange and the teacher - student and student - teacher are co-investigators each reforming their thinking through reflecting with each other. Knowledge is created or re-created through critical reasoning.

Part two *problematization*, which is a process of drawing attention to situations that require action or change. The possibility of change is indicated by posing changes. Problem posing is a process of questioning deeper structures; of challenging commonly accepted ideas by posing more and more questions to dig beneath conventional or common sense explanations of reality; of raising and analysing contradictions (Kidd and Byram, 1982).

The final component is *conscientisation*, this he describes as 'a permanent critical approach to reality in order to discover it and discovers the myths that deceive us and help to maintain the oppressing dehumanising structures, (it) leaves nobody inactive' (Freire, 1971). Therefore conscientisation goes beyond consciousness raising or an awareness of reality to a critical development strategy from experience.

In Social Action we have developed a five stage process based on Freire's coding system - naming, reflecting and action.

1   What - are the issues, concerns, problems
2   Why - do they exist
3   How - can this be changed
4   Action - taken by group
5   Reflection - review process and action by repeating the five stages.

The Social Action model is elaborated more fully in Mullender and Ward (1991) and was adapted for training ourselves and others.

For research we also developed new methods which can measure the effectiveness of this approach. Social Action research begins from the premise that communities are not merely the object of research but become the subject of research. Treating people as subjects means they have the right to speak out and the right to be *heard*. This is part of the empowering and enabling process that is a principle of our work. This by itself is not innovatory. However, the Social Action research method involves subjects at all stages. This dialogue style of research provides a better understanding of different perceptions of community members and allows them to shape the parameters of the research.

Fleming and Ward (1995) explains this process:

The Social Action research process starts with an open ended enquiry rather than with an attempt to verify existing ideas. Social Action research does not start with preconceived ideas and concepts, rather we work with community members/service users, managers and practitioners to identify the focus of the research and the outcomes it is seeking. These groups are involved in the refinement of the objectives for research or evaluation, in the formation of methods and in the interpretation of the data collected. We look to establish a collaborative method with all people affected involved in the research process.

This research process creates new agendas for change. It reverses the traditional way of carrying out research. Traditional research methods use quantitative research methods at the enquiry stage and qualitative methods to analyse the data collected. Social Action research uses qualitative methods to establish with the community or group being studied, the parameters, areas and content for research and the questions to be asked. They are then surveyed using qualitative methods such as individual interviews and focus groups using guided interview schedules devised from the initial consultation process. Sometimes community members or group members are employed as researchers to facilitate this process, particularly when working with minority ethnic communities, supported by a Social Action research supervisor (Dyson, 1995, Harrison et al., 1996). They are trained, supported and equipped to carry out the process by the research supervisor, often using a workshop format.

The results of this enquiry are then analysed again using qualitative methods. These are fed back to the research subjects, usually again in the form of a workshop, to check findings and to ensure that the research process hasn't missed out any essential data or findings.

By involving research subjects at every stage, including devising recommendations, there is a much higher validity and ownership of the findings. It also means the research process is an empowering one and creates agendas for change which have meaning to both sponsors and subjects of the research. In this way the Social Action research process addresses the criticisms of traditional and conventional practices. It also offers practitioners and researchers a progressive and innovatory way forward.

The two research projects we will be discussing both used the Social Action research methodology.

Continuities and contrasts

Before turning to a critical examination of how these theories, principles and practices transfer from one setting to another, it seems appropriate to outline some immediate differences between the populations and settings of the two series of projects. One overriding factor the African-Caribbean and Asian communities in Leicester and the Somali communities in Tower Hamlets share in common is the experience of racism. However, there are several factors which suggest that the Somali communities are even more disadvantaged. Firstly, the Somali community comprises primarily those with refugee status, notwithstanding the very long history of Somali seamen in Britain. This leads to even greater insecurities of residency than might otherwise be the case for Britain's black population as a whole. Secondly, whilst patterns of postwar migration have led to African-Caribbean and Asian populations having a younger age structure than the white population (Smaje, 1995) with women and children in these communities being separated, in some cases for years, from their menfolk before being able to join them in Britain, the Somali community reflects an even greater degree of distortion of these structures due to much more recent migration and the violence of the civil war, which was the impetus behind the migration. It is for these reasons that it is particularly young men, ex-warriors in the civil war, who are over-represented as a proportion of the population. Thirdly, their high levels of unemployment, low levels of access to housing, welfare, health, educational and interpreting services in the Somali community are further compounded by the failure of statutory authorities to recognize them as a group with distinctive needs. In this respect basing service provision on the 1991 Census figures misrepresents them in several ways. Firstly, and most obviously, in many cases the migration simply post-dates 1991. Secondly, many would not have been eligible to complete the Census return, others may not have been accorded the appropriate opportunity to do so by interpreting services. Finally, they may have been subsumed in the generic Black (African) ethnic category.

On the other hand, notwithstanding the divergencies of structure and experience between Leicester and Tower Hamlets, one continuity is the importance of being sensitive to diversities within black and ethnic minority communities. The Leicester Asian community mainly comprises Gujarati Hindus and Moslems, but Punjabi Sikhs, Moslems and Hindus are also represented as are smaller proportions of Pakistani, Bangladeshi and Chinese communities. The Leicester African-Caribbean communities represent many different Caribbean islands, especially a number of smaller islands such as Montserrat. The Somali refugee community is predominantly Moslem, but is based around one particularly important divide. The West London Somali community is mainly drawn from refugees from Somalia, a former colony of Italy. The Somali community in East London comprises refugees from Somaliland, that is Northern Somalia, with Britain in the role of former colonial power. This divide is one major basis for determining the opposing factions in the civil war and not surprisingly proved an important source of tension in the data collection.

Black community members-as-researchers

Reflexivity in research

Reflexivity draws on the notion that people's reactions to being researched and the experiences of the research process may tell us as much about the situation studied as the 'official' data. So, for example, the high level of inaccuracies and omissions in the officially recorded addresses for the black and ethnic minority populations are arguably a reflection of the level of priority accorded to those communities by statutory agencies. In order that this evidence not be lost, one recommendation is that the community interviewers be asked to keep research diaries of their experiences during the course of the project, and that these diaries be the subject of focused de-briefing interviews towards the conclusion of the research. This may have to be completed using cassette tapes where there is lack of self confidence in writing skills. However, the importance of writing out one's thought should not be underestimated as a mechanism for stimulating critical reflection on one's own point of view (Plummer, 1983) and thus reinforcing the insights offered by the process.

In the Tower Hamlets research the supervision was carried out through regular meetings which were run as workshops where the participants were encouraged to talk about their experiences and observations from the research. With the Somali refugee community there is little or no official data. This placed a heavy responsibility on the young community members who were recruited as researchers. The observations of the researchers provided as much information about the community as the 'official' answers.

Without community members as researchers subtle changes in circumstances would not have been picked up or understood. For example, at one point in the study the researchers reported that they were experiencing difficulties in obtaining interviews. The reason for this was a flare up in the civil war in Somalia. Without community members as researchers this subtlety would, we believe, not have been detected.

Delegation of organization of work

Within the broad parameters of the research design and funding there exists the potential for delegating many organizational features to the community members. This may include factors such as relative workload and the particular division of labour to be employed. Thus in the Leicester studies it was found to be beneficial to encourage this self-organization as it permitted decisions such as whether male-male match-ups for interviews were more or less appropriate than female-male; to enable a married couple to interview jointly as a team when interviewing other married couples; and to decide whether, within the particular culture in question, in cases where an community interviewer was well known to a potential respondent, it was more appropriate for the interview to be conducted by someone well-known, someone not immediately known, or to leave the decision to the respondent.

In the Somalian study the decisions about who should interview whom in the community were once more left to the community researchers. The assumption was made that they were the experts in knowing their own community, and the role of research supervisor was restricted to areas of research methods. Questions of gender, age and tribe were discussed with the supervisor acting as a sounding board. A great deal was learned about the community by this process and community cynicism (about whether the interviewers represented a particular local political faction) and suspicion (related to the civil war) seemed to be more significant than gender in gaining successful interviews. In fact the young female interviewer experienced some difficulties in obtaining interviews from older women (who enjoy higher status in the community) and eventually concentrated on interviewing men. The male interviewers interviewed women. Decisions about who would interview whom were again made on the basis of who knew whom.

Contrasting the 'hired hand' mentality

The use of community members as part of a research team lends itself to potential criticism by researchers (and indeed research funders) for 'when community groups generate their own research their methods are seen as idiosyncratic and often cause concern to the more experimentally inclined practitioner' (Daly and McDonald, 1992, p. 4). In fact, as Roth (1966) has argued, using professional but disinterested interviewers as 'hired hand' researchers brings with it quite systematic data collection avoidance and fabrication. This poor quality data can be seen to be the product of a hierarchical division of labour in which those responsible for collecting data have no vested interest in the procedures and research outcomes. As has been pointed out in the realm of official statistics, ostensibly neutral 'hired hands' do not have the motivation to identify implausible data to the research team, nor the initiative to get the issue resolved (Government Statisticians Collective, 1979). The Leicester experience suggested that community volunteer researchers have precisely that motivation. They returned to an address several times rather than give up; they traced people to new addresses where the original one listed was out of date, and they persevered in the face of full-time jobs, child-care commitments or both.

For the Somalian study to be successful it had to be carried out by an institution and Somali researchers who had credibility in the community. If this had not been achieved, access and information would have been denied and we believe even where access was gained the information gathered would not have been accurate. The combination was critical in this instance. Without the outside institution, there is the strong possibility that the Somali community would have been concerned that a Somali only initiative represented a particular sectional interest group as some local projects had, in the absence of proper statutory authority support, collapsed and monies been misappropriated. But an outside agency acting alone would have been viewed with the suspicion that information gathering was being employed as a substitute for services and the provision of infrastructure and support to local projects. This is an important reminder that we need to move beyond sterile dichotomies of insider v outsider or community v institution.

Critical commentary on validity and threats to validity

Following from the previous point, there exists the potential for community members to comment on their perceptions of the validity of data they are engaged in creating. They may be privy on the one hand to a shared experience of racism and sensitive to local community strategies for dealing with racism which may affect what people are prepared to say and to whom. Equally they may be attuned to internal divisions within a community who may appear to professional outsiders as an homogeneous grouping, divisions which may well influence what people say or claim at interview. For instance, in Leicester, especially in the thalassaemia research, interviewers provided insights to the effect that couples appeared to be hiding their knowledge of thalassaemia in front of their mother-in-law, or the wife from the husband because of the perceived stigma the inherited condition might bring on the family.

In the Somalian study checks on validity also came from the workshop format for supervision where through open discussion the researchers debated responses and findings and consensus was achieved. The important distinction from the work of Roth (1966) is that the negotiated meaning of responses took place with community researchers. This meant they held the dual roles of data collector and data interpreter (not separate as in Roth's experiences) and the collector-coders were also people who could themselves have been respondents and were not outsiders to the situation studied, again in contrast to Roth. Where there were still unresolved questions, these were checked out with other Somali community professionals who formed an informal support group to the study.

Personal rewards of research

Whilst it must surely be the aim of any collaboration with community members to secure professional rates of pay for comparable work where the worker so desires, there do seem to be important extra-monetary rewards which may motivate community researchers. From the Leicester experience these appear to include escape from social isolation; acquisition of new skills such as interviewing; self-clarification of views; increased confidence; and an opportunity to challenge community stigma. Payment may, in some instances, rob the activity of its symbolic meaning to the community, and this certainly echoes the concerns of Illich (1978) that professional work strips the community of its folk skills and lay strategies. Seeing the value of work only in monetary terms may indeed be the first step in crystallizing a community activity into professional work.

In the Somali community older, higher status women respondents tended at first to undervalue the contribution of the young interviewers who were in their mid-twenties. However, the process of research eventually appeared to entail an enhancement of community status for these young interviewers. Because status in the Somali community is related to age as well as to tribe, the work of the young interviewers helped to break down these age-related status divisions within the community. As there was a general lack of understanding about the basics of the British Welfare System, such questions about the accessibility of that system were not meaningful to respondents. For instance where the elder concerned did not know about Britain's welfare services they deferred to the researchers to complete the questionnaire on their behalf. In situations such as these the questionnaire format was to some extent abandoned as the researchers took on an educational role in explaining to their community the meanings of service provision such as social services and education. On the other hand the Somali interviewers were paid at professional rates of pay (University Research Scales). In retrospect the research supervisor felt that it would have been more appropriate to set the level of payment at a lower level (as the researchers were neither qualified nor experienced in research) but to pay longer hours (which would more closely reflect the real amounts of time spent on the study). Lower levels of researcher pay would also leave more monies for research supervision to support the community interviewers.

Valuing community researchers

The Leicester projects underlined what should have been apparent namely the importance of demonstrating to the community how their contributions are valued, not only by words but by the actions of the professional members of the research team. This means such things as having in place strategies for ensuring the personal safety of community researchers in terms of freedom from physical or sexual violence, or health and safety regulations covering unfamiliar buildings community members are asked to frequent. It also means that any tangibles of community researcher status (clipboards, pens, folders, notebooks, identity badges, typed guidelines) are of good quality, and do not convey the hidden message that cheap, second-hand, used or hand-written materials are 'good enough'. If training workshops are to be part of the process, then the basic minimum would seem to be to provide appropriate refreshments, and to dovetail the timing with the cycle of community religious or cultural commitments (e.g. collecting the children from the mosque).

These lessons from the Leicester study were raised with the Somali interviewers. Issues of personal safety were raised in the preparatory workshop. The interviewers felt that the work did not expose them to dangers over and above the very real threats to well-being attendant upon being black in an area of London infamous for the level of racial attacks on black people. Meanwhile the researchers were supplied with University business cards and official documentation to ensure their status as bona fide interviewers was not questioned. All supervisory meetings were scheduled around pre-existing commitments of the community members. A wide range of equipment needed for the research was supplied including clipboards, tape recorders, maps, pads of paper etc.

Different truths

The expectation that respondents will speak freely and truthfully to members of their own ethnic group, but hide at least parts of those truths away from white researchers is at best a simplistic assumption (Rhodes, 1994). Relative success in securing agreement to be interviewed must be conceptually distinguished from degree of commentary elicited concerning people's views of the research taking place and from eliciting their views on a sensitive subject which is the substance of the interview. In Leicester, African-Caribbean interviewers while appearing to enjoy good co-option rates, elicited expressions of anger from the community about research which gave nothing back to the community, but also met some resistance to an open discussion of the sensitive issue in question, namely sickle cell anaemia. A discussion the one African-Caribbean interviewer felt would have been more open to someone outside the community.

The Somali interviewers experienced difficulties in eliciting responses from some community members in a number of respects. This took the form of cynicism concerning the value of research born of the perception that there existed corruption within the community. This can be traced to the 'failed' initiatives where monies had gone missing following the collapse of a community project, where neither the buildings nor skills development of workers had been adequately resourced. Having the University as an outside research institution provided the researchers with an identity distinct from any local vested interest group. This allowed them to proceed more openly than might have been possible if a local agency or community organization had been the employing body.

Building trust over time

In Leicester two community conferences (Leicester OSCAR, 1988, Williams, 1990) are just part of the legacy of a ten-year collaboration between the community groups and the author. It is uncertain how successful any collaboration with community researchers can be as an initiative starting cold. Questions such as can people trust you as a professional worker? will only really be answered by actions over a considerable period of time. It may be judged on factors such as will you attend community meetings in your own time? will you become involved in self-help activities? will you make professional resources such as photocopying available to communities? It may also be judged by the success of smaller joint ventures and by your willingness to share professional expertise (eg. to make and disseminate notes in plain language where professional information is only available in jargon). This does suggest that a major joint research venture would be difficult, if not impossible, as a first initiative.

A proven track record and credibility within the community were essential for the Tower Hamlets research. The Centre for Social Action had been working in the Somali community for three years and were originally invited in by a professional/voluntary body that enjoyed the respect of the local community. The results of this first piece of work had a high degree of community involvement and produced tangible results for the community. The housing feasibility study developed a range of housing for the Somali community and led to the appointment of a part-time Somali Housing Development Worker. These successes meant that the researchers identified with the research as did the wider community such that the interviewers were able to gain access to all sections of the Somali community.

Feedback

A major complaint raised with interviewers in the Leicester projects was the absence of feedback or action from previous research involving the communities. Once more the basic minimum would seem to be a willingness to make results known in accessible formats (community newspapers, self-help newsletters, community centre conferences etc.), to discuss the meanings of any results found with the communities themselves (which is in any case a well-established feature of qualitative social research - Miles and Huberman, 1994) and to conceive of research as engaging with change, a conception which, in contradiction to Reed and Proctor (1995), can and is the legitimate concern of those who work in academic institutions. In Tower Hamlets consultation with key community members was carried out before, during and after the completion of the research. A follow-up workshop was held with community professionals and leaders to check out the findings and make additions and amendments as appropriate. A conference is being planned to feedback the results of the study to which the community and local agencies will be invited. Whilst the research process is seen by the community as being very successful the research will ultimately be judged on whether anything changes and whether additional resources and services are secured. Failure to deliver the recommendations will increase the community's disillusionment and make future research more difficult to carry out.

If the research enterprise is conceived of as making a contribution to the community whose members participate in the research process, then the policing of timescales, completion rates and the like begin to seem Draconian if they are at the expense of personal illness, family and community commitments and the work schedules of the community researchers. It seems that the supreme effort involved in fighting back needs protecting from a willingness to take on over ambitious demands, and this requires mutual clarification of anticipated commitments from the outset.

All the anticipated timetables and targets overran in the Tower Hamlets study. However, they were renegotiated by the Centre for Social Action with the commissioning organization. The reasons for the delays were in the main outside the control of the researchers. We saw it as our main job to take on as much of the management pressure as possible in order to free the workers to undertake their roles. All the commitments were met but in double the original timescale. This has provided valuable lessons for future projects of this nature, namely to allow more time to complete the research tasks.

Conclusion

Notwithstanding the important differences in context that we have outlined, many lessons about working with community members in research seem to have been transferable between situations.

Firstly, the possibility of learning lessons through thinking reflexively about the research process was confirmed in both cases. Difficulties in accessing the respective populations highlighted in Leicester the lack of care in health service record keeping for black clients, as well as an unwillingness to trust information provided by the communities themselves, and in Tower Hamlets the invisibility of the Somali communities to welfare services in the absence of a commitment to seek more up-to-date information than the 1991 Census. We have therefore come to the conclusion that research diaries and debriefing workshops should be an integral part of any community research.

Secondly, it appears that decisions about the division and organization of labour and about who interviews whom should be devolved to the community themselves. This recognizes that they are the experts in their own community dynamics. It avoids a rather programmatic imposition by the researchers about the meanings of social differentiations such as age and gender to respondents and interviewers. And it allows judgements about the importance of personal networks in securing interviews and obtaining appropriate match-ups to be made on the ground.

Thirdly, it is important to assert that employing interviewers who might be regarded as partisan appears to strengthen rather than weaken the quality and completeness of the data collected. On the other hand it is equally vital that the attempt to flatten the hierarchy of research relationships does not leave the community members unsupported. In this respect we recommend that ongoing supportive workshops are arranged throughout the period of data collection and beyond, and that community leaders other than those directly engaged in the research should have an acknowledged role in providing a complementary sounding board to the one also offered by the research supervisors.

Fourthly, we recommend that the critical reflections of the community interviewers on the validity of the findings they themselves generate should be an integral part of the data presentation. At the same time it is incumbent on the research supervisors to ensure that, for example, these validity checks are not misinterpreted by commissioning bodies as evidence of poor quality data, but to draw attention to the equivalent missing (or even suppressed?) checks in other data that a commissioning body may be relying upon.

Fifthly, we recommend that the pros and cons of monetary payments for community research work should be discussed with the community members at an early stage of planning. Where those members themselves feel that the team should be paid, and that payment is not compromising an important voluntary service ethos, then we feel that the following points should be addressed. The rates of pay should be on professional scales, but at a point on such scales reflecting the level of research experience of the community members, and the real numbers of hours worked, with proper allowance made to adequately fund research support and supervision.

Next, we recommend that particular attention be paid to health and personal safety issues at the planning stage, and that community members are given the minimum protection of identification and official documentation to carry with them in their work. Even within restricted budgets we feel that an important informal message of valuing people is conveyed by the allocation of good quality research materials to community members.

Additionally, we feel that an awareness is required of the manner in which research evidence is a product of a particular context rather than regarding different contexts as more or less likely to provide a privileged access to an external truth. Again this places a responsibility on research supervisors to expose to commissioners of research the productive processes in the production of other research information upon which they may base planning judgements.

Notwithstanding the tendencies of academic developments in social research to dismiss the possibility of progress on the basis of truths established by social research (Fox, 1993), the possibility of developing collaborative work with community members does depend on establishing a long-term relationship with community groups. Factors thought likely to help establish trust include demonstrating a commitment to work beyond professional boundaries; to work outside 9-5 hours; to contribute unpaid work of your own; to be accessible to researchers (eg. giving home telephone numbers as contacts as in Oakley, 1992); to make offers to contribute your expertise (eg. in Leicester this involved 'translating' a form rich in medical jargon into plain English for the self-help group) not to wait to be asked and to maintain contact over a long time-scale.

The penultimate point concerns the importance of providing feedback to the community at large. This involves not only disseminating results widely in accessible formats (community conferences; newsletters etc). It also means having regard to the possible consequences of revealing information about less powerful groups to powerful decision makers where this is not in the interest of the community themselves; providing opportunities to check the interpretation of results with community members before dissemination; and demonstrating a commitment to see action taken on the basis of the results.

Finally, we have identified the importance of not replicating the failures of statutory funders of services in using small, inadequately-funded and supported projects as a means of buying off community discontents. In other words it is vital to have and to show an appreciation of the place of research in the lives of community researchers, to tailor the pace of the research to their work, and to their family and community responsibilities. Ultimately this may mean, as in the Leicester project putting desired developments on hold so as not to unduly pressurise those who already live in challenging circumstances.

Acknowledgements

The authors would like to thank the following community members whose hard work we hope we have properly documented here: Carol King, Winston Nurse, Erskine Cave, Theo Badu, Pauline Samuel, Monique

Pinks, Nila Kataria, Viresh Kataria, Hanif Ebrahim, Soraya Ebrahim, Hina Patel, Jyoti Thakkar, Daxa Parmar, Mohammed Ismail, Rhodda Saeed, and Abdirashid Gulaid. We should also like to thank and acknowledge the participation of the community respondents in the various projects.

References

Bourdieu, P. and Passeron, J.C. (1977), *Reproduction in education, society and culture*, Sage: London.

Bourne, J. (1980), 'Cheerleaders and ombudsmen: a sociology of race relations in Britain', *Race and Class*, Vol. 21, No. 4, pp. 331-352.

Daly, J. and McDonald, I. (1992), 'Introduction: the problem as we saw it' in Daly, J., McDonald, I., and Willis, E. (1992) (eds), *Researching health care: designs, dilemmas, disciplines*, Routledge: London, p. 1-11.

Daly, J., McDonald, I., and Willis, E. (1992) (eds), *Researching health care: designs, dilemmas, disciplines*, Routledge: London.

Dyson, S. and Goyder, E. (1994), *Sickle cell anaemia: current carrier and community awareness in Leicester*, No. 1 in the DMU Haemoglobinopathy series, De Montfort University: Leicester.

Dyson, S. and Goyder, E. (1994), *Beta-thalassaemia: current carrier and community awareness in Leicester*, No. 3 in the DMU Haemoglobinopathy series, De Montfort University: Leicester.

Dyson, S. (1995), 'Clients-as-researchers: issues in haemoglobinopathy awareness', *Social Action*, Vol. 2, No. 4, pp. 4-10.

Dyson S. and Harrison, M. (1996), 'Black Community members as researchers: two projects compared', paper presented at conference: *Racism and Welfare*, Preston.

Fleming, J. and Ward, D. (1995), 'The ethics of community health needs assessment: searching for a participant centred approach', paper presented at the International Conference *Ethics and Community*, Blackpool, October 1995. (Publication forthcoming).

Fox, N. (1993), *Postmodernism, sociology and health*, Open University Press: Buckingham.

Freire, P. (1971), 'A few notions about the word conscientization', *Hard Cheese*, 1, pp. 23-8.

Government Statisticians Collective (1979), 'How official statistics are produced' in Irvine, J., Miles, I. and Evans, J. (1979) (eds), *Demystifying social statistics*, Pluto Press: London, pp. 130-151.

Harrison, M. (1993), *Housing Feasibility Study on behalf of Praxis Housing Committee*, Centre for Social Action: Leicester.

Harrison, M., Boulton, I, Abdirashid Gulaid, Mohammed Ismail and Rhodda Saeed (1995), *Research into the needs of the Somali Community in the Challenge area of Tower Hamlets*, Centre for Social Action: Leicester.

Illich, I. (1978), *Disabling professions*, Marion Boyars: London.

Irvine, J., Miles, I. and Evans, J. (1979) (eds), *Demystifying social statistics*, Pluto Press: London.

Leicester OSCAR; Leicester Thalassaemia Society and Leicestershire Health Promotion Department (1988), *The First Community Conference on Sickle Cell and Thalassaemia*, Leicestershire Health Promotion Department: Leicester.

Miles, M. and Huberman, A. (1994), *Qualitative data analysis*, Second edition, Sage: London.

Mullender, A. and Ward, D. (1991), *Self-Directed Groupwork - Users Taking Action for Empowerment*, Whiting and Birch: London.

Oakley, A. (1992), *Social support and motherhood*, Blackwell: Oxford.

Oliver, M. (1992), 'Changing the social relations of research production', *Disability, Handicap and Society*, Vol. 7, No. 2, pp. 101-114.

Plummer, K. (1983), *Documents of life*, Unwin Hyman: London.

Reed, J. and Proctor, S. (1995) (eds), *Practitioner research in health care*, Chapman and Hall: London.

Rhodes, P.J. (1994), 'Race-of-interviewer effects: a brief comment' *Sociology*, Vol. 28, No. 2, pp. 547-558.

Roth, J. (1966), 'Hired hand research', *American Sociologist*, 1, pp. 190-196.

Smaje, C. (1995), *Health, 'Race' and Ethnicity: making sense of the evidence*, King's Fund: London.

Williams, J. (1990), 'The second Leicestershire conference on sickle cell and thalassaemia', *MIDIRS Midwifery Database Information Pack*, 15, December 1990.

10 Black and White Women Working Together: Transgressing the Boundaries of Sisterhood

Margaret Ledwith and Paula Asgill

Introduction

This chapter was engendered by the coming together of two very different women. We are a Black Caribbean woman and a white British woman brought together by our working in a middle-class institution of higher education. We are both community workers and now teachers, committed to employing feminist and Freirean principles in our praxis. Our shared concerns include the way in which individualism has increasingly defined the socio-political context, thereby fragmenting a sense of the collective; and an unease at the unequal distribution of power and resources. In addition, we are acutely aware of the need to avoid essentialised definitions of the sources of hardship in Black and white working-class communities.

As colleagues in dialogue we discovered mutual excitement in the work of Kathleen Weiler (1994, 1995) and bell hooks (1993, 1994, 1995) who, in their separate work, raised critical questions around the nature of *difference* and its centrality in analyses of power and domination. We are interested in the potential of both educational practice and community work as catalysts in the emergence of feminist theory and politics in a way that engages actively with *difference* and seeks a structural social change which moves towards justice and equality.

This initial discovery led to our collaboration in writing a paper for the *Welfare and Racism Conference* at the University of Central Lancashire in 1996. We outlined our theoretical framework and formulated a basic hypothesis that sustainable structural transformation is improbable without alliance between women of difference, as well as with other social movements. That paper constitutes the first half of this chapter.

The result of our shared thinking drew us into further research which investigated the many complex questions which had been raised for us. Consequently, the second half of this chapter addresses the structured dialogue we have embarked upon in an endeavour to gain insight into the deeper aspects of the experience of Black and white women working together, and how this understanding may contribute, in turn, to a radical politics of alliance, located in an analysis that is acutely aware of the interface of gender, 'race' and class in women's lives.

Part I: Black and white women transgressing boundaries

Disparities and divisions cleave society in the most complex of ways, and we have witnessed a period where these divisions have become increasingly polarised. Any commitment to anti-oppressive practice must be founded in critical analysis in order to inform a practice equipped to address issues of social justice. For these reasons, a critical feminist community work praxis which addresses alliances of Black and white women working together for change is long overdue. This is a vital component in the struggle for social justice. Yet it can only be achieved through the disentangling of socially and politically ascribed roles which form barriers hindering this coming together. We suggest that patriarchal and racist assumptions have underpinned welfare policies, thus circumscribing women's lives. The result has been that women's needs have either been overlooked or marginalised and existing inequalities have been reproduced. An analysis of poverty illustrates how welfare policies have helped to marginalise and pathologise those whose lives do not fit the acceptable face of white, middle England family life. We are excited by the potential of *human agency;* that is the extent to which women themselves experience, shape, challenge and change welfare policies. We identify community work praxis as an important site for these activities. The full extent to which collaborative, collective action can generate energy for transformative social change can only be manifest if we identify the obstacles to creating this potential. By identifying some of the forces in this process, we attempt to transgress the boundaries which divide us; in coming together with an understanding of our *difference* we can tap into the energy of alliance without diluting identities formed in struggle. We choose to adopt the use of Albrecht and Brewer's definition of alliance as being beyond coalition; as being 'a new level of commitment that is longer-standing, deeper, and built upon more trusting political relationships' (Albrecht and Brewer, 1990:4).

During the long years of the ascendance of the New Right women as lone parents were targeted relentlessly. The moral debate pointed a victim-blaming finger at some of the poorest families in society, engendering a popular fear that lone mothers were not only welfare scroungers, but that they were undermining the moral fabric of society. As a result, children growing up in such families were labeled deviant - as the media were quick to portray. A preoccupation with going *back* to family values struck a chord of fear and nostalgia in the hearts of the nation, which firmly located the white, heterosexual two-parent, two-child nuclear model at the heart of the debate. Of course, in this process, anything other was labeled deviant and amoral. Statistically 90 per cent of lone parents are female, which, according to this argument, levels an inordinate accusation of deviancy at women. However, a deeper analysis reveals that 70 per cent of all lone parents have been married or in a previous stable relationship (OPCS, 1995). Phoenix (1990) poses the question that if these arguments have no statistical truth, then maybe there is evidence of class, 'race' and gender prejudice. For example, working-class women are less likely to have abortions and more likely, particularly at a younger age, to give birth alone than middle-class women. Although the harshness and the moral exactitude of radical New Right welfare attitudes (which at their height called for unmarried mothers to be dependent on their families rather than the state, and, failing that, that their babies should be put up for adoption [*The Guardian*, 14th August, 1995]) is not mirrored in New Labour, nevertheless there is still a cross-party focus on the image of the traditional family as embodying the moral highground of the nation. These attitudes do not pay attention to the welfare and well-being of children, neither do they address the implied costs to society of adopting such punitive measures of control. Exclusive rather than inclusive models of the family marginalise and socially exclude the vast numbers whose experience lies outside this form of social organisation.

Rigid emphasis on the role of the family, in its narrowest interpretation, has justified policies which have in built notions of the unpaid role of women in the home and the community. This includes major policy changes such as the National Health Service and Community Care Act, 1990, which has implicit expectations of the support role of women in community; and the Child Support Act, 1991, which purports to act in the interests of women at the same time as offering women on benefit no financial gain at all. In fact, the power contained in the Act often operates against the interests of the mother by threatening a reduction of benefit if the name of the child's father is withheld without 'due cause'. It is a contradiction of some concern to recognise that, whilst 90 per cent of all new jobs since 1970 have gone to women, 58 per cent of these women are working part-time (Campaign Against Poverty, Action Sheet 60, March 1994). Increasingly, women find themselves employed in part-time, low paid, casual employment attempting to keep their families from the worst ravages of poverty. There has been a change in trends since 1981 when 45 per cent of lone mothers with a child under 16 were in work, to one in 1990 where this figure had fallen to 39 per cent; whilst during the same period married mothers in employment increased from 47 per cent to 60 per cent (Oppenheim, 1993:97).

Glendinning and Millar (1992) clearly demonstrate that as welfare workers, as users of welfare services and as claimants, changes in welfare provision have influenced women's lives acutely. However, this goes largely unrecognised because of the invisibility of women's issues in official discourse. Government policies to deregulate the labour market have disproportionately affected women, most particularly Black women (Glendinning and Millar, 1994). The state is the largest employer of women workers and most of these are found in health, education and the social services. Deregulation has often resulted in job losses, reduction in pay due to competitive tendering, and reduced pension rights for the support staff working in these welfare agencies.

When risks of gendered poverty are subjected to an analysis which includes 'race', the complexity of oppression can be teased out. The unemployment rate for Black women is nearly twice that for white women - 7 per cent as opposed to 18 per cent respectively in the period 1989-91, and within this Pakistani and Bangladeshi women are most at risk with an unemployment rate of 14 per cent. For young women (aged 16-24) the figures are 19 per cent (Black) and 9 per cent (white). On all indices of poverty the evidence suggests Black women are more at risk of unemployment, low pay, poor conditions at work, and diminished social security rights (Amin and Oppenheim, 1992, Anthias and Yuval-Davis, 1992).

Given that risks of poverty are much higher amongst lone mothers than in two-parent families, analysis of risk according to ethnic groups reveals major variations (Oppenheim, 1993: 124):

1 6% of Indian families are headed by a lone-parent;
2 8% of Bangladeshi and Pakistani families are headed by a lone-parent;
3 15% of white families are headed by a lone-parent;
4 18% of all ethnic minority families are headed by a lone-parent;
5 30% of African families are headed by a lone-parent;
6 49% of African-Caribbean families are headed by a lone-parent.

So, examined at the interface of 'race', class and gender, the risks of poverty can be seen to be most acute for women in the lone-parent category, and most particularly for those who are African-Caribbean, yet the contradiction remains that women in this group have been scapegoated for being deviant whilst at the same time being amongst the most active in their communities, struggling for change.

Women have always been politically active in their communities; a fact which is so implicit that it has largely been taken for granted. Except for such feminist writers as Mayo (1977) and more recently Dominelli (1990), this taken-for-grantedness has eluded the consciousness of most community workers. Sexual politics pervades every aspect of work with women in community, yet those theories which are seen as fundamental to community work practice have largely ignored a feminist analysis. For example, Freirean pedagogy is acknowledged as the most outstanding contribution to critical or liberatory education. However, the work of Paulo Freire has been criticised by feminists as attempting a universal analysis of oppression which overlooks the complexity of lived experience (Weiler, 1994, Weiler, 1995). Emergent feminist theory has raised not only this lack of recognition of women's roles in their communities, but has also led to an awareness of the assumptions underlying the unproblematic and unitary category 'woman' (hooks, 1993, Lorde, 1984, Dominelli, 1990). What, perhaps, is overlooked is that Freirean pedagogy and feminist pedagogy have much in common. Certainly, there is a common vision of transformation within an analysis of consciousness and social change. In order to provide a framework within which a Black and white feminist praxis might develop from women's experience of the public and private, the state and community, we suggest that Freire's work be revisited, recognising that a Freirean-feminist model of community development would deepen the levels of analysis (Ledwith, 1997).

Paulo Freire has been a source of inspiration to many community workers in this country since *Pedagogy of the Oppressed* (1972) was published. He achieved a synthesis of theory and practice which offered not only an analysis of oppression, but a practical route to empowerment. In the United States, his work has become synonymous with *critical pedagogy* (McLaren and Lankshear, 1994, McLaren and Leonard, 1993, McLaren 1995, Shor, 1992). Yet, whilst feminist educators have cited Freire's pedagogy as profound in its influence of feminist consciousness from a perspective of identity, grassroots reality and a vision of transformative change (hooks, 1993), feminists in general have criticised its dualism, its emphasis on a universal truth (Weiler, 1994). Whilst Freire was criticised for his assumptions about a single category of 'oppressed' defined in relation to its opposite, 'oppressor', in turn, early second-wave feminism was challenged for its inherently racist assumptions of a unitary category 'woman'. The most prominent Black feminist proponent of Freire is bell hooks who highlights the issues relevant to the apparent tension between Freire's work and feminist pedagogy in the following way:

> There has never been a moment when reading Freire that I have not remained aware of not only the sexism in the language, but the way he ...constructs a phallocentric paradigm of liberation - wherein freedom and the experience of patriarchal manhood are always linked as though they are one and the same.

But she goes on to say:

> Unlike feminist thinkers who make a clear separation between the work of feminist pedagogy and Freire's work and thought, for me these two experiences converge. Deeply committed to feminist pedagogy, I find that, much like weaving a tapestry, I have taken threads of Paulo's work and woven it into that version of feminist pedagogy I believe my work as a writer and teacher embodies...Freire's work (and that of many other teachers) affirmed my right as a subject in resistance to define my reality (hooks, 1993: 148-150).

By contesting the partial or incomplete aspects of Freire's work, yet not rejecting the profound insights, bell hooks demonstrates the impact he has had on her own development. She stresses that it was impossible for her to ignore the value of his insight, since so much spoke to her experience; that of being a rural African American who had gone through the struggle of gaining an education so she could be part of the process of Black people reading, writing and reinterpreting the world for themselves made sense as the practice of freedom. Freire provided her with a language to understand and give voice to the 'construction of an identity in resistance'. In short, hooks suggests that by emphasising *conscientisation*, Freire assisted in the process of her developing the skills with which she is able to identify the sexism in his work.

Black feminists and postmodernists have opened up understanding of the way in which universal categories hide more than they reveal when failing to address the complex ways in which oppression overlays and interlinks in our lives; the ways in which multiple and contradictory sites of oppression exist and are reinforced on different levels (Anthias and Yuval-Davis, 1992, Walby, 1997). These theoretical challenges have called for the recognition of *difference* as a central category of analysis.

Like hooks, Weiler (1994: 16) calls for a 'critical feminist re-reading of Freire [which] points to ways in which the project of Freirean (like that of feminist) pedagogy can be enriched and re-envisioned'. She offers three key areas of analysis: the role and authority of the teacher; experience and feeling as sources of knowledge; and the question of *difference*.

Concerning the power invested in the role of educator, Weiler suggests that Freire's vision of a horizontal, reciprocal relation between students and educator can prove to be problematic if issues of power according to 'race', gender, class and status are not addressed. By failing to address the issue of differently experienced oppressions, we are dealing with partial understandings which, with the best will in the world, render the analysis incomplete. Education and the transmission of knowledge in society is one of the most powerful and insidious determinants of class and status. In order to understand the complexity of the educative process in reinforcing power and privilege, whether it be located in mainstream schools, in community or in colleges, it is vital that we move towards a more complete analysis of if we are to challenge the process effectively. It is insufficient to challenge a competitive and individualistic culture by adopting a horizontal model which does not offer the tools with which to make sense of the diverse and disparate realities of being 'woman'. The authority of the feminist educator as intellectual and theorist can with the essential contribution of Freire's concept of *conscientisation* move through the naming of difference to a more critical insight into the forces which have shaped difference. In doing so, this moves us closer towards an informed position for action for change.

Secondly, knowledge has long been presented as an uncontested, pragmatic truth - denying feeling and experience as legitimate aspects of reality. An underlying tenet of Freirean pedagogy is trust in the infinite potential of people to be intellectuals in naming and knowing their world, and in doing so to recognise their own power to transform the world. Thus, experience and feeling as fundamental aspects of a female paradigm must be a central part of reclaiming feminist knowledge and therefore informing social change based on a more balanced view of the world. The process begins with a questioning of experience. A traditional paradigm locates 'feeling' in the private domain, the world of women, thus not valid or rational in the view of a Western consciousness legitimised by pragmatism. Feminist pedagogy has emphasised feeling and emotion as a guide to women's knowledge of the world, as a link between the inner self and the outer world, between the public and the private, the personal and the political. Lorde (1984) captures the essence of feelings as a guide to

217

analysis and action, keeping us in touch with our humanity and compassion:

> As we begin to recognise our deepest feelings, we give up, of necessity, being satisfied with suffering and self-negation, and with the numbness which so often seems like their only alternative in society. Our acts against oppression become integral with self, motivated and empowered from within (Lorde, 1984: 58).

There are strong links here with Freire's emphasis on humanisation: dehumanisation as ways of being in the world. In identifying how our experience of power relationships is structured, the act of knowing, of critical insight, generates energy and motivation for action. Out of a state of dehumanisation, we are freed to rehumanise ourselves.

Thirdly, the question of *difference*. The assumptions of a unitary category 'woman', as already addressed, has led to major challenges by both Black women and postmodern feminists. Narratives of lived experience have been used in groups of women to focus on the social and historical forces which have shaped this experience. For instance, Weiler cites Sistren, a 'collaborative theatre group made up of working-class Jamaican women who create and write plays based upon a collaborative exploration of their own experiences' (Weiler, 1994: 31). The collective sharing of experience is the key to the knowledge of our socially and politically given identities, and is the process by which we discover our power as subjects in active, creative process in our world, rather than as objects which are fixed, defined and static. This is the process of conscientisation which Freire envisaged unfolding in such culture circles, where people can come together to question realities which have previously been taken for granted. 'The most radical politics come directly out of our own identity, as opposed to working to end someone else's oppression' (Combahee River Collective in Weiler, 1994: 32).

We are aware that identity politics is a highly contested area and so, there is a need for some clarification. Anthias and Yuval-Davis (1992) eloquently identify the role of the state in the rigid recreation of an essential multi-culturalism, where individuals are reduced 'to an all encompassing category both in terms of their treatment as well as their identity and empowerment'. This is problematic. Rather, we would argue that it is possible to reflect on one's separate identity, or as Brunt (1989) terms it 'return to the subjective' and, in doing so, locate the grids of power and resistance which are horizontal, not just vertical, at the same time as keeping political action heterogeneous and inclusive. Therefore, as Brah states:

218

'White' feminism or 'black' feminism in Britain are not essential categories but rather they are fields of contestation inscribed within discursive and material processes in a post-colonial terrain. They represent struggles over political priorities and modes of mobilisation but they should not, in my view, be understood as locating 'white' and 'black' women as essentially fixed oppositional categories (Brah, 1991 : 39).

It is valid that Black women should organise autonomously in terms of deciding priorities of struggles and to handle internal dissent. However, given the nature of discrimination faced by women in Britain, we believe that opportunities for alliances should be sought and established. Black and white women have and continue to work together to tackle issues which affect their lives and the lives of their children, and thus the future of humanity as a whole. These collaborative efforts have not been without deep conflict. We are located in a context where 'race' and class incorporate both differing access to privilege, and where experience of gender leads not to sameness, but to tensions of an articulation of difference (Weiler, 1995). These tensions referred to by Weiler locate our thesis: that it is through an analysis of the lessons learnt from the attempts of Black and white women to work together that we can find the way forward into alliance.

The period between 1970 and the mid-1980s saw Black and white women coming together. It is instructive that many of these joint struggles centred on women's access to safe contraceptives, abortions and the right to form a family. The development and availability of contraceptive and reproductive technologies have undoubtedly provided women with greater control over their lives, but at the same time these have been used by the medical profession and the state as a form of control over women. The Abortion Act, 1967, decriminalised abortion and was a landmark for women (Williams, 1995). However, no sooner had this been achieved than the pro-life lobby and other patriarchal forces threatened to restrict its scope. These threats became one of the focal organising issues of the women's movement, couched initially as 'the right to abortion'. However, while middle-class white women were campaigning to secure abortion rights, many Black women were being sterilised without their consent and having their fertility curtailed through the use of injectable contraceptives (Bryan et al, 1985, Williams, 1995, Mama, 1995). Although many Black women also needed access to safe abortions, they were aware that the state viewed *their* fertility as problematic. Klug argues that:

The question of the reproduction of the nation had a profound effect on the development of social policy with regard to women and reproduction. Whilst at various stages the state has encouraged white women to reproduce it has often set out to curb the black population by discouraging the fertility of black and ethnic minority women (Klug, 1989: 22).

The input of Black women to the movement was not only to acknowledge the general rights of women, but to highlight the fact that access to rights or denial of rights is racialised. The ensuing dialogue resulted in the terms of the debate shifting to 'a woman's right to choose'. Through a collaborative approach to this issue, feminist theory and practice was expanded to include an analysis which appreciated and informed the understanding that access to abortions, sterilisation and long-lasting contraceptive injections were not experienced as a right by all women; more often they were imposed as a form of control by state professionals operating with a pathological and eugenicist view of Black and poor women's fertility (Bryan et al., 1985: 103). It was this analysis that shifted the debate to focus on the feminist struggle for 'reproductive rights' that addressed the need for all women to have freedom of choice and control over every aspect of their reproductive capacity (Davis, 1990: 202-21).

In a similar way, the dialogue, or angry exchange, between Black and white feminists has led to shifts in feminist theorising unthinkable fifteen years ago. It is now possible to read a proliferation of texts on Black feminist subjectivity and to a lesser (but important) degree white women are now engaged in the process of examining whiteness and rejecting racist definitions of white femininity (Ware, 1992, Helen (Charles), 1992, Allen, 1994). In the process 'the truth about [this] subject...[comes] when all sides of the story are put together, and all their different meanings make one new one...' (Walker, 1983: 49). In 'unfixing' identity and creating the opportunity for women to explore difference white and Black women 'can unite...against the combination of gender, class and 'race' relations that forbids cultural difference and fears that the dominant culture will be 'swamped' by an Other one' (Ware, 1992: 253). This argument is taken further by Annette Kilcooley in the following way:

That sisterhood can be recognised as problematic, it has to be said, comes more out of the advances in feminist movement than it does from failures in feminism (Kilcooley, 1997: 31).

An example of the potential of this approach can be seen in the *Women in Community Work* training manual produced by the Federation of Community Work Training Groups (FCWTG, 1994). Between 1990 and 1992, the Federation of Community Work Training Groups supported five two-day training courses in four regions of the country for Black and white women community workers to come together to explore experience, identities and gender relations. From these events, a mixed group of Black and white women, lesbian and heterosexual, got together to explore collective strategies for overcoming oppressions. Although focusing on sexism and racism, they draw attention to the complex matrix of oppressions which interact through age, disability, class, ethnicity and sexual orientation and offer a framework of exercises for use with groups - including 'black and white women working together'.

Other examples of Black and white women working together and discovering new insights would include the campaigning of women in the 1970s and 1980s for housing rights for women fleeing domestic violence, the late 1980s and the 1990s has seen Black women leading the collaborative efforts to change the criminal justice system's assumptions about the nature of 'self defense or loss of control' as applied to women who have killed violent and abusive partners.

An important lesson that emerges from this brief review of Black and white women forming alliances or collaborating on issues is the extent to which praxis becomes transgressive. Hill-Collins (1990) observes that whilst dialogue within Black feminism is crucial to growth, so is dialogue with other groups. Coalition, she argues, can be the basis for 'exploring how relations of domination and subordination are maintained and changed, parallels between black women's experiences and those of other groups become the focus of investigation'. We would add, the basis for action. Within community work where the focus of action is the day to day experience of women, alliance means that groups must work out the 'dynamics of 'race', class and gender in every situation that demands a political response - adopting what some have called 'strategic identities' which allow opposition to one form of domination without being complicit in another' (Ware, 1992 : 254). In the words of Fiona Williams:

What is interesting about many women's struggles is that the process of struggling has been as significant as the aims of those struggles... This necessity to combine personal struggle with political struggle has given rise to two significant features. The first is the attempt to organise in ways which are themselves anti-sexist, anti-hierarchical, anti-racist and anti-bureaucratic... The second general important point which emerges

221

from the nature of women's struggles is that, in so far as these struggles are often situated in the community rather than the workplace and are battling over questions of reproduction and not just production, they begin to break down the distinction between work and the home... The idea that reproduction and production are seen as interdependent forms of equal importance and not separate forms in which the organisation of reproduction follows in the wake of production has important implications for welfare analysis and welfare strategy (Williams, 1992 : 196).

Reflection on lived reality offers the foundation for an analysis and practice which moves towards a critical praxis. By exploring the way that *difference* determines reality, it is possible to gain insight into the nature of interlocking systems of oppression. This is vital for the development of any critical, coherent, integrated praxis. This process of understanding will help to transgress the boundaries of *difference* that divide us and which dilute our combined potential for change. By alliance building around common goals we can establish Black and white alliances of difference where, under modernism, there were notions of collective consciousness. A Black and white Freirean-feminist pedagogy would generate energy for change on a much deeper level in our communities, leading to real possibilities of social justice and liberation.

Part II: Creating Critical Dissent Dialogue

Initially, we had founded our argument on the concept of sisterhood and coalition to capture both the challenge and potential that characterises the earlier debates that occurred between Black and white women (Carby, 1982, hooks, 1994). However, as we developed our thinking, *critical dissent dialogue* (hooks, 1994) and alliance has come to represent the intimacy of sisterhood and the political goal of social justice.

The process of writing the first paper raised a myriad of unanswered questions. Most notable are, what do we mean by *alliance*? What is the relationship between *autonomous* organisation and *alliance*? What is the process that evolves when, through mutual struggle and dissent, women become motivated to theorise and engage in a politics that is based on an analysis of 'race', gender or class, etc? At what point are we motivated to extend our analysis to 'others' oppression, and the ways in which different types of oppression interact' (Alperin, 1990). Finally, under what condition is critical dissent dialogue possible, and how do we work through the anger or rage (hooks, 1994, 1995) that inevitably emerges when Black and white women dialogue?

The above questions are now central to our current research. The first stage has been for us to engage in structured dialogue and thereby use our experience to map out what are tentative answers. The following are extracts from transcripts of us in dialogue:

Is it possible, then to take on the notion that in becoming so conscious of the insidious nature of multiple, complex oppressions they become our own pain, and at what point we can transcend the whole nature of injustice as a complexity and act together. (This process) has a parallel between Gramsci's concept of the traditional and organic intellectuals. Maybe, as organic intellectuals we're fighting our own oppression, we become aware of it and we act on it. But is there a point where we become global intellectuals because of our understanding... (Margaret, March, 1997).

No. My understanding of Gramsci's notion of the organic is that you are rooted, you are coming from somewhere - out of an experience; but nothing stays the same. There has to be change. So if it is organic that means it grows and changes all the time. The individual is coming from a state of 'Oh God, I didn't realise!' then there is thought and mobilisation around that particular experience, there is also theorising of the experience. But sooner or later, in the nature of things, growth has to occur, usually there is a stimulus. Sometimes it comes as an attack... (Paula, March, 1997).

From our dialogue, it became evident that being able to create alliance depended on the ability of white and Black women to understand the specific nature of their experience, not only in order to overcome internalised oppression, but also to be able to overcome internalised domination (Pheterson, 1990). 'Black women, at various points, have been asked to explain ourselves and our experiences of oppression by those that have a stake in power, those who seemingly don't have to explain their advantage. It is the basic imbalance of power that makes sisterhood suspect as a political stance... We are indeed unequal sisters ...' (Simmonds, 1997 : 27). Alliance can be characterised as a state of knowing, having respect for, and commitment between persons who are essentially different but whose interest in social justice is similar. This spoke to the two of us very clearly about our own coming together and the complexity evident in our relationship. For dominant groups, alliance is about preparedness to share

223

power and resources in creating structures that are equitably responsive to the needs and interests of all people. In doing this, *the drive to superiority* is relinquished, prejudices and assumptions are given up in return for a more tolerant and flexible relationship with self, with others and with society as a whole. For oppressed groups, alliance is a preparedness to engage with dominant groups for the right to an equal share of power and resources. This requires recognition of and indignation against oppression, thus generating the confidence and energy to bring about change. Furthermore, this state requires recognition and acceptance of, *never gratitude for,* alliance (Pheterson, 1990: 36). Both internalised oppression and internalised domination operate to undermine the possibility for alliance, therefore a rooted starting point is (perhaps) the precursor to alliance.

A discussion with Diane, a Black woman and friend, about this research led to an animated exchange about what the priorities should be for Black women. Diane believed that women of African and Caribbean descent do not engage in enough dialogue between themselves 'Why', she questioned, 'should we be devoting energy to dialoguing with those who are already privileged, and as far as I can see have little interest in entering into 'true' dialogue.' Eventually, the argument identified that Black women do dialogue with each other. Certainly, *more* dialogue is necessary, but as bell hooks (1995) suggests one way to turn rage against white women into energy for change is to engage critically in dialogue, initiating and responding to overtures for alliance. This was a living example of critical dissent dialogue. The discussion had a profound impact in sharpening and focusing our thoughts. Is this an either/or situation: should women *either* concentrate on dialogue for alliance *or* concentrate on overcoming internalised oppression? This questioning came at a critical point in the research. Examination of Diane's dissent raised questions about the *fear* that operates when considering difference, and the need to clarify what alliance would mean in practice. We had been alerted to the potential for this research to become locked into the dominant paradigm of binary opposites. In seeking to analyse alliance, would experience be 'diluted' and political goals become less focused? Alternatively, we began to consider whether autonomous organisation was not only the precursor to alliance, but also *necessary* in sustaining alliance.

> ...every once in a while there is the need for people to...bar the doors ...and say 'Humph, inside this place the only thing we are going to deal with is X or Y or Z.' And so only the Xs or Ys or Zs get to come in... Most of the time when people do that, they do it because of the heat of

trying to live in this society where being an X or Y or Z is very difficult to say the least... It gets too hard to stay out in society all the time. And that's when you find a place, and you try to bar the door and check all the people who come in. You come together to see what you can do about shouldering up all of your energies so that you and your kind can survive...that space while it lasts should be a nurturing space where you sift out what people are saying about you and decide who you really are (Reagon, 1983: 357-8).

Particularly, for those who are subject to the day to day experience of marginalisation and mis-representation, autonomous organisations are essential for the affirmation and identity which is a precursor of critical alliance. For those whose day to day experience does not comprise the same level of harassment, autonomous organisation may still remain essential to finding the consciousness necessary for effective alliance. Hill-Collins (1990) argues that alliance is the basis for 'exploring how relations of domination and subordination are maintained and changed'.

One must possess a sense of personhood before one can develop a sense of sisterhood...not one sisterhood but many (Anzaldua, 1990: 225).

In our dialogue, we borrow the term of *being* from John Rowan to characterise the state from which an individual becomes aware of *why* their difference has social importance and consequences (Rowan, 1985: 98). Anzaldua employs the term *personhood*. We agree this is the point from which an event or a series of events brings us into confrontation with our internalised oppression and internalised domination. Pheterson describes internalised oppression as:

...the incorporation and acceptance by individuals within an oppressed group of the prejudices against them within the dominant society. Internalised oppression is likely to consist of self-hatred, self concealment, fear of violence and feelings of inferiority, resignation, isolation, powerlessness, and gratefulness for being allowed to survive (Pheterson, 1990: 35).

Internalised oppression maintains structures of domination by securing the complicity of the oppressed in the present arrangement. This, of course, is never completely achieved, but is effective enough to maintain the *status quo*.
Pheterson describes internalised domination as

...the incorporation and acceptance by individuals within a dominant group of prejudices against others. Internalised domination is likely to consist of feelings of superiority, normalcy, and self-righteousness, together with guilt, fear, projection, denial of reality, and alienation from one's body and from nature. Internalised domination perpetuates oppression of others and alienation from oneself by either denying or degrading all but a narrow range of human possibilities. One's own humanity is thus internally restricted and one's qualities of empathy, trust, love and openness to others and to life-enhancing work rigid and repressed (Pheterson, 1990: 35).

There are clear echoes here of Freire's concept of *conscientisation*. Wrestling with these new understandings increasingly faced us with the complexity of the notion of alliance as the key component in transformative social change. The process is clearly neither spontaneous nor inevitable. It cannot be seen as a linear form of development which is made possible by intent. There are, however, certain clearly-defined stages. At the point of internalised oppression and domination the individual is uncommitted and without roots. In fact, both aspects of the internalised condition are alien to collective action; in the pure form they represent alienation from self and from others. An event or series of events may lead the individual to seek answers to new questions, and what was deemed to be personal failure or (in)effectiveness comes to be viewed as more systematically distributed than the law of chance would allow. At this point, in our experience, there is a seeking out of others like us - the process so eloquently described by Reagon above. Here, there is a process of consciousness raising - which identifies self and its 'other'. Pheterson (1990) labels this process *visibility*. *Pride* usually accompanies self identification, the search for self-love, self respect, the digging out of heritage and indignation against the denial of personhood to one's group and ultimately to any other group. Pheterson's linear representation of this process suggests a continuum; but, our experience suggests it is more complex. There is progress and at the same time new dimensions of internalised structures emerge. The entrance to *separate* organisation is a salient point in the search for personhood. The collective can provide this, but there are some dangers. For example, in relation to Black women in Britain, Felly Simmonds draws our attention to the following:

The cultural and political construction of Blackness in Britain is still fraught with contention. At its most basic, the question still remains: What is the basis of this identity? Who, for example, are the 'Black

226

women' we speak of in Black feminist theory?... My concern here is, as Black women, our sisterhood must rest on our ability to speak about our difference and our different experience of...this category 'Black' and the consequences of living in a white society...I want to ask the question: What does it mean to be African in Britain, when the Black politics continues to overshadow the particularity of being African, as opposed to being of the African Diaspora... (Simmonds, 1997: 25-26).

Within the separate group, the drive can be towards 'sameness in our difference'. An essentialised notion of self, which polices boundaries with a vigour that mirrors structures of domination in the wider society. Perhaps this is evidence that internalised oppression and internalised domination do not just manifest in one person or the other; but rather can and do exist intrapsychically within one person. At the point that we become locked into an essentialised mode of organising and operating, then we are ineffectual as agents of structural change.

How do we move deeper into the meaning of the overlapping, entwining complexity of oppressions and domination which will lead us to 'understand that the oppression of others hurts (us) personally' (Moraga in Adams, 1981) in order to forge principled coalition? 'Any kind of separatism is a dead end. It's good for forging identity and gathering strength, but I do feel that the strongest politics are coalition politics that cover a broad range of issues. There is no way that one oppressed group is going to topple a system by itself' (Smith and Smith, 1981: 126 in Adams) (Margaret and Paula, March, 1997).

It is our argument that when separate organisation works to create a sense of personhood, sustains the indignation against oppression and becomes focused on the need for structural change, the condition of autonomous organisation is realised. Autonomous organisation is central to creating the conditions for critical dissent dialogue within as well as with others. New questions are brought under scrutiny, leading to the risk-taking necessary to engage in critical dissent dialogue.

The lived experience of developing alliances hurts: it is painful at an existential level. So, if alliances are vital to transformation, how do we help the process along? Certainly, in order to overcome avoidance of this pain, we need to identify these experiences, and in the naming of them expose them as integral components of change. Below, we attempt to represent our initial conclusions in a diagrammatic form which maps the potential for *critical dissent dialogue* and captures the complexity that must inform autonomous development and *alliance* building.

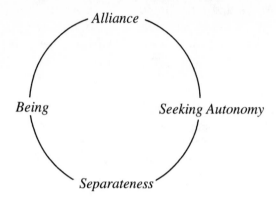

Figure 10.1 Cycle model of alliances in process
(with acknowledgment to John Rowan, 1985)

Inspired by John Rowan's notion of the cycle model as a dialectical process of engagement with the world (Rowan, 1985), we began to explore the possibility of a model of process. This model starts in *being*. There is a point at which personal experience is questioned, a point of dissonance. It is no longer possible to accept explanations which rest on a concept of the essentialised self. There is recognition of aspects of one's own alienation. There is realisation of *difference*.

Motivated by a quest for understanding, there is a move into an inner stage of *seeking* which requires new thinking. This action may be prompted by a negative experience (such as racism) or a positive experience (an encounter with new ideas/perceptions). It is not necessarily a solitary stage, but can be creative and collective. It is a process of 'adding and combining the new information into unfamiliar relationships' (Rowan, 1985 : 98); a stage where expanded possibilities are allowed into the consciousness, and where contact is made with new people and groups in order to explore these thoughts. This leads to a reaching outwards to seek belongingness in being with others of the same identity. Although *separateness* is an outer movement, it is in essence a withdrawal from mainstream society because there is a need to challenge the hegemonic ways of making sense of personal experience. A need to separate self from the context in which it has originally been defined; the need to extricate self from the forces which have limited truth, if self is to be redefined according to a new understanding. It is a stage at which membership of separate groups is

228

sought, and is characterised by a search for identity and respect, a sense of pride, driven by a quest for self-love and self-respect, a need for safety, a sense of rage, and a fear of dilution.

At this stage of the cycle there may be a marked choice to remain separate in order to gain strength from identity and group cohesion. There may even be a denial of difference within the group in order to maintain an undifferentiated identity. However, if the group or some members of it move into a strong sense of personhood, the potential is moved on towards *autonomy*. This stage may be characterised by a strong sense of identity, an increase in confidence around that identity, and a development in *critical consciousness*.

Autonomy is a stage at which *difference* is explored from an inner conviction. There is an active desire to reach out in confidence, and of recognising that conflict may be inevitable. At the same time, we remain organic to our separate identity; indeed, it is the very strength of this identity which gives us the courage and conviction to look outside. This move is motivated by a deep level of understanding of our own oppression, and in this developing critical consciousness we are compelled to understand the oppressions of others. This is a bridging stage. In dialogue with others, there is a reaching out to understand difference, not as a division but as a strength, as a way of moving forward in commitment to a more fair and just society. We recognise that the stage of *alliance* must be entered in order to achieve the potential for collective action for change. This awareness precipitates us into an inner stage of *seeking*. It is one of risk taking; of reaching out to others who may not reciprocate and of recognising the inevitable conflict which results from transgressing boundaries. We explore new possibilities in *alliance* which may be characterised by deep listening, a sense of indignation, and of painful new understandings; a stage at which empathy, trust, love, openness and receptivity are vital components. This is a stage of risk-taking, but there is a preparedness to struggle because we are beginning to identify the power and resources necessary for transformation. Through the creation of committed alliances we 'embrace a more flexible relation to ourselves, to others and to society as a whole' (Pheterson, 1990: 36). This is the stage at which we take on the oppressions of all as the pain of our own.

As with all cycles, withdrawal to previous stages is not only possible but expected and, at times, even desirable. There may be occasions when there is a need to nurture self alone, away from the group; there may be times when we, as a group, need to withdraw from alliances to explore our own issues in greater depth. By the same token, we never reach a point of arrival; we are always in process. Thus, there comes a time when the *alliances* we have established are not enough, the dominant hegemony is ever-changing and reforming and so we need to be in constant dynamic. This moves us into multiple cycles. It is this constant process of change which makes it possible to envision a feminist politics that is based on alliance and adopts what Ware (1992) calls *strategic identities* where as women we can oppose domination in it various guises without becoming complicit in another.

The need for this process is so poignantly captured in the following words of Audre Lorde. It is the fractured nature of identity and experience that she presents here that underpins the importance of *critical dissent dialogue* and the radical potential of *alliance*.

> *Who Said it was Simple*
> There are so many roots to the tree of anger
> that sometimes the branches shatter
> before they fall
> Sitting in Nedicks
> the women rally before they march
> discussing the problematic girls
> they hire to make them free
> An almost white counterman passes
> a waiting brother to serve them first
> and the ladies neither notice nor reject
> the slighter pleasures of their slavery.
> But I who am bound by my mirror
> as well as my bed
> see causes in color
> as well as sex
>
> and sit here wondering
> which me will survive
> all these liberations

Audre Lorde, 1973 (in Wilson and Russell, 1993)

Faced with a socio-political context characterised by individualism, the possibility of transformative social change through collective action is undermined. For this reason, it is crucial that our understanding of *difference* addresses alliance building. Separate organising inevitably leads to partial and incomplete attempts to confront the issues related to the marginalisation of women. We believe that our research identifies a way

230

forward in alliance building, thereby harnessing women's collective potential for sustainable change. Alliance building, far from diluting identities formed in struggle, offers a real possibility of attaining a future defined by 'committed and trusting political relationships' (Albrecht and Brewer, 1990: 4).

Bibliography

Adams, M. (1992), 'There's No Place Like Home: On the Place of Identity in Feminist Politics' in Humm, M, *Feminisms: A Reader*, Harvester Wheatsheaf.

Albrecht, L. and Brewer, R.M. (1990), *Bridges of Power: Women's Multicultural Alliances,* New Society Publishers.

Allen, S. (1994), 'Race, Ethnicity and Nationality: Some Questions of Identity', in Afshar, H. and Maynard, M., *The Dynamics of 'Race' and Gender: Some Feminist Interventions,* Taylor and Francis.

Alperin, D. (1990), 'Social Diversity and the Necessity of Alliances: a Developing Feminist Perspective' in Albrecht and Brewer, *op cit.*

Amin, K. and Oppenheim, C. (1992), *Poverty in Black and White: Deprivation and Ethnic Minorities,* Child Poverty Action Group.

Ang-Lygate, M., Corrin, C. and Henry, M. (eds) (1997), *Desperately Seeking Sisterhood: Still Challenging and Building,* Taylor Francis.

Anthias, F. and Yuval-Davis, N. (1992), *Racialised Boundaries; Race, Nation, Gender, Colour and Class and the Anti-racist Struggle,* Routledge.

Anzaldua, G. (1990), 'Bridge, Drawbridge, Sandbar or Island: Lesbian-of-Colour, Hacienda Alianzas' in Albrecht and Brewer, *op cit.*

Brah, A. (1991), 'Difference, Diversity, Differentiation' in Allen, S, Anthias, F. and Yuval-Davis, N. (eds), *Special Edition of Revue Internationale de Sociologie,* New Series, No. 2, April.

Brunt, R. (1989), 'The Politics of Identity' in Hall, S. and Jacques, M. (eds), *New Times,* Lawrence and Wishart.

Bryan, B., Dadzie, and Scafe, S. (1985), *The Heart of the Race: Black Women's Lives in Britain,* Virago.

Campaign Against Poverty (Manchester) (1994), Action Sheet 60, March.

Carby, H. (1982), 'White Women listen! Black feminism and the boundaries of sisterhood' in Centre for Contemporary Cultural Studies, Routledge.

Clarke, J. (ed.), *Comparing Welfare States: Britain in International Context,* Sage.

Davis, A. (1990), 'Racism, birth control and reproductive rights' in Gerber Fried, M. (ed.), *From Abortion to Reproductive Freedom: Transforming a Movement,* South End Press.

Dominelli, L. (1990), *Women and Community Action,* Venture Press.

Federation of Community Work Training Groups (1994), *Women in Community Work: A Feminist/Womanist Perpective,* FCWTG.

Finch, J. and Groves, D. (eds) (1983), *A Labour of Love: Women, Work and Caring,* Routledge and Kegan Paul.

Freire, P. (1972), *Pedagogy of the Oppressed,* Penguin.

Glendinning, C. and Millar, J. (1994), 'Still on the Margins of Welfare' in *Poverty,* No. 88, Summer.

Glendinning, C. and Millar, J. (eds) (1992), *Women and Poverty in Britain in the 1990s,* Harvester Wheatsheaf.

Goodman, A. and Webb, S. (1994), *For Richer, For Poorer: The Changing Distribution of Income in the United Kingdom, 1961-91,* Institute for Fiscal Studies.

Helen (Charles) (1992), 'Whiteness - The Relevance of Politically Colouring the 'Non'' in Hinds, H., Phoenix, A. and Stacey, J., *Working Out: New Directions for Women's Studies,* The Falmer Press.

Hill-Collins, P. (1990), *Black Feminist Thought: Knowledge, Consciousness and the Politics of Empowerment,* Routledge.

Holub, R. (1992), *Antonio Gramsci: Beyond Marxism and PostModernism,* Routledge.

hooks, b. (1993), 'bell hooks Speaking About Paulo Freire - The Man, His Work' in McLaren, P. and Leonard, P., *op cit.*

hooks, b. (1994), *Teaching to Transgress: Education as the Practice of Freedom,* Routledge.

hooks, b. (1995), *Killing Rage, Ending Racism,* Penguin.

Kilcooley, A. (1997), 'Sexism, Sisterhood and Some Dynamics of Racism: A Case in Point' in Ang-Lygate et al., *op cit.*

Klug, F. (1989), 'Oh to be in England' in Yuval-Davis, N. and Anthias, F. (eds), *Women-Nation-State,* Macmillan.

Ledwith, M. (1997), *Participating in Transformation: Towards a Working Model of Community Empowerment,* Venture Press.

Ledwith, M. and Asgill, P. (1997), 'Transcribed notes' in *Critical Dissent Dialogue Research,* University College of St Martin: Lancaster.

Lorde, A. (1984), *Sister Outsider,* The Crossing Press.

Lorde, A. (1993), 'Who Said it was Simple' in Wilson, M. and Russell, K., *Divided Sisters, Bridging the Gap Between Black Women and White Women,* Doubleday.

232

Mama, A. (1995), *Beyond the Masks: Race, Gender and Subjectivity,* Routledge.

Mayo, M. (ed.) (1977), *Women in the Community,* Routledge and Kegan Paul.

McLaren, P. and Lankshear, C. (eds) (1994), *Politics of Liberation: Paths From Freire,* Routledge.

McLaren, P. and Leonard, P. (eds) (1993), *Paulo Freire: A Critical Encounter,* Routledge.

McLaren, P. (1995), *Critical Pedagogy and Predatory Culture,* Routledge.

Offices of Population Censuses and Surveys (1995), *Conceptions in England and Wales, 1992,* OPCS.

Oppenheim, C. (1993), *Poverty: The Facts,* Child Poverty Action Group.

Payne, S. (1991), *Women, Health and Poverty: An Introduction,* Harvester Wheatsheaf.

Pheterson, G. (1990), 'Alliances Between Women: Overcoming Internalised Oppression and Internalised Domination' in Albrecht and Brewer, *op cit.*

Phoenix, A. (1990), *Young Mothers?,* Polity.

Reagon, B. (1983), 'Coalition Politics: Turning the Century' in Smith, B. (ed.), *Home Girls: A Black Feminist Anthology,* Kitchen Table Press.

Rowan, J. (1985), 'A Dialectical Paradigm for Research' in Reason, P. and Rowan, J. (eds) *Human Inquiry: A Sourcebook of New Paradigm Research,* Wiley.

Rowan, J. (1995), 'Transformative Research' in Reason, P., *Collaborative Inquiry,* No. 4, Jan, 1995, Centre for Action Research, University of Bath.

Shor, I. (1992), *Empowering Education: Critical Teaching for Social Change,* University of Chicago Press.

Simmonds, F. (1997), 'Who are the Sisters? Difference, Feminism and Friendship' in Ang-Lygate, M. et al., *op cit.*

Walby, S. (1997), *Gender Transformations,* Routledge.

Walker, A. (1983), *In Search of Our Mothers' Gardens,* Harcourt Brace and Jovanovich.

Ware, V. (1992), *Beyond the Pale: White Women, Racism and History,* Routledge.

Weiler, K. (1995), 'Freire and a Feminist Pedagogy of Difference' in Holland, J. and Blair, M. (eds), *Debates and Issues in Feminist Research and Pedagogy,* Multilingual Matters with the Open University.

Weiler, K. (1994), 'Freire and a Feminist Pedagogy of Difference' in McLaren and Lankshear, *op cit.*

Williams, F. (1992), *Social Policy: A Critical Introduction,* Polity.

Williams, F. (1995), 'Gender, 'Race' and Class in British Welfare Policy' in Cochrane, A. and Clarke, J. (eds), *Comparing Welfare States: Britain in International Context,* Sage.

11 Race, Gender and Class in Child Sexual Abuse Research

Claudia Bernard

Introduction

This chapter explores the intersection of race, gender and class in child sexual abuse research and examines power relations in the research process. It centres on the notion that an investigation of the relationship between race and gender in the research process is necessary to understand the complex ways power relations are manifested, thus heightening a number of ethical concerns. The chapter draws on a study of black mothers whose children have been sexually abused, to examine the factors influencing power relations in the research process and will discuss the broader theoretical and methodological issues raised in my work. In combining an analysis of race as it intersects with gender, I will articulate a black feminist perspective of researching child sexual abuse, and shall explore the possibilities for empowering research practice. After a brief review of the literature on the practice of doing research, I will explore some issues associated with gathering data in research on child sexual abuse in black families. I will then look at some specific dynamics relating to power in negotiating with gatekeepers to identify research participants for the study. Finally, I will move on to consider some issues concerning power relations between the researcher and the researched in the context of negotiating consent. My discussion will be located within feminist and anti-racist discourses on research.

The research

The work on which this chapter is based is a qualitative piece of research of black mothers' emotional and behavioural responses to the sexual abuse of their children. The study is primarily concerned with examining the help-seeking behaviour of black mothers on discovery of the abuse, and seeks to explore how factors of race and gender influence their help-seeking and protective strategies. A unique element of the research is its examination of the intersection of different oppressions and their impact on child sexual abuse. My primary interest was in asking mothers themselves to articulate their experiences in their own terms and from their own frames of reference. The starting point of the research is that whilst child sexual abuse transcends race and class boundaries, an examination of the issues affecting black families must focus on the specificity of their experiences. The study draws on a sample of 30 black mothers of African, Caribbean and South Asian origin and utilises loosely structured interviews with open-ended questions. Participation in the study is voluntary and the respondents were recruited through a number of social services departments, voluntary agencies, community groups and through publicity material distributed in medical centres. To be eligible for the study, mothers had to have acknowledged that the sexual abuse had occurred, and discovery of the abuse had to have taken place at least six months before the interview.

Whilst there are a number of advantages to my method of selecting respondents for the study, there are also limitations. My sample is small, not randomly selected, and mothers were asked to self-report. Clearly, broad generalisations about black mothers as a whole cannot be made, particularly as participants are self-selected. This means that the bias already inherent in the sample will be aggravated, leaving the work open to criticism of validity and reliability (Reinharz, 1992, p. 256). Notwithstanding these limitations, this discussion can provide insights into the nature of some important factors that influence the research process.

Researching child sexual abuse

Current debates on researching sexual abuse centre on the methodological and conceptual problems inherent in researching the phenomenon (Barnet et al, 1997, Bradley and Lindsay, 1987, Finkelhor, 1986, Ghate and Spencer, 1995, Geffner, Rosenbaum and Hughes, 1988, Kinard, 1994, Levanthal, 1982, Wescott, 1996). Much of this work focuses on the problems of defining and measuring the extent of child sexual abuse. Such analyses indicate the complexities of studying child sexual abuse, an entity that is not easily definable because of its social, cultural, and political underpinnings (Herzberger, 1993, Kinard, 1985, Weis, 1989, Widom, 1991). Herzberger, in particular, suggests that the most prominent themes that emerge in the literature on child abuse research are 'definitional problems, the lack of appropriate control or comparison groups, the failure to address child abuse from a multitheoretical and multivariate perspective, and the difficulties imposed by retrospective designs' (p. 34). Works like these clearly provide important theoretical and practical insights into what is already known about child abuse research, and help us to consider to what extent research can help predict its occurrence in particular groups (Dingwall, 1989). What has been highlighted very succinctly by existing literature is that there are many methodological problems of researching in this area, and also that there is a great deal we can learn from what is already known about studying the phenomenon.

Although there is much we can draw from these existing works, few studies have examined the nature of the relationship between race and gender in researching child sexual abuse. This lack of attention means that the complexities of race and gender and its relationship to power in the research process have not been fully explored. As a consequence, ways in which research can replay and reproduce dominant power relations are absent from or marginal to the debates on research processes in child sexual abuse research.

Feminist and anti-racist perspectives on research

Undoubtedly, feminist and anti-racist discourse on research methodology has been at the forefront in redefining our understanding of the dynamics of research processes (Eichler, 1991, Finch, 1984, Harding, 1987, Lee and Renzetti, 1993, Marshall, 1994, Reinharz, 1992, Roberts, 1981, Yllo, 1988). The significance of feminist and anti-racist analyses on research methodology is their challenge to the claim that a disinterested, value-neutral perspective exists in research (Mama, 1995, Maynard and Purvis, 1994, Phoenix, 1994, Stanley and Wise, 1990). The central tenet of much feminist and anti-racist scholarship is that all research is socially constructed and historically embedded. In taking such a stance, these thinkers have radically challenged prevailing ideas about the objectivity and neutrality of research.

Significantly, feminist scholarship has sought ways of conceptualising the experience of doing research and has been insightful in addressing a number of pertinent questions. In particular, feminist perspectives have addressed questions of experience, knowledge, and the construction of objects and subjects in research. Most notably, feminist thinkers have examined the significance of the relationship between the researcher and the researched, as well as the impact of particular contexts upon research, and the likely influences of these factors upon research production (Reinharz, 1992). As Reinharz has pointed out, in striving to uphold the notion of objectivity, much mainstream writing on research methodology either ignores or downplays the interaction of gender and power as important contributory factors to the research process (p. 249). In particular, feminist theorising on research in the area of violence against women and children has provided important insights into the dynamics of doing research in this sensitive and controversial area (Burton et al, 1994, Kelly, 1988, Moran-Ellis, 1995). These works have been ground-breaking in charting the ways research methodologies can draw on feminist theory and insights to gather data on women and children's experiences of living with male violence.

Arguably, feminist scholarship has been at the forefront of drawing attention to gender and power dynamics in research processes and in developing empowering research paradigms. However, whilst white feminist writers have had much to say about the nature of the link between gender and class, much less attention has been paid to the relationship of race and gender in the research process. There has been a tendency to focus almost exclusively on the commonalties of women's experiences, disregarding the ways in which gender has been constructed through class and race (Brah, 1992). Clearly, a further set of questions concerning race in the context of gender needs to be addressed in feminist debates.

By contrast, anti-racist discourse on research has taken race as the starting point of its analysis. Thinkers from this standpoint have interrogated the dynamics of race and power in research paradigms and have surmised that traditional research paradigms are Eurocentric in their orientations and underlying theoretical formulations (Barn, 1994, Butt, 1994, Franklin, 1994, Hammersley, 1995, Stanfield II and Dennis, 1993, Uehara et al., 1996). Central to their analyses is the proposition that much social science discourse is from a deficit model that has constructed a pathological exploration of the black experience. Moynihan's (1968) influential study, in which the black family is constructed as weak and inherently pathological because of its supposedly matriarchal family structure, is a good example of this fallacy. As a result, anti-racists scholars contend that the validity of much mainstream research on race and ethnicity has to be questioned because of its possible distortion by Eurocentric paradigms. Most importantly, anti-racist thinkers have brought insights and explanations to further an understanding of the political use and abuses of 'race' research. They have called attention to the ways mainstream research involving black subjects typically emphasises a deficit perspective that reaffirms racism rather than counteracting it. In this regard, anti-racist thinkers provide important insights into the multiplicity of factors underlying the debate of 'race' and research and the limitations of Eurocentric frameworks to accurately reflect the black experience.

Notwithstanding the strong contributions noted above, much anti-racist discourse on research tends to focus on race but gloss over or obscure its relationship to gender. As the question of race and its complex relationship to gender is not given prominence in anti-racist debates, the specificities of black women's concerns are typically not explored. Thus, black women have been paradoxically rendered invisible by both anti-racist and feminist discourses.

Black feminist standpoints and research

Black feminists have done much to redress the imbalance between anti-racist and feminist debates about race and gender dynamics (Bhavani, 1994, Brah, 1992, Hill-Collins, 1991, hooks, 1984, Mama, 1989, Mama, 1995, Pheonix, 1994). Their scholarship has been instrumental in deepening our understanding of the interconnectedness of race and gender and the ways in which a focus on gender can obfuscate and marginalise race and vice versa (Crenshaw, 1989, Smith, 1990). In particular, black feminist thinkers have examined the framework of interlocking oppressions and have explored the need for constructing new models of research. Most notably, Kimberlie Crenshaw argues effectively that the experiences of black women cannot be explained by race alone but require a multi-layered analysis. She contends that black feminism presumes 'the intersectionality of race and gender in the lives of black women thereby rendering inapplicable to the lives of black women any single-axis theory about racism and sexism' (Crenshaw cited in Smith, 1990, p. 272). Taking this argument further, I would suggest that unless due consideration is given to the intersection of race and gender in both feminist and anti-racist frameworks then their wider applicability to black women is questionable.

Though these scholars' work is not specifically concerned with the researching of child sexual abuse, their contributions to extend our understanding is enormous. We can draw from their analyses and frameworks to inform research in this complex and sensitive area. For example, the theoretical formulations of Mama, (1989a and b, 1995) in the area of researching black women's experience of domestic violence is insightful in that she calls attention to developing a research paradigm that is sensitive to the subtleties of gender and race oppression of black women. According to Mama, rather than claim objectivity, scholars should strive to make explicit the values, motivations and commitments that are central to the production of research. She attempts to translate these principles in her research practice by developing a framework that can capture the specificity of black women's experiences of domestic violence. Her goal is to generate data to enhance our understanding of the lives of black women living with the experience of domestic violence. In taking such a stance, she has utilised research tools that would enable the participants to 'articulate their experiences in their own terms and from their own frames of reference' (Mama, 1989, p. 29).

Mama's thesis has served as a guide in helping me to develop an appropriate research paradigm for my study. The ideas of Mama and other black feminists have provided me with a framework to conceptualise the multi-faceted ways race and gender intersect in child sexual abuse research with black families. A starting point for me has been that studying black women's experiences of welfare intervention essentially means approaching the research from an explicitly political standpoint. Drawing on black feminist insights has therefore facilitated my development of a framework to locate my work within its broader context, by considering the significance of the interconnectedness of race, gender, and class factors in the research process. This essentially means being able to see and interrogate gender dynamics in the context of racism (Mama, 1995).

My work has sought to build upon the knowledge of black feminist thinkers and has enabled me to frame questions that would be better able to capture the lived experiences of mothers, by bringing an understanding of the effects of oppression on black women. Additionally, it has allowed me to consider the likely impact the research process may have on them, and consider ways to minimise potentially negative aspects. Of particular significance is the capacity for developing awareness of the ethical concerns that attention must be given to in order for the research experience not to disempower participants (Bernard, 1994). On a concrete level, this has meant giving much careful thought to how I negotiated access to respondents, and how I negotiated their consent. My starting point was to ensure that my approach was sensitive to the multiple layers of oppression the mothers have experienced in order not to reproduce oppressive systems in the research experience (Martin and Humphries, 1996).

Researching child sexual abuse in black families

In discussing research frameworks for examining child sexual abuse in black families, it is important to remain aware of the context of that research. In Britain, there is a paucity of original research that has addressed the specific experiences of sexual abuse in black families. This lack of existing research to draw on means that the methodological and conceptual issues that are inherent to this area of study have not been fully explored.

Additionally, one of the major problems associated with gathering data on sexual abuse in black families is that there can be a great deal of fear and mistrust on the part of the respondents. It has been noted elsewhere that research on child sexual abuse is potentially stigmatising to those being researched (Lee, 1993). Furthermore, because of the sensitive and private nature of the subject, it is not always easy or straightforward to get accurate and reliable data. The threatening nature of a topic like child sexual abuse may make some people hesitant to participate in research. Concerns about the use and abuse of research findings may be predominant in people's mind.

The context in which the research is taking place is vital as this involves levels of threat or risk to participants. Most significantly, the problems of doing research on sexual abuse in black communities are compounded by the possibilities that the findings may be interpreted in ways to reaffirm racist myths and misconceptions about the scale of sexual abuse in black families. Respondents might be fearful of raising the topic of sexual abuse in public as this might invite a racist backlash. It could be argued that the more marginalised the group, the more likely they will be inclined to protect their image (Ritchie, 1996).

A major methodological problem in child sexual abuse research in black communities is the under-reporting of the problem (Jackson, 1996, Mtezuka, 1996). Many aspects of sexual abuse are not reported to official agencies such as the police or social services departments and thus do not appear on official registers (Bernard, 1997, Wilson, 1993). For instance, black people may feel alienated from the whole notion of law enforcement. Often the reason sexual abuse is not discussed openly is the fear of exposing the black community to coercive intervention by statutory agencies. The reporting of sexual abuse in black communities generates fear of reprisals and could incur marginalisation or even exclusion from families and communities (Bernard, 1997). As hooks has so cogently argued: 'Black people have been raised to believe that there is just so much

241

that you should not talk about, not in private and not in public' (hooks, 1989, p. 2).

These factors contribute to the vast under-reporting of sexual abuse in black communities and reinforce the idea that it is not an issue (Bernard, 1997). Furthermore, a combination of under-reporting and unsubstantiated cases of child sexual abuse makes it difficult to uncover the true scale of the problem in black communities. By implication, the under-reporting of sexual abuse in black communities means black families are not accurately reflected on the official registers that are often the first port of call for many mainstream researchers when selecting participants for their research projects (HMSO, 1995).

The importance of considering these factors is crucial as such an understanding would heighten awareness of some ethical concerns that need exploring (for example, how access to participants, confidentiality, and anonymity is negotiated). Failure to take on board such concerns could mean that finding research participants who are able to make an informed choice to be part of research can be a slow process fraught with difficulties. As Andersen (1993) observes, black people have more reason to expect they will be exploited by researchers than white people (Andersen, p. 41). According to Andersen, researchers conducting studies with black families should examine their research frameworks for the influence of racism and consider the ways it may shape the formation and development of their research rather than assume a colour-blind stance (Anderson, 1993, p. 43). As Lee has also stated, 'where the members of some groups to be studied are powerless or disadvantaged, they may fear exploitation or derogation...or be sceptical about research' (Lee, 1993, p. 7). Clearly, the more marginalised the group being studied, the more likely they will be wary of researchers.

Negotiating access to respondents

The gatekeepers to respondents are key elements in shaping the research process. Indeed, because of the sensitive and threatening nature of the subject being investigated, access can often be a problem (Lee, 1993). Negotiating access through gatekeepers can involve a complex set of power relationships that have to be explored. The significance of power relationships in influencing access to research participants cannot be underestimated. Barn (1994) has highlighted very succinctly the way access to respondents through powerful bureaucratic organisations can influence the shape and form of the research. For example, gatekeepers to research participants may have vested interests in the research, or may have their own agendas. Their values, political agendas, and current priorities will be key factors in deciding whether they take the research seriously and grant permission to do the research within their organisation. Clearly, gatekeepers have to weigh up the risks and benefits not only to their organisations, but also to participants - their service users. Organisations may have particular concerns that the research findings might be critical of their practice. Explorations of these issues are important because the researcher has to be mindful of how her ideas and values might be compromised in the process of negotiating access.

One avenue for gaining access to black women to participate in the research was through statutory sector agencies with responsibility for working in the area of child protection. I initially wrote to a number of senior managers of statutory and voluntary agencies seeking their permission to approach their front-line practitioners who might have been in contact with black mothers who fitted the study criteria. The information I sent out to organisations thus explicitly stated the goals and objectives of the research and I clearly outlined the methods, values, and assumptions that informed and underpinned my research. I also indicated my own racialised and gendered identity, and gave some other details about myself and my professional background. I explained why I was interested in this area of study, and mentioned my previous social work experience with mothers of sexually abused children. I felt it was important to explicitly state what personal and professional perspectives I would bring to the study to allay any concerns about the potential harm to or exploitation of respondents.

Foremost in my mind was my desire to reach black women who matched the study criteria. I also thought that such women might be more inclined to take part in the study if they knew from the outset that the researcher was another black woman. Although I hoped being explicit about my stance might encourage women to come forward, I was also aware it might discourage some social services managers from involving their agencies in the study as a possible outcome could be critiques of their social work practice.

I subsequently found that my access to black women was mediated through an agency hierarchy structured around race, gender and class. Of the twenty-five senior managers with whom I made contact, all were white and only two were women. One has to bear in mind that the hierarchical structures of welfare agencies in Britain are largely middle-class preserves, dominated by white men, and that black women's voices are largely absent from policy development and decision making (Mama, 1989). That the gatekeepers were predominantly white middle-class males created a further barrier for me. It raised questions about the extent to which my study would be taken seriously by the organisations' senior managers. I was concerned that the research would be judged mainly by white males, few of who would be familiar with, let alone sympathetic to, black feminist thought. I particularly feared that my requests for access might be refused or ignored as the women I was hoping to interview are often low on the agenda of service providers in welfare agencies.

A number of senior managers (or their representatives) responded and questioned me at length about the study. I had no difficulties with this course of action, as I was asking them to pass on information to users of their services, and clearly they had a right to know with whom they were dealing. However, it is interesting to note that of the twenty-five managers who replied, only two agreed to circulate the information to the relevant staff. The remainder either declined to be involved, or did not contact me again, thus cutting off my access to potential participants for the study. Of course, it is possible that these agencies did not have any black women who matched my study criteria. However, all the agencies I approached were located in geographical areas that served large, multi-racial communities, and some of the agencies ran groups specifically for mothers of sexually abused children (my reason for approaching them in the first place). I was mindful here of the politics of research, and can only question whether the stance made explicit in my research design may have seemed too threatening. As Lee (1993) points out, 'outsiders whose values are thought …to be different may be feared or greeted with suspicions' (p. 9). I would go even further and concur with Stubbs (1993) who argues that there may be resistance to black-led initiatives in research, as they are seen to be challenging to existing orthodoxy.

Negotiations with gatekeepers may not only determine access, but may also influence how black respondents perceive the research and the researcher, particularly when that negotiation has been mediated through what is perceived to be a white organisation. The structural location of the researcher may mean she is relating to multiple constituents simultaneously. Black respondents may view a black researcher as a member of what they perceive to be the white establishment, and even as a threat to their position. She may also be seen as removed from the black community and there may be mistrust of the researcher's motives. Respondents may thus not see black researchers as having credibility in the community. Thinking through the implications of these issues was important, as I was seeking to ensure that my research did not become part of the problem for black mothers rather than part of the solution (Reinharz, 1992, p. 12).

The relationship between the researcher and the research participants

Negotiations between the researcher and the researched are also an important locus of power. The interaction between the researcher and the researched in the data collection process is of significance, and unequal power relations between them are of key importance in shaping the process. For example, Moran-Ellis argues that the self-reflective method of child abuse research is more likely to produce research that does not reproduce dominant power relations. For Moran-Ellis, reflecting on research topics that are sensitive and controversial provides researchers with the tools of analysis to ensure that participants are not objectified or further disempowered by the research process. Ethical practice requires that researchers remain self-reflexive and attuned to processes and power issues (Reinharz, 1992, p. 269). Through reflection we will develop insight and awareness of the political implications of research (Atkinson and Shakespeare, 1993, p. 6).

Choice and control

My commitment to promoting ethical and sensitive research meant finding ways to ensure that the participants, who were central to the research, were empowered by the process. Translating my intentions into actual practice during the research required giving careful consideration to my research tools. For example, I devised a leaflet giving brief details of the research and to answer questions and concerns that respondents might have. Meeting with the participants beforehand was also important to give them opportunities for clarification and discussion, and for them to ask questions about my motivation and the ideas informing the study. I thought this approach facilitative to the women in making informed choices about their participation. Particularly as I was doing research in a sensitive and controversial area, I saw this as an opportunity to give the respondents some choice and control whether to take part in the project. I also felt that giving the participants the space to voice their concerns would be a further opportunity for me to reflect on ways that the research experience might not disempower them. Foremost in my mind was that some of the respondents who were suggested to me by their social workers may not have felt strong enough to refuse to be part of the research. Additionally, 'where families have experienced investigation from child protection agencies, they may resent any further intrusion from outside sources' (Kinard, 1994, p. 651). As black women experience multiple-layers of

245

oppression, knowledge of the personal, structural and political forces that shape their lives is necessary to understand their interactions with welfare agencies. It was important for me to consider that these women may have understandably felt defenceless in the face of powerful institutions such as social services. Such factors would influence how women participate in the research, so I wanted to ensure that the process did not reinforce the very same power relationships I was seeking to challenge. I concur with Reinharz (1992) who proposes that the goals of non-exploitative research relationships with respondents are relations of respect, openness, and clarity of communication (p. 267).

Additionally, as I would be asking probing questions about the abuse that would be painful to respondents, I needed to be aware of the level of stress that this might incur for them. The subject matter of child sexual abuse is laden with emotion and I wanted to be sensitive to the impact of my questioning on the research participants. I therefore wanted tools that would enhance my ability to pay attention to the emotional content of the research so that I could be attentive to the feelings that arose, whilst at the same time minimising the stress brought to the participants.

Central to my thinking were ideas drawn from feminist scholarship purporting that research by women researchers with women is potentially less exploitative to respondents (Finch, 1980, Roberts, 1981). I was concerned to explore what factors inform the research relationship when both the researcher and the research participants share the same race and gender. How do issues of power change in the context of the different relationships? Are power imbalances between them lessened, or do they become more complex? It was illuminating to see how these issues manifested themselves in my research.

Here is an extract from one respondent who interviewed me very rigorously before consenting to participate in the research:

Why are you doing the research? Why are your employing organisation funding you? How can I be reassured that my story and other black women's stories will not be used in ways to reinforce stereotypical myths about black women and their families?

First hand accounts such as this diffuse the suppositions that being the same race and gender may presume similarity. In reality, the situation may not be experienced as such by the respondents. Whilst on one level I was aware of why it was important for these questions to be asked, on another level I was surprised at my discomfort at being questioned. I had taken it for granted that the information I had sent out was sufficient to convey my good intentions. On reflection, I recognised the wisdom beneath the healthy caution this respondent expressed. After all, she would be trusting me with private and personal information about herself and her family, and this was her way of assessing whether or not this trust would be misplaced. It could also be argued that this was her way of exercising some control over the process.

What became apparent at this point is that it mattered little to this participant that we shared the same gender and race. Whilst we may have some shared experiences of racism as black women living in a predominantly white society, education, income, and socio-economic status are important markers for differences between us. Moreover, participants have to weigh up the risks and benefits of participating in the research and consider what the potential costs to them and their families will be. Where research is threatening, 'the relationship between the researcher and the research participants is likely to become hedged about with mistrust' (Lee, 1993, p. 2). Black researchers must also be concerned not only with their representation of the research participants, but with the contradictions resulting from their positioning and perceived identification with those in power (Martin and Humphries, 1996). An exploration of these issues can further our understanding of the way power operates on different levels to influence the process of negotiating consent with participants. Given that research has contributed to the pathologisation and stigmatisation of the black community, it was not surprising that this participant responded with suspicion.

Perhaps most importantly, it cannot be assumed that because the researcher and the researched share the same race and gender that concerns about the uses and abuses of research are lessened in the minds of black respondents. Research could be carried out by a black researcher utilising frameworks which are Eurocentric and reproduce racist discourses about the black community. Ken Pryce's ethnographic study of West Indian life-styles in Bristol is a case in point (Pryce, 1979). Moreover, as Burton, et al. (1994) have argued, the fact that the researcher is of the same race or gender does not necessarily mean it will be easier for the respondent to speak freely:

> There is the possibility...that similarity may limit disclosure, since it may incur judgement from 'inside' knowledge, or that there is a presumption of similarity which may not be experienced as such
> by the individuals concerned (Burton et al., 1994, p. 46).

As Andersen (1993) contends, feminist epistemologists have argued that the relationship between the researcher and her subjects is a social relationship, and is bound by the same patterns of power relations found in other social relationships (p. 51). I would argue that even though both the researcher and her respondents may share a marginalised position in society, the power dynamics between them in the research process are not lessened. On the contrary, I believe these become more complex. Mama (1995) has argued that 'choosing to study a multiply oppressed group does not in itself ensure that one's research does not affirm the status quo' (p. 67). As Phoenix (1994) points out: 'It is also important to recognise differences and commonalities between people who are socially constructed as belonging to the same group' (p. 70). Regardless of the many commonalities that may exist between the researcher and the participants in her study, the relationship is one that is still based on unequal power to the advantage of the researcher.

As the researcher, I also become the interpreter of the respondents' stories. I can interpret the data and construct the respondents' stories in ways that may not represent their lives accurately. As Fine (1992) has observed, researchers are not 'vehicles of transmissions with no voices of our own' (p. 211). Therefore, '...power relations in the research process need to be recognised and made overt' (Holland and Ramanzanoglu, 1993, p. 132). By acknowledging the power imbalance inherent in the research relationship, the researcher will be better able to recognise her particular responsibility to make sure that her findings will not be interpreted or used in ways that reinforce racist and sexist stereotypes about black women and black communities.

Conclusion

Throughout this chapter, I have explored the intersectionality of race, gender, and class in research processes, seeking to understand how these dimensions shape power relationships. Drawing on black feminist thought, I have attempted to convey something of the way power relations influence research on child sexual abuse in black families. I have suggested that mainstream theorising on researching sexual abuse often overlooks or gives scant attention to race. As a result, the ethical and methodological challenges that arise for researchers attempting to place the interlocking nature of race and gender at the core of their work remain largely unexamined. Whilst anti-racist and feminist critiques of research methodology have examined constructions of race, gender and power relations in research, neither approach offers adequate attention to understanding the intersectionality of these variables in influencing the research process. Having argued throughout that race, gender and class are important markers for experience, I would contend that these dimensions need to be at the centre rather than the margins of research if we are to ensure that research participants are not objectified or disempowered by the research process. Unless there is an exploration of the interconnectedness of race and gender in research processes, we run the risk of reproducing in our research the very same powerlessness that research participants may experience as service users in their interaction with welfare agencies.

Furthermore, I have examined some key issues that are central to an understanding of power relations between the researcher and the researched, particularly when they are both members of a marginalised group. I have suggested that the effects of commonality as well as heterogeneity of experience need to be fully explored in the context of the research. I contend that in particular, black feminist researchers studying the lives of other black women will experience a number of dilemmas and contradictions. Perhaps most significantly, it cannot be assumed that similarities around race or gender will automatically mean that issues of power in the research relationship will be less apparent. Indeed, I believe the research relationship becomes more complex. This essentially means that we are continually forced to reflect on the research process to ask questions of ourselves about not only who we are accountable to, but also how our work is relevant to those working for social change. Most importantly, it places an onus on researchers to understand the ethical responsibilities we have to consider the impact of our research on research participants.

Finally, an understanding of the ways in which the wider socio-political context in which research takes place is crucial. This extremely important factor not only influences which research projects are funded, but also what problems are investigated, and how research findings can be interpreted and used. Most specifically, in the area of child protection work, broader questions are raised about the role of research and its impact on social policies. Research is playing an increasing role in influencing the nature and direction of policy and practice. The recent debate on 're-focusing' child welfare is a good example to illustrate this point (HMSO, 1995). This increasing use of research as the rationale for policy direction in child protection work means that it is imperative that research paradigms are grounded in a greater knowledge of the simultaneity of race and gender oppression and their impact on the construction of child sexual abuse. Interrogation of these issues will result in a better understanding of the complex processes involved, and present a more accurate and complete picture of black families' experiences of welfare practice in the area of child protection. Ultimately, to begin to integrate these concerns into research requires a better understanding of discourses around race and gender as they impact on research processes.

References

Andersen, M.L. (1993), 'Studying Across Difference: Race, Class and Gender in Qualitative Research', in J.H. Stanfield II and R.M. Dennis (eds), *Race and Ethnicity in Research Methods*, Sage: Newbury Park, CA, pp. 29-52.

Atkinson, D. and Shakespeare, P. (1993), 'Introduction', in P. Shakespeare, D. Atkinson, and S. French (eds), *Reflecting on Research Practice*, Open University Press: Buckingham, pp. 1-10.

Barn, R. (1994), 'Race and Ethnicity in Social Work: Some Issues for Anti-Discriminatory Research', in B. Humphries and C.Truman (eds), *Re-Thinking Social Research*, Avebury: London.

Barnett, O.W., Miller-Perrin, C.L., and Perrin, R.D. (1997), *Family Violence Across the Lifespan*, Sage: Thousand Oaks, CA.

Bernard, C. (1994), 'The Research Process: Dynamics of Race, Gender and Class', *Research Policy and Planning: Journal of Social Services Research Group*, Vol. 12, No. 2, pp. 20-22.

Bernard, C. (1997), 'Black Mothers' Emotional and Behavioural Responses to the Sexual Abuse of Their Children', in G. Kaufman Kantor and J. Jasinski (eds), *Out of the Darkness: Contemporary Perspectives on Family Violence* Sage: Thousand Oaks, CA, pp. 80-89.

Bhavani, K-K. (1994), 'Tracing the Contours: Feminist Research and Feminist Objectivity', in H. Afshar and M. Maynard (eds), *The Dynamics of "race" and Gender*, Taylor Francis: London, pp. 26-40.

Bradley, E.J. and Lindsay, R.C.L. (1987), 'Methodological and Ethical Issues in Child Abuse Research', *Journal of Family Violence*, Vol. 3, pp. 239-255.

Brah, A. (1992), 'Difference, Diversity and Differentiation', in J. Donald, and A. Rattansi (eds), *"Race", Culture and Difference*, Sage: London, pp. 126-145.

Burton, S., Kelly, L. and Regan, L. (1994), 'Researching Women's Lives or Studying Women's Oppression? Reflections on What Constitutes Feminist Research', in M. Maynard and J. Purvis (eds), *Researching Women's Lives from a Feminist Perspective*, Taylor & Francis: London, pp. 27-48.

Butt, J. (1994), 'Exploring and Using the Black Resource in Research', *Research Policy and Planning: The Journal of Social Services Research Group*, Vol. 12, No. 2, pp. 9-12.

Dingwall, R. (1989), 'Some problems about predicting child abuse and neglect', in O. Stevenson (ed.), *Child Abuse: Public Policy and Professional Practice*, Harvester Wheatsheaf: Hemel Hempstead.

Eichler, M. (1991), *Nonsexist Research Methods: A Practical Guide*, Routledge, London.

Finch, J. (1984), '"It's great to have someone to talk to": the ethics and politics of interviewing women', in C. Bell and H. Roberts (eds), *Social Researching: Politics, Problems, Practice*, Routledge & Kegan Paul: London, pp. 70-87.

Fine, M. (1992), *Disruptive Voices: The Possibilities of Feminist Research*, The University of Michigan Press: Michigan.

Finkelhor, D. (1986), *A Sourcebook on Child Sexual Abuse*, Sage: Beverley Hills, CA.

Franklin, A. (1994), 'Anti-Racist Research Guidelines', *Research Policy and Planning: The Journal of Social Services Research Group*, Vol. 12, No. 2, pp. 18-19.

Ghate, D. and Spencer, L. (1995), *The Prevalence of Child Sexual abuse In Britain*, HMSO: London.

Geffner, R., Rosenbaum, A.J. and Hughes, H. (1988), 'Research Issues Concerning Family Violence', in V.B. Van Hassett, R.L. Morrison, A.S. Bellack and M. Hersen (eds), *Handbook of Family Violence*, Plenum: New York.

Hammersley, M. (1995), *The Politics of Social Research*, Sage: London.

Harding, S. (ed.) (1987), *Feminism and Methodology: Social Science Issues*, Indiana University Press: Bloomington.

Herzberger, S.H. (1993), 'The Cyclical Pattern of Child Abuse: A Study of Research Methodology', in C.M. Renzetti and R.M. Lee (eds), *Researching Sensitive Topics*, California: Newbury Park, CA, pp. 33-51.

Hill Collins, P. (1991), 'Learning from the Outsider Within: The Sociological Significance of Black Feminist Thought', in M. Fonow and J. Cook (eds), *Beyond Methodology: Feminist Scholarship as Lived Research*, Indiana University Press: Indiana, pp. 35-59).

Holland, J. and Ramazanoglu, C. (1994), 'Coming to Conclusion: Power and Interpretation in Researching Young Women's Sexuality' in M. Maynard and J. Purvis (eds), *Researching Women's Lives from a Feminist Perspective*, Taylor Francis: London, pp. 125-148.

hooks, b. (1984), 'Feminist Theory: From Margin to Centre', South End Press: Boston.

HMSO, (1995), *Child Protection: Messages From Research*, HMSO: London.

Humphries, B. and Truman, C. (eds) (1994), *Re-Thinking Social Research*, Avebury: London.

Jackson, V. (1996), *Racism and Child Protection: the Black Experience of Child Sexual Abuse*, Cassell: London.

Kelly, L. (1988), *Surviving Sexual Violence*, Polity Press: Cambridge.

Kinard, E.M. (1985), 'Ethical Issues in Research with Abused Children', *Child Abuse and Neglect*, Vol. 9, No. 3, pp. 301-311.

Kinard, E.M. (1994), 'Methodological Issues and Practical Problems in Conducting Research on Maltreated Children', *Child Abuse & Neglect*, 18 (8), pp. 645-656.

Lawrence, E. (1992), 'In the Abundance of Water the Fool is Thirsty: Sociology and Black "pathology"', in *The Empire Strikes Back: Race and Racism in 70s Britain*, Centre for Contemporary Cultural Studies, Race and Politics Group, Hutchinson: London, pp. 94-142.

Lee, R. (1993), *Doing Research on Sensitive Topics*, Sage: London.

Lee, R.M. and Renzetti, C.M. (eds) (1993), *Researching Sensitive Topics*, Sage: Newbury Park, CA.

Levanthal, J.M. (1982), 'Research Strategies and Methodologic Standards in Studies of Risk Factors for Child Abuse', *Child Abuse & Neglect*, Vol. 6, pp. 113-123.

Mama, A. (1989a), *The Hidden Struggle: Statutory and Voluntary Sector Responses to Violence Against Black Women in the Home*, Race and Housing Research Unit: London.

Mama, A. (1989b), 'Violence Against Black Women: Gender, Race and State Responses', *Feminist Review*, Vol. 32, pp. 30-49.

Mama, A. (1995), *Beyond The Mask: Race, Gender and Subjectivity*, Routledge: London.

Marshall, A. (1994), 'Sensuous Sapphires: A Study of the Social Construction of Black Female Sexuality', in M. Maynard and J. Purvis (eds), *Researching Women's Lives from a Feminist Perspective*, Taylor & Francis: London, pp. 106-124.

Martin, M. and Humphries, B. (1996), 'Representation of Difference in Cross-Cultural Research: The impact of Institutional Structures', in S. Wilkinson and C. Kitzinger (eds), *Representing the Other*, Sage: London, pp. 119-123.

Maynard, M. and Purvis, J. (eds) (1994), *Researching Women's Lives from a Feminist Perspective*, Taylor & Francis: London.

Moran-Ellis, J. (1995), 'Close to home: the experience of researching child sexual abuse', in M. Hester, L. Kelly and J. Radford (eds), *Women, violence and male power*, Open University Press: Buckingham, pp. 176-187.

Moynihan, D. (1968), *The Negro Family: The Case for National Action*, Washington D.C. GPO.

Mtezuka, M. (1996), 'Issues of Race and Culture in Child Abuse', in B. Fawcett, B. Featherstone, J. Hearn and C. Toft (eds), *Violence and Gender Relations: Theories and Interventions*, Sage: London, pp. 171-177.

Phoenix, A. (1994), 'Practising Feminist Research: The Intersection of Gender and "Race" in the Research Process', in M. Maynard and J. Purvis (eds), *Researching Women's Lives From a Feminist Perspective*, Taylor & Francis: London, pp. 49-71.

Pryce, K. (1979), *Endless Pressure: A Study of West Indian Life-styles in Bristol*, Penguin: Harmondsworth.

Reinharz, S. (1992), *Feminist Methods in Social Research*, Oxford University Press: New York.

Ritchie, B.E. (1996), *Compelled to Crime: The Gender Entrapment of Battered Black Women*, Routledge: New York.

Roberts, H. (1981), *Doing Feminist Research*, Routledge & Kegan Paul: London.

Smith, V. (1990), 'Split Affinities: The Case of Interacial Rape', in M. Hirsch and E. Fox Keller (eds), *Conflicts in Feminism*, Routledge: London, pp. 271-287.

Stanfield II, J.H. and Dennis, M. (eds) (1993), *Race and Ethnicity in Research Methods*, Sage: Thousand Oaks, CA.

Stanley, L. and Wise, S. (1983), *Breaking Out: Feminist Consciousness and the Reproduction of Patriarchal Relations*, RKP: London.

Stanley, L. and Wise, S. (1990), 'Method, Methodology and Epistemology in Feminist Research Process', in L. Stanley (ed.), *Feminist Praxis: Research, Theory and Epistemology in Feminist Sociology*, Routledge, London.

Stubbs, P. (1993), '"Ethically Sensitive" or "Anti-Racist"? Models for Health Research and Service Delivery' in W.I.U. Ahmad (ed.), *Race and Health in Contemporary Britain*, Open University Press: Buckingham, pp. 34-47.

Uehara, E.S., Sohng, S.S.L., Benkding, R.L., Seyfried, S., Richey, C.A., Morelli, P., Spencer, M., Ortega, D., Keenan, L. and Kanuha, V. (1996), 'Towards a Values-Based Approach to Multicultural Social Work Research', *Social Work: Journal of the National Association of Social Work*, Vol. 41, No. 6, pp. 613-630.

Weis, J.G. (1989), 'Family Violence Research Methodology and Design', in L. Ohlin and M. Tonry (eds), *Family Violence*, University of Chicago Press: Chicago.

Wescott, H.L. (1996), 'Practising ethical and sensitive child protection research', *Practice*, Vol. 8, No. 4, pp. 25-33.

Widom, C.S. (1991), 'Sampling Biases and Implications for Child Abuse Research', *American Journal of Orthopsychiatry*, Vol. 58, No. 2, pp. 260-270.

Wilson, M. (1993), *Crossing the Boundary*, Virago: London.

Yllo, K. (1988), 'Political and Methodological Debates in Wife Abuse Research', in K. Yllo and M. Bograde (eds), *Feminist Perspectives on Wife Abuse*, Sage: Newbury Park, CA, pp. 28-50.